# Dimensions of Public Communication

**John F. Wilson**

*Herbert H. Lehman College of the City University of New York*

**Carroll C. Arnold**

*The Pennsylvania State University*



**Allyn and Bacon, Inc.**

*Boston • London • Sydney • Toronto*

*All illustrations were prepared for this book by Leonard N. Boylan.*



**Library of Congress Cataloging in Publication Data**

*Wilson, John Fletcher, 1923-*
*Dimensions of public communication.*

*Includes index.*
*1. Public speaking. I. Arnold, Carroll C., joint author. II. Title.*
*PN4121.W457 808.5'1 75-25546*

*ISBN 0-205-04917-6*

*Second printing . . . August, 1976*

# Contents


*Preface* **ix**

**CHAPTER 1** **Speaking to Your Public** **1**

*Misconceptions about Speaking* 3
*The Capacity to Choose* 7
*Human Communication and Rhetorical Situations* 9
*Summary* 15
*Exercises* 16

**CHAPTER 2** **First Considerations** **18**

*Listening* 19
*Basic Procedures in Speech Preparation* 23
*Preparing a First Assignment* 29
*Modes of Delivery* 32
*Stage Fright* 34
*Rehearsal and Attitudes toward Speaking* 37
*An Overview of Preparation* 38
*Summary* 39
*Exercises* 40

**CHAPTER 3** **Understanding Your Rhetorical Situation** **41**

*Observing Responses* 41
*Adjusting to Listeners' Preferences* 42
*Rhetorical Situations* 45
*Getting Attention* 50
*Achieving Change* 51
*Features of Attention and Interest* 56
*Summary* 60
*Exercises* 60

CHAPTER 4 **Locating Ideas That Will Communicate** 63

*Choosing Subjects* 64
*Discovering Lines of Thought* 67
*General Research* 75
*Humanizing Ideas* 84
*Summary* 87
*Exercises* 87

CHAPTER 5 **Invention: General Tactics** 89

*Reviewing Purposes and Goals* 90
*Proofs* 91
*Summary* 110
*Exercises* 111

CHAPTER 6 **Invention: Clarifying and Reinforcing Ideas** 113

*Introducing Anecdotes* 114
*Comparing and Contrasting* 115
*Defining* 117
*Describing* 119
*Exemplifying* 121
*Quoting* 122
*Repeating and Restating* 123
*Quantifying* 124
*Audio-Visual Aids* 126
*Summary* 128
*Exercises* 130

CHAPTER 7 **Invention in Relation to Purposes** 132

*Speaking to Inform* 133
*Speaking to Persuade* 137
*Other Purposes* 142
*Classifications Other Than by Purposes* 146
*Summary* 146
*Exercises* 147

CHAPTER 8 **Disposition: Organizing Materials** 149

*Main Components of a Speech* 151
*Useful Patterns of Organization* 156
*Outlining* 165

*Sample Outlines and Speakers' Notes* 172
*Summary* 178
*Exercises* 178

CHAPTER 9 **Choosing Language** **183**

*Improving Your Personal Style* 184
*Goals in Choosing Language* 188
*Oral and Written Style* 195
*Summary* 198
*Exercises* 198

CHAPTER 10 **Delivery** **201**

*Delivery as Adaptation* 202
*The Resources of Delivery* 206
*Delivery and Rhetorical Settings* 217
*Summary* 222
*Exercises* 223

Appendix: The Biography of a Speech 227

Special Index for the Study of Types of Speeches 246

Index 249

# *Preface*

We all speak to someone every day. On most days we talk to many people individually, and on many days we say things to groups of people. We speak to our "publics" – to groups small and large who "give us the floor" for brief or extended talk. In our daily lives, the behavior we call human communication is unavoidable!

We can all speak to our "publics" better than we do. But how? How shall we make our public messages and the way we present them more effective?

For at least 2,400 years men have been engaged in three major ways of trying to improve their speaking. First, there are those who have tried to learn about speaking by studying human behavior and social processes, and then attempting to speak according to the rules or principles supported in their theory. Second, some have learned rules or steps of speaking, as a teacher or other authority has laid them down. The learners then speak according to rules, following the sacred steps rigidly and often imitatively. A third way of studying speaking has been to locate the problems that communicators have had to solve, identifying the choices people have made in solving them, and reasoning to conclusions about which choices seem best for specific communicative situations.

A trouble with the first method is that many people cannot make the leap from *knowing about* to *doing*. The fact that you have passed the written test for an airplane pilot's license will not, in itself, guarantee that others will trust you at the controls during flight.

You may have seen advertisements inviting you to learn by the second method. The advertisements promise "Ten Steps to Successful Speaking," to successful salesmanship, or to successfully investing in the stock market. The best speakers, salesmen, and stock brokers we know would all but unanimously agree that "there's more to it than that." Just following rules, it seems, will not quite do. Because situations change and people change, rules or steps that work in some circumstances fail to work in others. Recipes do not always serve, especially in human affairs. New conditions make flexibility imperative.

The third approach to improved speaking seems to us the surest. It recognizes that speaking is something you do in so many different settings that your needs can never be fully predicted by any general theory or met by any single set of rules.

Speaking is a way of adjusting yourself to circumstances, is it not? Whether you greet a friend or give a formal talk, the action is an attempt to make ideas and feelings you have fit with what and who you are, and both of these with what a set of circumstances calls for. General theories and specific sets of rules do not describe or prescribe what needs to be done in *particular* circumstances. Yet problems you face from day to day have unique qualities. They arise from who you are in the eyes of *those* listeners whom you meet in a unique situation, seeking to accomplish special goals with a particular set of ideas and feelings. You cannot predict the exact requirements of a speaking situation until you can foresee the situation. That is why we shall try everywhere in this book to think with you about reasoning out how you can, in the future, adjust yourself to circumstances neither you nor we can as yet identify in detail.

This book is about "public speech," though much of what is said applies to all speaking. By "public speech" we mean *speaking where you need to make continual talk for the purpose of accomplishing some task with listeners.* We shall not be thinking only about platform speaking. What we shall discuss are your choices when you talk briefly or at length in any imaginable, practical set of circumstances where you have responsibility for speaking to others without much interruption. Because you cannot predict all those circumstances, our questions throughout will be: how shall you *think about* yourself, your ideas, and your circumstances – when you talk continually to accomplish something with people; and how shall you *choose* what to do on some future day?

Answering the above questions requires us to explore (1) how to think about speaking situations and audiences; (2) how to think about finding and choosing ideas that will do practical, purposeful work; (3) how to think about giving ideas clear and influential arrangements; (4) how to think about language as a resource for clear, telling, oral communication; and (5) how to think about presenting or delivering spoken messages. These are the five points of special questioning and choosing every speaker confronts when planning and presenting public speech. They are the topics of our major chapters.

Chapters One and Two are introductory. Chapter One defines "public speech," and misconceptions about it are discussed. The key concepts, that communication is human relationship and that rhetorical situations are unique, are then discussed. Chapter Two treats "first considerations" that need to be understood if first experiments in public speech are to be made before all recurring problems in speaking have been studied in detail.

Chapter Three gives you basic facts about audiences and situations. From these you can reason out what can probably be expected of your listeners. Chapters Four, Five, Six, and Seven treat the most important set of problems speakers face: trying to find what can and ought to be said, and how to adjust those ideas to your purpose, audience, and particular situation. Chapter Eight deals with the choices you have in organizing ideas so they will be clear, strong, appropriate to the conventional ways of analyzing things in our culture, and still appropriate to your purposes with audiences. Chapter Nine considers language as a resource. There, we have also described how you can develop habits that will allow you to use words effectively. Finally, Chapter Ten treats problems you are probably already more concerned about than you ought to be: how to think about delivering a public speech. We put this chapter last for a reason. If you can solve the problems presented by audiences and situations, if you can find and select the right ideas (*invention*), if you can get those ideas in order (*disposition*), and if you can evolve effective language (*style*), you will have solved the most important problems about delivery almost without knowing it. Most problems of delivery come from thinking wrongly about yourself, your hearers, and your plans. The only way we can prove this to you is to ask you to solve the other kinds of speaking problems first; you will then see that carefully solving those problems makes you less worried than you were about the private bugaboo of all speakers, *delivery*.

Speaking to publics, the actual *doing*, is solving problems. You will solve them intelligently or mistakenly, but in the doing you will deal with them somehow. To show that college students *can* analyze and solve their problems intelligently, we have drawn upon a large number of examples of students' achievements in speaking. Randy Cohn, formerly an undergraduate at Herbert H. Lehman College of the City University of New York, has let us use her complete record of how she prepared and presented a short speech. We use this record throughout our chapters as an extended example of problem solving. Ms. Cohn's diary, covering her preparation, all her preparatory papers, the text of the speech as she gave it, and critical comment about it, makes up our Appendix. The example fairly and truly illustrates practical solutions—for the most part successful — of the problems of classroom speaking. This example and most others come from our own classrooms, allowing us to give background information about the students and their situations.

Special exercises are provided at the ends of chapters. Our students have found these interesting and sometimes fun. Each is designed to make one or more points concerning the nature, resources, and opportunities of practical speaking.

Saying requires choosing. If you choose ideas, arrangements, language, or personal behaviors without forethought, you may "luck out" and get your job done. But will luck be with you next time, and the next, and the next? Not for most of us. Meanwhile, some basic facts, about people as listeners and about situations in which people speak more or less formally, can be known. Other facts, about what speech and language are and are not as means of communication, can be known too. Knowing them, you can diagnose difficulties in public speech and solve many problems by planning and self-control. To understand what you can reasonably do in a speaking situation does not deny Lady Luck. We all need her, too. But being able to estimate what will *probably* happen in speaking adds a considerable margin on the side of success. It is that margin—that edge—that we have tried to show you how to get. We cannot give it to you, but we can explain and illustrate how you can gain it for yourself. That's what this book is about.

For special assistance we gratefully acknowledge help from: Bie Arnold, Joseph Aurbach, Randy Jill Cohn, Robin D. Meyer, and Susan May Wilson, and the following personnel of Allyn and Bacon, Inc.: Wayne A. Barcomb, Vice-President and Director of the College Division; Jane Richardson, Production Editor; Frank Ruggirello, Editor; and Allen Workman, Basic Book Editor.

**John F. Wilson**

**Carroll C. Arnold**

# Dimensions of Public Communication

# 1

# Speaking to Your Public

*Although language is often confusing, it is the easiest way to exchange information.*

English, like other languages, is often confusing. Meters, flashing lights, and Morse code signals would communicate more exactly. Why, then, do businesses and governments and other organizations spend billions of dollars to set up *vocal* communication between headquarters and such people as deep sea divers, airplane pilots, drivers of taxis, trucks, buses, police cars, and so on? There are good reasons. It is hard to ask questions of meters and lights. You cannot learn easily about people's feelings through strictly mechanical means. The simple fact is, it is easiest to *exchange* information through verbal communication, and face-to-face, oral communication allows the most accurate and feeling-full exchange. This is why few organizations of any kind can do without direct talk among workers, supervisors, executives, and all other members.

Despite the obvious importance of direct talk, people often overlook its role in their daily lives. Not long ago, some specialists studied the beliefs and the behaviors of clerks, secretaries, technicians, and engineers who worked in a research laboratory. The staff actually spent more than a third of all working time carrying on face-to-face talk with individuals and groups.

But when these people were asked to estimate how much time they spent in these ways, they *under*estimated by about forty percent! And they *over*estimated the time they spent in writing and reading by about forty percent![1] The study showed only too clearly how easy it is for highly intelligent, practical people to disregard the importance of informal and formal speech in their workaday affairs. If you will carry out Written Exercise 1 at the end of this chapter, we think you, too, will be surprised at the importance talk plays in your everyday affairs.

*Making a public speech is a common occurrence in everyone's life.*

It is also commonplace to believe that only "leaders," such as politicians, preachers, and lawyers, engage in *public* speaking. That is a mistake. As one of our colleagues recently remarked, "Every time a physician sits down with a patient after completing the standard diagnostic tests, he makes something like a three-minute speech—and to a very uneasy audience." Take another case. What was it the service manager of a garage did when he called one of your authors on the telephone and spent nearly five minutes explaining why what your author had hoped was ignition trouble was actually *valve* failure, requiring grinding the valves, keeping the car for three days, and a payment of $125 instead of the $20 the author had hoped for? Did the service manager make a *speech,* or just chat? The fact is that service managers, physicians, scientists, building supply brokers, airline hostesses, and virtually everyone else make far more *speeches* than they usually recognize.

We are suggesting that whenever one person is responsible for continuing a relationship with others for longer than a

[1]E. T. Klemmer and F. W. Snyder, "Measurement of Time Spent Communicating," "*The Journal of Communication,* XX (June, 1972), pp. 142–158.

few moments, then that person makes *a speech*. When we get such responsibilities, most of us feel they are special. As soon as we sense that others expect us to "carry on" continuously, our attitudes toward what we are doing become somewhat like those most people associate with the phrase "public speaking." A doctor or service manager knows he has to carry through on his own when he reports his diagnosis and tries to win acceptance of what he believes must now be done. He may speak to only one person at a time, but his tasks and responsibilities are not fundamentally different from those the President of the United States shoulders when he goes before Congress to report the state of the national economy and ask for the legislation he thinks Congress should pass. Nor does the doctor, service manager, or President undertake tasks basically different from those a teenaged adult has when he or she makes a case that the family ought to approve and help to buy a car "for me." When you have the responsibility to influence others through *systematic* talk, the literal size of your audience is only a secondary factor affecting the problems you face.

*Responsibility is the major element of "public speech."*

We shall thus use the term "public speaking" in what is perhaps a slightly unusual way. When a person has responsibility for maintaining communicative relations without much interruption, we think that person makes *public* speech. The time involved may be long or short. It is the special responsibility that, to us, seems important, that makes the speaker's task unique. When we cannot predict who has responsibility for carrying on social relations, as in ordinary conversation of a chatty kind, we shall call the speaking *private*. It is to help you get better results in the first kind of situation that we have written this book.

## MISCONCEPTIONS ABOUT SPEAKING

We just pointed out that much more speaking than we usually realize is carried on under "public" responsibilities. One of the reasons we fail to notice how much speaking is of this kind is that most of us take all of our talk for granted until we find we have failed to get the social effects we hoped for when we talked. It is not surprising that we think this way. Most of us learned to speak from the people who were around us, and our learning was largely unselfconscious because it occurred so early that we cannot now remember how it happened. The notion that effectiveness in talk just "rubs off on you," or fails to, is so widespread that we doubt you could ask ten people "What

*Good public speakers are not "born that way."*

makes an effective speaker?" without getting several answers such as "They're just born" or "They have a gift."

No doubt some of us are endowed with greater abilities in language than others, but we can all develop what abilities we have. On the day this paragraph was first composed its author was introduced, in a student cafeteria, to a young undergraduate who just a year before had been in a special class for "reticent speakers." She had wept at her inability to speak with other people. Now, this day, she had given a very successful lecture to a class of graduate students on how she had moved from having "no ability" in even private speech to confident effectiveness in public. She is an exception, and she probably had an exaggerated idea of her original inabilities, but by education and practice she *did* discover and develop capacities she had not known she had.

What happens in industrial training programs is more representative of what study and practice can do. Several years ago the authors taught substantially what we are putting in this book to more than sixty office managers for a large utility company. Afterward the company made its own checkup on the men's speaking abilities and concluded that all but one was a better communicator—by the company's definition—than before training. There was nothing unusual about this. Other businesses have found the same improvement from public speaking programs taught by other people. The point is that although talent for speaking exists, just as talent for mathematics or sports exists, study and practice can improve speaking just as they can perfect natural mathematical and athletic abilities. You don't "just have it or not."

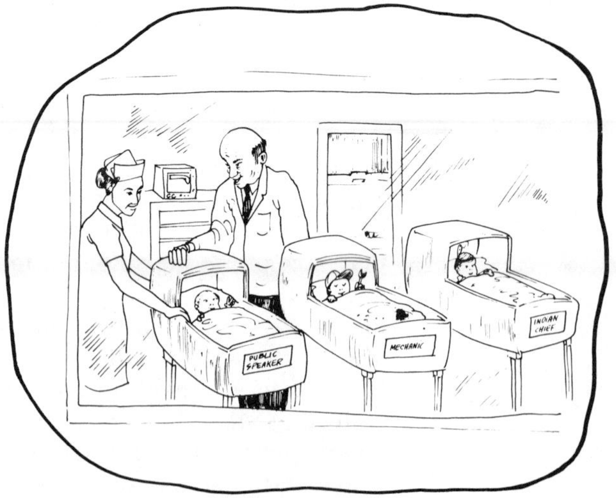

A second misconception about speaking is as old and mistaken as the first: if you know your subject, you needn't worry about how to present it. This idea dies hard, but doesn't every well-informed but boring professor you have had refute it? Nelson Rockefeller is an interesting person in this respect. He is experienced and well informed, yet he is sometimes very hard to understand because he strings ideas together in clause after clause until it is hard to know what his point is. This may not make trouble in informal situations, but it does limit his formal, extemporaneous speaking. He does not lack knowledge, certainly. Apparently he has not *learned* to think ahead carefully to see how his statements are going to come out before he begins them. For him, for you, for everyone, knowing what you are talking about is essential, but knowledge alone teaches no one how to *adapt* ideas and themselves to particular, differing, rhetorical situations.

*Knowledge alone does not make a successful speaker.*

A third misconception about speaking is equally unfounded. It is contained in the saying, "It isn't what you say, it's how you say it." We all know some speakers who seem to get away with "smooth talk" that has little substance behind it. Notice, first, that the very fact that we think like this is proof that as listeners we do look for *what* is said as well as how. Notice, second, that it is from *what* is said that we take the measure of a speaker's *brains*. A former Harvard University faculty member has illustrated this, recalling a politician's failure with a group of students. In 1968, the former Governor of Michigan, George Romney, was seeking nomination for the presidency. At one point he visited Harvard

*Style alone does not make a successful speaker.*

> . . . where he met with students privately. When the Governor agreed with everything suggested at the meeting, the students voiced disappointment with his malleability. In their consensus, he was a "limp dishrag," who "lacked backbone," and "never would become President." . . . A major reason interest lagged was his failure to take a stand on issues and to support it without second thoughts.[2]

The Governor was too smooth and too agreeable for the students to believe he really *knew* much and could make decisions on important matters. Everywhere, it takes content *and* "ways of saying" to achieve goals consistently in public communication.

A fourth misconception concerns what is important to study to become an effective speaker. Many people—including many students entering speech courses—think delivery is the most important thing to work on. This is a dangerous over-

[2]Irving J. Rein, *The Relevant Rhetoric* (New York: The Free Press, 1969), p. 30.

emphasis on what is just one aspect of successful speaking. That it is a dangerous notion is illustrated by the experience of a young college teacher. In the second teaching position he held, the basic course in speaking emphasized getting information, adapting it to audiences, organizing thoughts, and finding the most direct language for easy communication. Delivery was seldom discussed except in reference to how students could *improve* their natural habits of speaking. In the midst of teaching this course for the first time, the young instructor told the author of this paragraph, "I don't understand why it is that I haven't had a 'crack up' in mid-speech, or a student who said he or she couldn't get up on the platform." He was perplexed, he said, because in the basic course he had taught in his first job, a number of students "broke down" in early speeches. When syllabi of the two courses were checked, it turned out that in the course he formerly taught weeks had been spent discussing and practicing aspects of delivery before students prepared and delivered their own talks. Apparently this emphasis on manner instead of *matter* unnerved students by making them excessively self-conscious. This danger is one reason we defer discussion of delivery until late in this book.

*Good delivery alone does not make a successful speaker.*

Disciplined, adaptive delivery is important in all speaking, but in either public or private speaking, voice and gesture can only *support* ideas if delivery is to seem and be natural. Much of the support delivery can give develops without direct attention when your ideas and goals have been carefully thought out in advance of speaking. Because we want to minimize your self-consciousness and because we hope ideas and attitudes will, themselves, generate improvements in your presentations, we concentrate first in this book on choosing and adapting ideas. When you achieve those things, it will be time to give thought to how your best, natural manner of presenting ideas can be further improved.

The fifth and final misconception about public speech that we shall consider is the notion that speakers are pretty much like actors in a play or like people pretending to their friends. This is a mistaken idea because in most circumstances listeners will expect you to communicate your *own* thoughts and feelings about whatever you discuss. Consider yourself as a listener to others. Don't you begin to distrust people when you suspect they are not saying what they mean or are "not being themselves"? Except in very special circumstances, you do not want people to *pretend* to you. You want "straight talk." Most listeners to public speech are like that. You will lose their serious respect if you pretend to them—if you "act" instead of talking *as yourself*. "Be yourself, but your *best* self" is the safe rule in speaking publicly.

*A good speaker is not an actor.*

None of us can be his or her "best self" if we do not know what our options are and what distinguishes a wise from an unwise choice in whatever we happen to be doing. What good is a football player who does not know *all* the plays in which his position is involved? Would you want to fly with a pilot or hire a racing car driver who did not know *all* that his machine can and cannot do? Would you really want to buy a house constructed by an architect who understood design but not the safe use of different kinds of metals, concrete, plastics, lumber, and so on? If such people would seem inadequate to their tasks, what should we say of speakers who do not consider the possibilities and the limits of speaking as a way of communicating? No speaker can be his or her "best self" without understanding the opportunities, limitations, and probabilities of speaking in order to achieve personal goals. These are what this book is about, and a good point at which to begin thinking about them is with the question: what possibilities does studying speech, itself, open up to you?

## THE CAPACITY TO CHOOSE

*A speaker should be concerned with his listeners.*

If you watch and think about what goes on in your speech class, you will discover that studying public speech is actually studying yourself and others as people—especially as *listeners*. It usually makes no sense to talk unless someone pays attention. If you approach it thoughfully, all the talk that takes place in your classroom invites you to learn what other people like most to think about, what interests them, why, and in what circumstances. The student who chose to talk about the nature of sleep in an 8 A.M. class had a very fitting subject. Why? Because most listeners at that hour wished they were still sleeping, and they woke up to learn about what they were missing! There's a general idea to be learned here: people are always ready to think about what has recently been pleasurable for them. You can learn dozens of other general principles of human behavior from how people speak and react, as we shall show in later chapters. The point just now is that it is intelligent to approach your study of public speech as a study of *people*.

Your study of public speech can also be a study of how to put together in your own head the kinds of special knowledge that are important to you, personally. If concepts of engineering, or music, or broadcasting, or anything else are going to be important in your own life, make them clearer in your own mind by talking about them to your friends in speech class. If you can be clear to them, you will be clear in your own head and can use those ideas better. If you have some special interest in acoustics, physiology, the psychology of perception, languages, the sociology of groups, or clothing design, you can develop that knowledge by talking about the ways any of these collections of ideas explain why oral communication works as it does. They *do* add explanations. Listening successfully depends on a host of acoustical and physiological conditions. Attending to speech depends on the nature of human perception and the nature of language. An audience is a group that sociologists can help us understand better, and a speaker "speaks" through clothing as well as by mouth. The ways other sciences and arts help to clarify what it is to communicate could be multiplied; our examples are intended to emphasize that your speech class can become a genuine laboratory for the study of speech *and* social sciences, linguistics, physical science, and other topics.

*Making speeches provides good opportunities to learn about many topics.*

We are really urging you to ask "Why?" about all that happens to you as a student of public speech. Discovering *why's* lets you think outward toward your entire life from particular experiences and observations you are bound to have in a speech class. Consider two simple examples.

From studying public speech you will learn the importance of making *purpose* clear to listeners. Why is that important? Because people have a need to know what you want from them. Now, take that notion with you to a meeting of some organization you belong to and watch for moments when your group seems confused. The reason is very likely to be your old friend, *purpose*. The confusion is almost sure to exist because people are not seeing the group's immediate purpose in similar ways. People's need for clear purposes does not occur just in speech classes or among general listeners. (One reason the movement for black people's rights has seemed so disorganized since the death of Dr. Martin Luther King is that there has been, and is, disagreement over what the main *purpose* of civil rights organizations should be.)

*The purpose of a speech must be clear.*

You will learn that speeches tend to be organized in one or another of about eleven standard ways, and that each way has certain advantages and disadvantages. But choosing and analyzing *patterns* are not problems just for speakers. Poets must choose among patterns. So must automobile designers and people who lay out housing developments. "Lifestyle" is a popular phrase, but what is it really about? It involves *patterns* of living from day to day. Everywhere, including in the devising of public speeches, we have to identify our options among patterns, find their advantages and disadvantages, and choose in informed ways—or else we will simply bumble in speaking, and in life.

Look, then, for the ways in which speaking reflects living.

# HUMAN COMMUNICATION AND RHETORICAL SITUATIONS

## Human Communication

*Communication is both necessary and enlightening.*

There are two good reasons for studying how we communicate. First, communication is necessary to human beings' healthy development. Solitary confinement is severe punishment just because it ends association and communication with others. Experiments have shown that people even begin to have hallucinations when deprived of the company of other humans. Second, understanding how we communicate reveals a great deal that is widely useful for understanding all social behavior, as we suggested in the previous section.

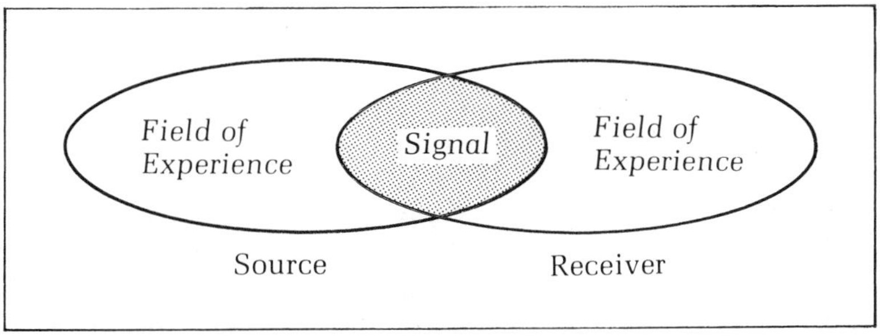


**FIGURE 1.**

Scholars have represented how we communicate in a number of ways, but Figure 1 is a graphic representation we like because it is simple and shows some basic features of all of our satisfying relationships with one another.[3] The major points made by this figure, which we have adapted from one originally drawn by Wilbur Schramm, are:

1. Each human being engaged in communication lives within his or her *own* "field of experience." You and everyone else know what experience has taught. You understand soccer, but I don't, so you must teach me about soccer—put it into my experience—before we can communicate about it as equals. So it is in all communication and in most other social relationships; for understanding, there must be *shared* experience. But it is not possible for us to sense and know everything exactly alike. Some of our awarenesses and understandings are *always different* from those our partners have. In the figure these unshared aspects of our experiences

[3]Wilbur Schramm, "How Communication Works," in W. Schramm, ed., *The Process and Effects of Mass Communication* (New York: Holt, Rinehart and Winston, Inc., 1960), p. 72.

are represented by the unshaded portions of the two ellipses. For most people there is more unshared than shared experience.

2. We communicate by signaling one another. The source chooses one kind of signal or another (speech, writing, waving flags, dressing in certain ways, etc.). Our signals represent our meanings, but they are not meanings in themselves. In communication we signal with *symbols*—behaviors that *stand for* specific meanings.
3. For us to understand each other, the signals of a source must fall within the experience of the receiver; the signals must be *mutually* understood. That we can only communicate through commonly understood symbols is represented in the figure by placing the "signal" within the shaded area of overlapping experience.
4. All you and I can really know about one another is what we can communicate to one another through experiences we have or can share. Each of us will remain ignorant of most of the other's experiences.
5. The most important point of the figure is this: the problem we face in making communication work is the problem of creating signals that (a) are understood by those we try to communicate with, and (b) have meanings that relate to experiences shared by both of us. Put differently, the problem is to keep communicative efforts constantly within the *overlapping* portion of our partners' and our own experiences.

We shall not go further into the subject of general communication theory because our concern is with a special kind of communication: rhetorical speaking—any speaking intended to get someone else to understand or agree to an idea or set of ideas. Obviously this kind of speaking will involve us in close study of the *ideas* speakers and listeners share or can be helped to share. Indeed, the basic task of public speakers is to discover the true natures of their listeners, as they listen in a situation shared with the speaker. But what can we say about the *situations* speakers and listeners share when rhetorical speaking occurs?

### Rhetorical Situations

*The particular speaking situation is most important.*

The most important single generalization about public speech which we can offer you is that effectiveness always depends on the extent to which the requirements and possibilities of a *situation* are met. *Public speech takes place in a particular place, at a particular time, with particular people present.* Whatever else a speaker and his listeners do or do not share as experience, they share their moments together, their place of meeting, and their mutual humanity. These, at the very least, are facts of shared experience and knowledge that make up part of the shaded, "overlapping" area in Figure 1. A term used in speech communication to identify these and all else that is shared because speaker and listeners *come together* is "rhetorical situation." We want to explain that concept further, because unless you understand it you are unlikely to see clearly what you have to *adapt* to, and what resources beyond yourself are available to you when you speak publicly. Let us begin with a simple example.

Suppose a group of people comes to hear a speaker who, it has been advertised, is prepared to speak on animal life in the Arctic region. Since the people are now in a place where this particular speaker is going to appear, there is a possibility for the speaker to, say, remind the listeners of what they know of polar bears and tell them things they did not know about the bears and other Arctic animals. The listeners can be changed because they have come to a place expecting to have new ideas given them. Now, the speaker appears. In a very real sense he is *entering* a situation where, by talking, he can *do* something that makes the world just a little different from what it was before he spoke. People are "out there" ready to become a little different from what they were. But these are not circumstances in which the speaker can simply open his mouth, say some words, and have the changes take place as though he had "stuck" something into the people's heads. Look at Figure 1 again. Though they share being together just now, with common interests in the Arctic, the listeners' knowledge of the Arctic is far less than the speaker's. The speaker must *connect* Arctic weather with weather that the listeners know about, polar bears with bears the listeners know about, Arctic seals with other seals or still other animals the listeners understand. He cannot *plant* what he knows into his listeners' minds. The best he can do is to stir up meanings. Only by using what is already there can he help listeners arrive at new concepts and fresh meanings. So, he must make a speech the listeners can understand *on the terms of their present and past experiences.*

There is more, however. Speaker and listeners are in a place, and things besides speech can happen in that place to change the experiences shared and used. Perhaps a train rumbles by outside making it hard for the speaker to be heard. That, too, will become a part of the general situation the speaker and the listeners have to cope with. Perhaps the season is winter and it is cold outside. That will be a fact of the situation which a speaker talking about the Arctic could *use*, because it is a fact of the situation which all share. So, *circumstances*, as well as what listeners have consciously in their minds, are included in the possibly useful features of situations in which speakers seek to change other people.

A less obvious example of speaking situations in which human change is possible occurs when you go to see a personnel officer of a business to be interviewed for a job. You and the personnel officer come together in a certain place. You exist together in a situation where the furniture is arranged in a certain way, the temperature is warm, cold, or just comfortable. There either have or have not been some previous arrangements which affect the character of *this* meeting between you and the personnel officer. The communication that takes place can create change. It is sure to make some difference in the interviewer's thoughts about your fitness for the job and in your thoughts about how much you would like the job. The situation is therefore a *rhetorical* one because it is one in which talk *can* create change. But you and the personnel officer can deal effectively with each other only to the extent that your talk concerns matters that fall within the experiences of *both* of you. Among those shared experiences is the experience of being together in this particular place, at this time, because a job is open.

*A speech must incorporate the shared experiences of speaker and listener.*

Every communicator must direct communication toward areas of shared experience. A peculiarity of *speech* as communication is that it takes place in a particular, shared time, at a particular location, and for particular reasons that bring speaker and listener together. To be successful, then, you as speaker are forced to direct your speaking toward the time and place and reasons for being together, as well as toward whatever other experiences your listeners share with you. In speech, time, place, and occasion give you special restraints and opportunities as you approach listeners. Let us put the point in a still different way, for it is crucial that you understand rhetorical situations if you are to understand the kinds of problems and opportunities public speakers always face.

*In the rhetorical situation lies the potential for change.*

There are many different kinds of situations in the world. There are situations in which we make idle talk, as when we meet by accident on a street. There are situations in which talk is inappropriate, as in the midst of a symphonic concert. There are situations in which changes, but not what we would call social changes, occur, such as football games, horse races, and work in scientific laboratories. But there are also situations in which something has made people ready to be changed in some degree. Our concern is with those situations where *speech* could cause the change. We are concerned with situations that are *rhetorical* because, if appropriate things are said in appropriate ways, the act of speaking can bring into being the changes for which readiness already exists. It can do so not just because there are people present but because they are subject to influences from all their circumstances. Of these, speaking is the force that brings other forces together in ways that make listeners want to understand and believe what the speaker proposes.

These are some dimensions of a "rhetorical situation" as Lloyd F. Bitzer has described it. We have simplified his description, but we have hoped to make clear that when you speak to other people in a rhetorical situation there is *more* to be considered and *more* to be worked with than just your own person and the bodies and minds of your listeners. Professor Bitzer defines a rhetorical situation as a "complex of persons, events, objects, and relations presenting an actual or potential exigence" that can be changed by "creation of discourse which changes reality through the mediation of thought and action."[4] As synonyms for "exigence" you could use "need" or "readiness." For "mediation of thought and action" you can read "creating social change" or "changing perceptions." Bitzer's notion is that when you speak, you move into a kind of social system where you and everyone else are influenced by everything that makes up what Schramm would call "fields of experience." You, a person with a past, enter a world which is someone else's. Can you make yourself understood and believed in this world of people who know only *their* pasts and what *this* moment in *this* place and *these* surroundings have taught them?

An old fashioned way of thinking is to ask, "*Who* is listening?" If the answer is, "About thirty-five people under the age of twenty-three, two-thirds male and one-third female, among whom fifteen are Black, fifteen are Caucasian, and five are Puerto Rican," what shall you say? You really have no answer. Professor Bitzer argues, in effect, that you must ask what this collection of people think they *need* from *you* as a *speaker*. You do not tell everyone what he or she wants to hear, as Professor Rein says Governor Romney did, to his loss, at Harvard (see p. 5). You *connect* what you feel *you* need to say *to* what they need at this moment, in this place, under these circumstances. All that is easy to say but harder to figure out. When you are about to enter such a situation, how shall you think?

Whenever you make public speech you need ways of thinking out what your opportunities and limits are. Figure 2 and an explanation of it may help you see the range of your possibilities. The *audience* in the figure represents all who com-

[4]Lloyd F. Bitzer, "The Rhetorical Situation," *Philosophy and Rhetoric*, I (January, 1968), pp. 1–14.

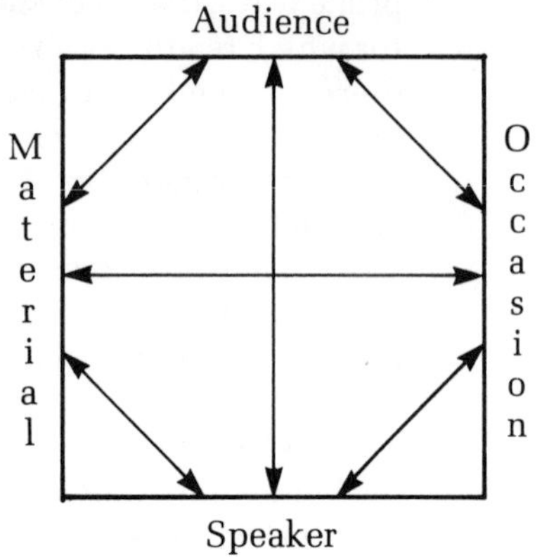


**FIGURE 2.**

prise the speaker's immediate "public." The *occasion* is the specific set of circumstances (psychological as well as physical) under which speaker and audience meet. *Material* is whatever the speaker knows about himself, the audience, his subject, and the occasion.

When you enter a rhetorical situation, all the relationships suggested by the double-headed arrows in the figure are yours to use, to secure the responses you need in order to create the change you seek in the communicative system that is represented by the entire figure. From the broadest point of view, the figure represents the resources you have to work with. These are resources *every* rhetorical speaker has in whatever speaking situation he enters. For example, if you are related to the audience as chairman to group members, you can use your "position" as something authorizing you to speak now *unless* the relation of audience to occasion is one that decrees that this is a time for conversation, not for formal speaking. Or, if you know the audience has assembled because this occasion might be one where the answer to an economic problem could be learned, you ought to infer that what you say ("material") must acknowledge and satisfy the audience's situational craving for economic answers.

The figure gives you the compass points of a rhetorical situation. By studying the different interrelationships that can exist, you can decide whether your situation is in fact a *rhetorical* one inviting public speech. If it is, you can see what you must do to adapt in order to create the changes you want. The figure suggests that you ought to review these questions before finally shaping and presenting any message as part of the rhetorical situation:

1. What is my relationship to the audience?
2. What is the audience's relationship to me?
3. What is the relationship between the audience and the occasion?
4. What effect does the occasion, the particular circumstance in which the speech is to be delivered, have upon the audience?
5. What influence does the audience exert upon my material, upon what I have to say?
6. What is the relationship of my speech content, my material, to the audience?
7. What is my relationship to my material? What do I as a person bring to my material to determine its final substance and form?
8. What effect does my material (my subject choice, the facts, opinions, and illustrations) have upon me as a person?
9. What is my connection with the occasion?
10. What is the effect of the occasion upon me as a speaker?
11. What influence does the occasion have upon my materials, upon what I intend to say?
12. What does the content of my speech do to modify the nature of the occasion?

In some situations some of these questions will be more important than others. Sometimes the best answers you can give to yourself will be only educated guesses. But in all public speech you will need to calculate the probable answers to as many of these questions as possible. Only by answering them can you understand *yourself* and your *ideas* as they are really going to be perceived in moments of actual talk.

## SUMMARY

In introducing this book we called attention to several very important but basic ideas about studying speech. We have tried, as we shall continue to do, to tell you the *why's* for whatever we suggest you do in studying and speaking. If you have understood us in this chapter, you know *why:*

1. Most of us overlook how much of our speaking takes place in situations where we "carry" the responsibility for creating particular kinds of social relations by means of talking for what turns out to be more than just a few moments.
2. It is not practical to act on the notions that effectiveness in speaking is simply a gift or talent, or that knowing your subject will solve everything, or that smoothing delivery will solve everything, or that pretending to be what we are not

can get us through successfully in rhetorical situations.

3. Treating the study of speech as a search for rules and devices is not as profitable as trying to locate generalizations from which to think about the requirements of many speaking situations and even of more general social situations.
4. The only safe way to approach public speaking is to conceive of yourself as entering rhetorical situations in which the relationships within a "complex of persons, events, objects" determine what can be accomplished by directing speech to that "complex."

Everything that follows in this book deals in one way or another with how to analyze rhetorical situations, prepare to act influentially within them, and, thereby, create changes in the people who are part of them. Very briefly put, the business of public speech is to create change in situations that already are or can be made open to change. Therefore, as you proceed with your study and practice, the single most important section of this chapter will prove to be Figure 2 and the related questions on pp. 14–15. We advise you to review those pages frequently.

## EXERCISES

*Written*

1. Keep a diary of two or three hours of your normal activities, noting all the occasions on which you found people, including yourself, speaking to others in relatively uninterrupted fashion with the aim of altering listeners' perceptions of their relationships to people, ideas, and things.
2. In anticipation of your first speech in your class, choose a subject you hope to speak on and analyze the class as a rhetorical situation for your speech. Answer the twelve questions posed on page 15 as far as possible. (Or form a group with four or five other members of the class and construct a general analysis of the class as a "system" in which rhetoric is going to occur.) Write a paragraph or two explaining what advantages and disadvantages you (or each member of your discussion group) will have in speaking in this situation.

*Oral*

1. Give a short talk in which you describe a specific rhetorical situation and point out aspects of it which you might have overlooked had you not attended a class or read this chapter.
2. Report to your classmates how many "public speeches" (as defined

in this chapter) you have given in the last twenty-four hours. Indicate where you were most and least successful and why.

3. Observe a public speaker. Describe his rhetorical situation and tell how well he met it.

# First Considerations

# 2

*Skill in public speaking comes from step-by-step practice.*

If you were learning to play billiards, write, play tennis, or perform a ballet step, your teacher and you would have a clear plan about how to proceed. You would consider what could be done in the "game" you were learning. Then you would set a goal for your first attempt at the game or art. Next you would make a try at doing what you decided to do. You and your teacher would then consider how close you came to your goal and, after that, you would set a new goal and try again. Again, you would consider "How did I do?" Following that, you would set still other goals and try another shot in billiards, write something different, work on a new move or stroke in tennis, or refine a familiar step in ballet or try a new one. Developing skill in public speech is the same. You consider what you might accomplish by speaking, set your goals, plan how to attain them, try out your plans, evaluate how well you did what you tried to do, and repeat the process. You learn from your successes and weaknesses. You study your possibilities anew and from this new understanding devise new goals and strategies for next time. In order that this essential process can begin early, you will no doubt be asked to make some talks very early in your speech course.

It would be easy to argue that you ought to know all that is in this book before trying to make a public speech, but that is not the way other arts and skills are learned. You can learn from doing if you begin early. That is why we shall in this chapter give some "first considerations" that will help you in first speeches. What we shall say here will be treated again later and in more detail, but at the beginning of your study-practice program you ought to think in a preliminary way about listening, basic steps in preparing a public speech, preparing first assignments, modes of delivery, stage fright, and oral rehearsals.

## LISTENING

People speak in public because there are listeners. This would be too obvious even to say if beginning speakers did not so often ignore their listeners. But they do. So, before you speak you need to give some serious thought to what listeners are like and how they listen. Because these are "first considerations," we shall focus on listeners in classrooms.

In a speech class you will be concerned with listening in three ways: (1) you will have to *adapt* your ideas to the ways people listen; (2) you will be listening to your colleagues both as an "ordinary listener" and as a fellow student who ought to help *evaluate* your friends' communicative skills; and (3) because speaking will be the main business in your class, you will have opportunities to train yourself as a listener, anticipating situations you will face outside your speech class.

*Listening differs from situation to situation.*

The first thing you ought to think about is general. People do not always listen in the same ways. Their reasons for listening differ from situation to situation, so their ways of attending and responding differ. When one of your colleagues or your instructor speaks in your classroom, will you listen to gain information? To absorb material on which you expect to be tested later? To be entertained? To assess arguments and interpretations of facts? To hear another "side" of an argument or case? To get information about a single point, or to understand a subject as a whole? To judge how far a speaker achieved all he or she could under the circumstances? Sometime in your life you have listened for each of these reasons, and your listening habits changed as your reasons changed.

It would make sense in some circumstances to say you listened for more than one of the reasons implied by the questions we have posed. But ordinarily some *one* of these reasons is *primary* when you listen seriously and closely. So it should be.

It is only when people have consciously or subconsciously determined a *primary* reason for listening that they listen efficiently. Haven't you listened to your parents to discover what was *behind* rather than *in* the words? Did you always get their real meanings that way? Probably not, and that says something about how one must speak to be effective.

In speaking you need to devise specific ways of getting your listeners to listen as *you* want them to. Accordingly, we are going to say something about matters like purpose statements, main points, and planning as we move through this chapter. How you handle such phases of speaking determines whether you can bring your listeners to hear you in ways that serve *your* purposes rather than their imaginations. And, of course, you are going to be a listener more often than a speaker, so you ought to think about how you can discipline your own listening, too.

What you will notice as a listener will generally depend on what you have allowed yourself to listen for. Isn't it true that if you listen to the "Johnny Carson Show" or some other comedy program on television, you keep asking yourself where the next "gag" is going to occur? Isn't it true that when you think someone is trying to give you advice you wait for answers to a question like "What should I *do*?" Whether you are conscious of it or not, you usually listen for particular kinds of content that you have "set" yourself to receive; other kinds of content seem irrelevant to your needs and interests in those moments. This is the way of all purposive listening; and if you are to train yourself to listen as efficiently as possible, you will need to discipline—to consciously control—your ordinary habits of listening.

*Listening comprehensively is a difficult task.*

You can, when you want to, decide what to listen for and discipline your senses according to your decision. It is hard work, but it is often worthwhile. Louis Nizer says, "So complete is this concentration [of listening comprehensively] that at the end of a court day in which I have only listened, I find myself wringing wet despite a calm and casual manner."[1] If you are to take in the information a speaker gives, weigh its sense, and consider whether it is best for your interests and/or the speaker's purpose, you, too, will have to exert effort to keep your attention from wandering. This is what we mean by "listening comprehensively." To listen comprehensively you will find you have to exclude certain stimuli that impinge on your senses. A flickering light, a noisy radiator, the sound of a truck are all stimuli that compete for your attention. Other distractions may come from the speaker. He may fidget, speak

[1]Louis Nizer, *My Life in Court* (New York: Doubleday, 1961), pp. 297-298.

monotonously, or present an imperfectly organized train of thought. Then, you will be tempted to think about the interfering stimuli and about the speaker's problems, or your own, instead of about what the speaker actually says. But if you do that, you cannot know how well what he said suited his purposes and why or why not. Those are the crucial questions you need to help answer in a speech class.

Interference in listening can also occur *within you*. An early study of students' listening, judged by how much data they took in from a series of ten-minute talks, showed that the following capacities significantly affected students' abilities to hear and remember:

1. Intelligence.
2. Linguistic capacities (like reading ability, grammatical knowledge, and vocabulary).
3. Ability to make inferences.
4. Ability to see organizational plans in talks.
5. Level of fatigue and energy.
6. Factors having to do with listeners' *attitudes* toward what they were hearing: (a) their interest in the subject discussed, (b) their emotional adjustment to the speaker's content, (c) their curiosity about the subject, and (d) their recognition of the significance of the subject.

It was also found that the students who tried to concentrate on improving their listening learned more than those who did not.[2] As far as we know, no evidence has since challenged these findings. The implications for you are that, whatever your natural intellectual and linguistic abilities, you will miss a good deal of the talk around you if you do not deliberately try to perceive the reasoning, the organization, the possible interest and significance of what is talked about. If you do not do these things, your own attitudes and careless thought processes will work against your awareness of what is really going on when colleagues speak.

As a listener-critic-helper in a speech class you need to think deliberately about each speaker's purpose, watch for *how* ideas relate to purposes and to each other, try as hard as you can to be interested and curious about the subject, and analyze *why* relations among ideas were not as clear as they could have been or the subject as interesting as it could have been. If you can report *how* and *why* you responded as you did to a friend's speaking, you will help him, because each speaker must

---

[2]Ralph G. Nichols, "Factors in Listening Comprehension," *Speech Monographs*, XV (No. 2, 1948), pp. 154–163.

improve by preventing specific weaknesses in the future and by reproducing his best strategies. He cannot know what those weaknesses and strengths are without the help of alert, friendly listeners who will report candidly. We once discovered a situation in which a professional speaker was heard by a full dozen very friendly listeners. Some unobtrusive research revealed that the dozen friends understood the speaker's main point in *eleven* different ways! Yet none of the "friends" was willing to tell the speaker he needed to be clearer about stating his purposes and organizing his speeches! In our opinion, that is not very friendly, candid listening and support for a speaker. We are simply saying you can do better than that for your colleagues if you discipline your listening, making clear to yourself what you are listening *for* and *how* you are affected.

By trying to discipline your listening in your speech class, you can also improve your alertness to speaking outside your class. In any speech class, many kinds of organizational patterns will be used. Notice the different ways you have to take notes to get quick records of these differently structured talks. When a speaker gives you evidence and *then* conclusions, you record what he said in one way. When he gives conclusions first and then supports or amplifies them, you have to take notes differently. It will be practical for you to study how you need to listen differently to these two styles of presentation because college lectures come in both, and other, forms, as do reports, essays, and books. You can train yourself to process different forms of information if you deliberately explore your alternatives in listening as you hear talks in a speech class.

You can also learn from observation how nonverbal behavior reveals attitudes, how it causes people to listen more

*Communication can also come through nonverbal behavior.*

attentively, or how it reflects levels of attention. Note the kinds of bodily actions that alert listeners to the importance of what is being said. What postures or stances do speakers use to hold attention? What gestures make listeners pay attention to especially important points? By watching, you can learn what you need to try to do as a speaker. As you watch, do you see listeners nodding their heads in agreement, closing their eyes as they think of what you are saying (or as they nap!), looking at the ceiling in boredom, or smirking or sneering when they disagree with what you are saying? From what you learn by carefully observing listeners you can prepare yourself to answer an important question about your own speaking: how will I know when I am succeeding and when the audience is slipping away? If you can answer that question *before* you speak, you will be better able to adjust to what you see *as* you speak.

To sum up, you and your colleagues will learn most in your speech class if you all listen to each other with clear, conscious purpose and seek to make clear reports to one another about *what* happened as you listened and *why*. Your key question as a listener needs to be: "*Why* did what was said affect me and others as it did?" Every answer you can make to that question will help other speakers acquire knowledge of how to speak more effectively, will show you what resources are open to you as a speaker, and will add to your capacity to take in all that is important when you listen to speaking that takes place outside your classroom.

## BASIC PROCEDURES IN SPEECH PREPARATION

In later chapters we shall explain fully how you can prepare yourself for occasions when public speech is expected of you. Here we want to consider some procedures that are important in preparing even the brief, first talks expected in most speech courses.

### Subjects and Goals

*Subject or goal can be chosen first.*

In classroom speaking it does not matter much whether you first decide to talk about drug abuse and then decide your goal is to make the *extent* of the problem clear, or settle first that you will make the extent of *some* problem clear and then decide that drug abuse will be the problem you will discuss. Outside classrooms your choices are not likely to be this "loose." There, subjects for speaking tend to be "assigned" in the sense that you are likely to be asked to speak on some specific topic or you will decide you must speak on a particular topic because the rhetorical situation requires it. In any case, *having a subject* and *setting a goal for your treatment of it* are unavoidable, first requirements in speech preparation. Since in this chapter we are trying to prepare you for first speeches in a course, we shall assume that finding a subject to speak about comes first in your preparation and setting your goal comes second.

*Choosing Your Subject.* A class assignment may simply say, "Talk about anything you want to." In that case there are several things you should consider in a deliberate way.

*Six factors must be considered in choosing a subject.*

1. The first thing to consider is your own experience. It is unwise, especially in first speeches, to try to talk about subjects concerning which you know absolutely nothing about before beginning preparation. But experience is not the whole answer. We think of the student who had much experience with turtles. He was a turtle expert. He spoke first on diamond-back turtles. The class was fascinated with his breadth of knowledge, enthusiasm, and thoroughness. Experience served him well. The second time, he chose to talk about snapping turtles. He was still interested in turtles and he was still experienced, but the audience had heard enough of turtles and turned its attention elsewhere. In this case experience and personal interest did not serve.

   We also think of the students who, told to consider their personal experiences in arriving at subjects, gave speeches on "my summer job as a milkman" and "my days as a lifeguard." Their subjects were not well received, though the speakers had experience and enthusiasm. What they had to say was trite and thus incapable of stimulating their audiences to think.
2. Prior knowledge is a second factor to consider. If you do not know your subject, you must learn before you have earned the right to take your listeners' time. Remember, 5 minutes spent before an audience of 20 people consumes 100 minutes of the world's time. You will need to choose a subject you already know about or about which you can know before your speaking engagement.
3. The availability of material becomes a third determinant in choosing a subject. Do not choose speech subjects without making a preliminary survey of the resources for obtaining the information you will need. We will mention possible

sources of speech materials on p. 29 and will discuss them further in Chapter Four. Unless you make a preliminary inventory you may find that there is just not enough material to warrant a speech.

4. Consider your audience as you choose any subject. Their expectations or special interests and past experiences may rule out some subjects. Remembering this could direct your thoughts to other subjects that would be of greater interest.
5. Consider other elements of the rhetorical situation. Review the questions on p. 15. Doing so may help you find a subject and help you evaluate the promise of subjects you are considering. Consider, too, special aspects of your classroom speaking: the time allowed, the assignment, and your colleagues' special expectations. These can both guide you toward subjects and give you grounds for evaluating subjects you have found.
6. Finally, consider that something ought to be gained by both you and your listeners from any public speech you make. Listeners want some "news." If you choose subjects carefully, you can stretch their brains a bit even in a very short talk. A really good subject ought to be intellectually challenging.

First speeches are usually short. Even so, if what you talk about is based on your experience, if you have investigated further in preparation, and if the subject is appropriate to your particular audience and the situation, there will be a possibility of giving listeners a bit of "news." Indeed, how you treat a subject is usually more important than what the subject is. If you have great difficulty finding something to talk about in your first speeches, look forward to Chapter Four, where some special suggestions for "digging up" subjects are given. Our next concern, here, must be with making clear in your own mind what responses you ought to seek in first speeches.

*Determining the Response You Want.* As soon as you know even in general terms what you would like to speak about, your thoughts should go to what kind of response you want from your listeners. Notice that, according to "The Biography of a Speech," which appears in the Appendix of this book, this was a very early concern for Randy Cohn. She chose her general subject early, but she reconsidered—indeed changed—her goal before she reported her settled subject and goal to her instructor. As with her, a very basic question you must settle early is: what do I want my listeners to *do* as the result of hearing me? Do you want them simply to understand and believe the information you will give? If so, your own personal sense of purpose will be: "I want to give information; it will be enough if they understand and believe what I tell them." On the other hand, you may want them to form beliefs they have not had before, or you may want them to *act* either on beliefs they already hold or on something new that you will say. Then, your sense of personal purpose will be something like: "I want to persuade them (that x is *true* or that they should *do* what I shall ask them to do)." These are the two most common kinds of purposes speakers have and the two kinds of responses they most often seek: to inform and to persuade.

*The most common goals are to inform and to persuade.*

These two goals and their associated purposes relative to specific audiences are not, of course, mutually exclusive. You may wish to inform listeners but hope to entertain them during certain moments of your talk. Or you may want to persuade them of something but find there are things you will have to explain in order to do so. It is not uncommon to have overlapping purposes even in short talks, but *one* kind of response ought to be the main one you seek. If a single purpose does not dominate your preparation and speaking, you are apt to confuse your listeners—as Randy Cohn confused her instructor and her listeners by including so much history (informing) that her persuasive goal was overshadowed. (See pp. 237–239.)

The reason you must become very clear in your own mind about exactly what response you want when you talk is a simple but basic and practical one: neither you nor your listeners can think clearly about a subject unless you and they understand the *chief* reason for thinking about it at all. The best way to clarify your own mind about these matters is to create and carefully phrase a *central idea* for every talk you give.

*Locating Central Ideas.* When you have decided what you want your listeners to *do* as the result of hearing you, your next step ought to be to frame a formal statement that expresses pointedly the main thought to which they are to respond. Whether you call this formal statement a "central idea," "a thesis," or a "subject sentence" is not very important. What is important is that you create a clear statement that says exactly what your subject is and what your speaking is intended to accomplish. You should be able to express an idea that will function within your talk as the hub of a wheel from which supporting spokes (main points of the speech) extend or as the apex of a pyramid supported by blocks of specific information.

*The central idea of every speech must be clearly stated.*

It is not because a pair of stuffy professors says so that you need to frame a clear central idea for each bit of public speech you utter. You must do it because of the ways people listen. In Chapter One and again in discussing listening we pointed out that what people listen *for* predetermines what they will hear. Your need as a speaker is to help your listeners to listen for what you want them to attend to. Whether you announce your central idea or let hearers know it indirectly, those who listen to you need to be clear about what thought and what goal are dominant in what you say. Phrase a subject sentence that covers your subject and purpose, and you can give listeners the guidance they need. If you do not, you may be unhappily surprised to learn that you said "Pick your teeth" when you meant to say "Care of teeth saves expense and pain."

*Phrasing Subject Sentences.* It is scarcely possible to frame a clear, guiding statement for talk without putting your central idea into a clear, complete sentence. We shall call that sentence a "subject sentence," though other names for it are also common. When you intend to inform listeners, your subject sentence ought to express a clear *assertion*. When you intend to persuade, your subject sentence ought to express a *proposition*—usually containing "ought" or "should." Suppose your subject is the community theatre in the United States. For the commonest rhetorical purposes you might formulate subject sentences like these:

*Informing* (to evoke acceptance or understanding): The history of the community theatre movement in the United States shows that its purpose has been chiefly cultural.

*Persuading* (to evoke support for a course of action): The federal government ought to subsidize community theatres.

*A subject sentence serves three purposes.*

Notice that each sentence does three things: (1) reveals the subject of the speech, (2) states the central idea clearly, and (3) clearly implies the kind of response sought. With this kind of subject sentence, you can scarcely become confused about what you need to do in building your talk; and if you are guided by such a statement, your listeners are unlikely to be confused about what you want from them. Since you are unlikely to try to entertain listeners in first speeches, we shall defer discussion of subject sentences for such speeches until Chapter Seven.

It is wise to tell your listeners outright what your subject sentence is unless there are special reasons for delaying this revelation. One such reason can be that the audience is doubtful or hostile and might be put off by learning your goal before you have an opportunity to give reasons for their acceding to it. In any case, it is as much for your own guidance as for your listeners' sense of understanding that you need to compose subject sentences carefully.

As you prepare first speeches you will need to remember two cautions about phrasing those statements. Some *one* idea ought to dominate in each of your talks, so beware of compound statements. An "and" or a "but" between two clauses in a subject sentence is a danger signal. They are signs that you may be stumbling into preparing two talks instead of one. And guard against mistaking a statement of a subordinate, supporting point for the *main* thought you want to develop in your talk. "Community action is important, as was shown by the Hill District's clean-up campaign" probably expresses a supporting example to be used within a talk on community action. Ask yourself, "Is *that* the *whole* idea I want to leave with them?" In the above example the answer would probably be that this is one of several ideas the speaker could use to make a major point like, "Encouragement of community action programs ought to be a major feature of our urban planning."

*Supporting Your Central Idea.* When you have chosen a subject, determined what response you want from your listeners, and phrased a clear subject sentence, you are ready to look for materials that will add detail to, or prove and reinforce your major thought. What kinds of materials amplify or prove? Generally speaking, the best are: (1) facts, (2) testimony, (3) examples, whether extended or brief, real or hypothetical, (4) stories, (5) statistics, (6) comparisons, contrasts, and analogies, (7) definitions, and (8) audio-visual aids. With your subject sentence framed, your next move is to find whatever of these materials you can and from them select those that most interestingly and sharply amplify or prove your central idea in ways that will get the response you want. This is a point at which you will do well to remember a French saying that runs in English: "The art of boring lies in saying everything."

*There are many kinds of supporting materials from which to choose.*

If you have not spoken very often, you will probably do well to begin with simple, one-point speeches. Your procedure will then be substantially as follows.

## PREPARING A FIRST ASSIGNMENT

1. Choose a subject that meets the requirements we have discussed on pp. 24–25.
2. Select from within that subject a simple, single idea which you can clarify for your audience or which you would like them to accept. Sometimes you can locate such an idea by sketching out a longer speech on the subject and then choos-

ing one main point for development in the talk you are going to give now.

3. Phrase your chosen idea in a clear subject sentence.
4. Use just one structural pattern (method of development). For example, amplify or support your main idea by a chronologically arranged series of subordinate ideas, or by cause-effect reasoning, or by describing a problem. The point is to keep your scheme of development as simple as you can in order to concentrate on "the basics" of speech preparation and presentation.
5. Consult at least some sources of information in addition to your personal experience as you search for pertinent supporting-amplifying information.
6. Make an outline of even this brief speech. It may consist of only six or eight items, but you will be getting useful practice in organizing clear units of thought.
7. Be sure that each informational item you put in the outline bears unmistakably on your subject sentence. As you check up on these relationships, begin to invent ways of *saying* to your audience what those relationships are and why they are important *to the listeners.*
8. Practice giving the whole short speech with an appropriate introduction and conclusion. Do not try to "learn" the speech. Practice to invent ways of expressing the ideas, in planned order, with their relationships clear, and their importance to the listeners emphasized. You ought to end practice with more than one way of doing each of these things. That will assure you that *some* effective way of speaking will come to mind naturally as you finally make the talk.

9. When you have given the talk to your audience, test your achievement by asking whichever of these questions is appropriate: "Does my audience understand my point better now that I have spoken?" "Does my audience more nearly accept my point as I proposed it?"

Let us back up now to see how these nine steps would be literally carried out with an actual subject. Let us suppose you have decided that a *major* speech might be given on the subject sentence: "We need to support mental health organizations better than we do." How would you find a single, simple main idea for a first speech? If you asked yourself what the main headings of a major speech on this subject would be, the following might occur to you:

I. Anxiety is a disturbing phenomenon.
II. Anxiety is widespread in our society.
III. Mental health organizations help people to reduce their anxieties.
IV. Mental health organizations deserve more help than we give them.

Any of these four points could be used as a central idea for a short speech, although the fourth is least promising because it depends for support on the other three. If you chose the first of these points for a one-point speech, you would need to prepare a simple outline or plan of its development. It might look like this.

**SUBJECT SENTENCE:**

*Anxiety is a disturbing phenomenon.*

**SUPPORTING MATERIAL:**

*Definition*

1. Harold Basowitz and Roy Grinker define anxiety as ". . . the conscious and reportable experience of intense dread and foreboding, conceptualized as internally derived and unrelated to any external threat."

*Statistics*

2. A recent article in the *National Observer* cited the estimate that from fifty to eighty percent of all visits to doctors are by people with complaints for which no physical cause exists.

*Example*

3. Dependence on drugs, psychotherapy, occult religions, and "cures" are all indicators that numbers of people experience anxieties they cannot explain physically or in reference to specific external dangers.

*Example*

4. The Kennecott Copper Corporation found unexplained absenteeism among employees so widespread and so severe that the corporation had to institute its own mental health program as an answer to the problem.

*Authority*

5. The admission rates of state and county mental hospitals, and their annual out-patient services for psychiatric problems, have risen steadily over the last twenty years according to reports of the National Institute of Mental Health published in the *World Almanac.*

A comparable plan for a one-point speech amplifying a proverb might be outlined like this.

**SUBJECT SENTENCE:**

*Ecological experience today exemplifies only too well Confucius's saying: "Those whose care extends not far ahead will find their troubles near at hand."*

**SUPPORTING MATERIAL:**

*Examples*

1. Our energy shortages can be traced to too little long-range care about:
   a. hasty depletion of oil reserves,
   b. research into clean combustion processes using coal, and
   c. development of safer processes of producing nuclear energy.

*Generally Accepted "Fact"*

2. Today's food shortages in the world result from yesterday's uncontrolled growth in population.

*Example*

3. The seriousness of air and water pollution was foreseeable more than a generation ago.

*Authority and Example*

4. Fortunately our Department of Transportation is investigating possible climatic effects of supersonic aircraft, according to Dr. Alan Grodercker.

**CONCLUSION:**

All nations must learn to be among those "whose care extends far ahead," or we can only expect new ecological troubles in the near future.

A finished outline for either of these imagined talks would, of course, show what would be said in both introduction and conclusion. If the talk were to have a title, that too would be shown in the outline.

*Outlines serve four purposes.*

Outlines like these will help you even in very short speeches. They (1) let you see quickly whether you have enough amplifying-supporting material to make your subject sentence clear and believable; (2) allow you to check and recheck different sequences of thoughts so they will be in the best order in your final plan; (3) make it easy for your instructor or a friend to examine your plan and make suggestions for further improvements before you speak; and (4) give you a handy, easy-to-read plan which you can review and rehearse from before speaking in public. First speeches can be a bit unnerving. One of the very best protections against "nerves" is to have a full, easy-to-comprehend plan that you can understand at a glance while speaking. Outlining is simply a way of making plans as *visible* as possible.

## MODES OF DELIVERY

Your early classroom talks are likely to be presented *extemporaneously.* Talks recited from memory or read like legal documents would sound silly, wouldn't they? Besides, speaking extemporaneously is the best way to begin learning to speak easily and directly. Other ways may seem to you easier or "safer," but they are not. You can deliver talk *impromptu,* by *reading* what you have to say, from *memory,* or *extemporaneously.* Memorizing puts an extra burden on your mind and most people read speeches badly. These are reasons enough to put aside memorizing and reading in first speeches. We shall discuss the proper use of these methods in Chapter Nine and consider here only the differences between impromptu and extemporaneous speaking.

*Extemporaneous speaking is the best mode of delivery.*

As the terms are used in speech communication, *impromptu* refers to speaking for which no formal preparation is made except at the moments of speaking; *extemporaneous* refers to speaking which has been planned with considerable care but not memorized or otherwise formally "set" in word-by-word fashion.

You will do considerable formal and informal impromptu speaking in your speech class—during class and group discussions, in short speaking exercises, in commenting on other people's speaking. The basic things you can learn from experience in impromptu speaking are how to focus quickly on a central idea, how to test amplifying ideas in a speedy if not very thorough manner, and how to adapt thoughts to people on the spur of the moment. But you are unlikely to develop these skills in speaking impromptu unless you have first trained yourself at greater leisure through extemporaneous speaking. Moreover, few impromptu speeches are as well designed as speaking can be, unless the speaker is thoroughly conversant with his subject and has already evolved sound, habitual ways of handling the ideas. These are reasons you will probably be asked to prepare your first regular speaking assignments for *extemporaneous* presentation.

The nine steps of preparation we outlined in the previous section of this chapter constitute your best course when preparing to speak extemporaneously. With this kind of preparation you can be at your best as a direct, thinking, interested communicator. The extemporaneous method of speaking gives you freedom to adjust to rhetorical situations and opportunity to be spontaneous, but not offhanded, in language. Most important, you can talk conversationally with your listeners while at the same time working from plans devised specifically for them.

The object in extemporaneous talk is to be yourself—in an efficient way. Come back once more to the analogy with sports, which we have used before. A tennis player *learns* certain moves that are required. He or she makes these moves *habitual*. The player also thinks about the next opponent and tries to devise specific strategies that will work against that opponent's habits, strengths, and weaknesses. Now the player is ready for the match. The moves originally established as habits will occur automatically when needed. The player will consciously use specially planned moves, foreseen and practiced for play with *this* opponent. But during the match the player will also be analyzing the opponent's play and consciously trying to devise new strategies. Perhaps he will even need to change or abandon some of his earlier plans or even try to change some of his habits. Overall, however, his play will be partly learned, partly planned but adaptable, and partly the result of instantaneous adaptations to unforeseen requirements.

This is precisely the character of expert, extemporaneous speaking. Your best oral skills, learned since childhood, are the bases of your talk. A plan for *this* rhetorical situation is the new resource you create and practice. But you must be tuned to the rhetorical situation and its unexpected features so you are ready to create new strategies as your relationship with your listeners requires.

The trouble with memorizing—which so many beginning speakers think is "safer"—is that it confines you to a single plan, usually to a single set of words, and restricts your capacity to adapt to what happens in your relationship with listeners. So does reading what you have to say. Besides, reading draws your attention to papers and away from your listeners. In impromptu speaking, you lack the advantage of a preplanned strategy "for this game" and are wholly dependent on your basic oral skills and on instantaneous adaptation. Extemporaneous speaking, based on planning such as we have described, is by far your best method of delivery in first speeches. You get the security of systematic planning, the freedom to change as you need to, and, most important, you learn quickly that you *can* deal with an audience in purposeful but natural ways. Actually, once you are used to speaking extemporaneously, you will probably come to like its freedom with security and the rapport you can develop with listeners.

## STAGE FRIGHT

We come now to a topic—stage fright—which, frankly, we would not even discuss as a "first consideration" if there were not so much mythology about it. Some candid talk about the subject seems necessary before you make your first efforts at public speech.

*Stage fright is not something to worry about.*

The first fact about "stage fright" or "speech fright" is that it is a universal experience. And the second fact about it is that the experience called stage fright is *not* something to *worry* about, however foolish that statement may seem to you at first.

Stage fright is something all serious speakers who care about what they are doing experience. One of your authors experiences it every academic term in the first moments of meeting each new class—and this after forty years of teaching! The real point is, however, that on the day when starting a new class no longer scares him at least a little, he will be the poorer teacher for it.

Just what is this experience? You have probably had it, and if not, you will. But have you *analyzed* what happened, and *why*? If you have experienced stage fright, the experience was probably something like this. Some situation demanded that you carry the burden for oral communication in a formal interview or standing alone before an audience. You then discovered that your knees were shaking, that your mouth felt dry, that your voice was a little unsteady, and that your heart beat more swiftly than usual. You may also have been aware that the palms of your hands perspired, and you may even have felt as if twenty-two butterflies were using your stomach as a football field.

Now, what did you *do* in those moments—whether they occurred before or during speaking? You probably did what most of us do until we learn better—became preoccupied with getting rid of the "shakes" and with such tasks as trying to get your tongue and lips comfortably wet again. You probably did *not* concentrate on doing anything about your fear—the cause of it all.

*Stage fright is partly physiological.*

Anyone who cares seriously about an important communication is anxious about it. That anxiety or fear causes certain physiological changes. What literally happens is that the flow of epinephrine (adrenaline) accompanying anxiety sets off additional changes. Blood pressure, rate of respiration, and nerve conductivity increase. More blood sugar furnishing energy enters the system. More thyroxine may be secreted, speeding up the burning of the blood sugar. More oxygen is taken into your blood. More poisons are removed from your system. As a result of these changes, fatigue probably lessens and you may experience the kind of increase in strength that athletes so often report experiencing when they get "psyched up" for a contest. The "problem" with stage fright is not that bodily changes occur. If stage fright has been a "problem" for you, it was because you *worried* about these physiological changes and you thereby *made* them "serious" annoyances and "causes" for more fear concerning your capacity to get on with your real business.

If you experience stage fright in anticipation of speaking or during speaking, a certain amount of the bodily change and the anxiety generating the change ought to be taken as natural evidence of being "psyched up" about the job to be done. To the extent you accept quivers, dryness of mouth, and a sense of unusual nervous energy as natural for you and everyone else, these consequences of proper anxiety become resources that actually help you along as soon as you plunge into the far more serious business of communicating earnestly. If you believe your physical experiences are caused by an excess of fear or anxiety—beyond that which ought to be there to make you as strong and alert as possible—*there are things you can do to allay fears* that are the causes of undue physical change.

*There are three ways to control stage fright.*

First, *planning* before speaking reduces the reasons for being afraid in speaking situations. We have indicated this before, but it is time to add that *preparing with your future listeners in your mind's eye* is a major way of combating fear. As with the tennis player we just discussed, a "game plan" is something tangible and rehearsable, so it gives security. More important, however, if you plan with your listeners and the actual situation constantly in your thoughts, the situation and the listeners will not seem new when you finally meet them in reality. This is no exaggeration. You *can* "have been there before" if your preparation takes your whole speaking experience into account in your imagination. Then, there will be a great deal less to be fearful of than if your preparation were otherwise.

Second, mere experience with speaking situations reduces fear of them. It does not eliminate all anxiety if you really care what you do, but it does equate the effects of anxiety with athletes' "psyching up" processes. One of the functions of a speech class is to give you the opportunity to get enough speaking experience so you will know that "making a speech" is not really as risky or laborious a task as inexperienced people usually think. Only experience can teach that lesson. When it is learned, more causes of fear will fall away, the sensations of stage fright will diminish naturally, and the positive strengths of normal tensions will reinforce communicative efforts.

A third way to control fear and its demoralizing effects is to expect some anxiety—some degree of stage fright. Every accomplished speaker, singer, actor, and most athletes *know* tension is necessary to be at one's best. You ought to be concerned about whether audiences will respond as your goals require, and you ought to be pleased that your body can and will produce a little extra adrenaline to help you enter upon important human relationships energetically. And, of course, if you *expect* to be "up" for speaking engagements, you will experience little anxiety that you cannot manage constructively.

By choosing wisely and carefully what you will say, you can approach speaking situations with confidence rather than fear. The right preparation is your best protection against disturbing stage fright. Practice will further reduce fears of taking responsibilities in significant speech situations. And by accepting anxiety as a reflection of your *proper* concern for your task, you can turn anxiousness into controlled motivation for communicating better. It is not at all cruel of us to say we hope you never reach a point where the prospect of speaking in public does not make you tense, at least in anticipation. And we are only being charitable to ourselves in saying that if you do reach that point of unconcern, we hope we, at least, will be spared having to hear you.

## REHEARSAL AND ATTITUDES TOWARD SPEAKING

*A good speech requires wise rehearsal.*

In this section, we shall discuss the *how's* of rehearsing for extemporaneous speaking. In several connections we have mentioned the importance of practicing extemporaneous speeches before presenting them to audiences. But *how* you rehearse makes a difference. Wise rehearsal yields command, confidence, and flexibility. The suggestions below will help you, if you follow them, in preparing for any extemporaneous speaking.

1. Read through your written plan, fixing your mind on the succession of main points. Reread it, this time concentrating not only on the main points but on the details supporting each.
2. Still referring to your outline, speak through the speech in whatever words happen to come. Talk out loud, not under your breath. You will find it helps to stand up and face an imaginary audience. Try out gestures as you verbalize. Get through the whole speech. If you bungle a part, go right on to the end without stopping to straighten out the troublesome section. Come back to that when you have finished running through the entire speech.
3. Without using your outline or any memoranda except those notes you will use on the platform, stand up and speak through the speech as before. If you can find a patient listener or group of listeners, so much the better.
4. When you can get through your total speech fairly well, time yourself and adjust the speech to the time allotted for your actual presentation. Such an adjustment may call for omissions or condensations, or it may call for additions or expansions of points. It is important to acquire a sense of time on the platform and develop the habit of keeping within time limits.
5. During preparation and just before speaking, renew your desire to share a worthwhile message with others. Remind yourself that the experience before you is not a "performance" but an opportunity. You have earned that opportunity through the knowledge you have acquired and your position as a respected human being in a communicating society.
6. Recall that your auditors are persons not very different from yourself, and that they want you to succeed.

7. Don't expect to avoid all tension. Some tension is good for you. Properly channeled tension can serve you positively by increasing your alertness and your available supply of energy.
8. As a general rule, avoid last-minute changes in your speech, especially during your maiden efforts. Do not add to uneasiness by entertaining misgivings about choices already made. Adapt to the moment and to other speakers but do not make changes that undermine the overall plan you established in your mind by systematic rehearsal.[3]

Oral rehearsal is insurance. Fluent discourse demands it. Speakers are often tempted to omit this important stage of speech preparation because of self-consciousness or because they are unwilling to take time for it. It is significant, however, that from ancient times to the present even the busiest of public figures who became known for effective speech have found the time to rehearse for major speeches. They have known what you should learn if you do not already know it: control over self and control over content are imperative when what you say is important, and both kinds of control are established through such oral rehearsal as we have described.

## AN OVERVIEW OF PREPARATION

In the foregoing pages we have emphasized the things a speaker ought to consider in preparing for a simple assignment requiring that he speak publicly. In concluding, we shall summarize the sequence of preparatory steps serious speakers have found it important to follow. Ordinarily you will need to do the following things in getting ready to speak to an audience:

1. Considering the nature of your audience and the occasion, decide what response you seek concerning the topic you have decided or been assigned to talk about.
2. Narrow or expand your topic until you have located the specific subject that will fit your capacities, your goal, and the requirements of the situation.
3. Wed your rhetorical purpose and your central idea in a clear-cut statement expressing unambiguously the coverage of what you will say and your reason for saying it.
4. Gather the variety of materials that will most strongly and

[3]Adapted from *Manual for Public Speaking, I*, p. 22, by H. A. Wichelns and others (1932) and *Manual for an Elementary Course* by H. A. Wichelns, G. B. Muchmore, and others, p. 19.

interestingly amplify or support what is expressed in your subject sentence.
5. Organize these materials into a structure which can be shown clearly and systematically in outline form.
6. Consider what kinds of language will best interrelate your materials to form a *whole* that interestingly asserts the basic message contained in your subject sentence.
7. If it is at all possible, prepare yourself to present your talk extemporaneously, so you can speak in an organized, informed way, yet spontaneously and adaptively.
8. As insurance for your plan and against stage fright, rehearse your speech orally to gain full control of the pattern of your ideas, alternative wordings, timing, and confident self-control.

By listing preparatory steps as we have, we do not mean you must invariably proceed in exactly the way our summary implies. For example, a speaker planning to talk about his recent experiences in a rehabilitation project in Peru need not pause very long over step 4, but he may have more trouble than some others in narrowing and focusing his discussion as called for in steps 1 and 2. A speaker assigned to report on the budget has step 1 settled for him, plus most of what is called for in steps 2 and 4. The speaker who has been in Peru may find it difficult to sift out irrelevant material to accomplish step 5. The speaker giving the budget report may find that there are standard forms for budget reports that accomplish most of step 5 for him. What we have presented are the normal preparatory procedures for *any* speaking in which you bear special responsibilities for creating and sustaining communication. The extent of your work in accomplishing each step will vary from subject to subject and situation to situation, but each of these eight speech problems must be settled somehow. Whether some have been taken care of by an "assignment" or by your own experience or by your listeners' expectations is something *you* must decide. That is your freedom and your burden as a communicator.

## SUMMARY

If you have read this chapter thoughtfully, you know the steps you need to take to prepare and give at least a short public speech. We have emphasized in a number of ways the importance of systematic preparation, and we have just made a final summary of the steps we have discussed elsewhere in detail. It is possible that our emphasis and your special interest in how to prepare *yourself* for speaking have obscured the fact with which we began this chapter: speakers have to function in certain predictable ways largely because *listeners* have certain special needs, desires, and problems when they hear a speech that continues over several minutes or longer. Planning helps you to keep "on track" when you speak, but that really would not be very important if listeners did not always need as much help as possible in *finding* the "tracks" their speakers lay down. A sharp sense of purpose helps you focus your effort, but that would not be very important if listeners did not constantly look for "the point of it all." Rehearsal and self-confidence make you more satisfied with your speaking efforts, but it is really less important that you be comfortable and confident than that your listeners see and hear in you someone who inspires confidence and trust because he seems to know what he is doing. In the final analysis all speaking is for the sake of listeners. We have concentrated on *you* in this chapter. That will get you started in your classroom speaking, but now it is time to turn again to the real reasons for all this effort—listeners and the situations in which we find them.

## EXERCISES

*Written*

1. Write down five simple, single ideas which you think would be good ones for development in a speech of two-three minutes.
2. Select a subject area. Frame a subject sentence for each of the rhetorical purposes: informing and persuading.
3. Listen carefully to a speech by one of your classmates. Take notes in outline form on what he is saying. Following the speech, compare your outline with the one the speaker used. Check to see (a) how accurately you noted what was said, and (b) how much you missed noting.

*Oral*

1. Deliver a three-minute speech in which you develop a single point that could be one of several main points in a longer speech. In developing your point use at least three different kinds of supporting material. In preparation, prepare a simple outline like that found on pages 30–32.
2. Prepare and deliver a brief speech on a proverb of your own choosing. Select at least five items to support its truth or falsity. In preparation devise a simple outline like that on pages 31–32.

# Understanding Your Rhetorical Situation

# 3

Whenever you speak seriously to someone, you expect some response. You speak because you want to be heard, understood, reacted to. So, if you are serious, you watch your listeners to "read" what they signal back to you. Such activity is often called "feedback." Everyone knows about this process, but many people forget it as soon as *responsibility* for speaking in public falls upon them. Few people stare out windows or study their shoes when in earnest private conversation, but many do just that while they make "reports" or give "public speeches." You have seen those people. You may have been one of them.

## OBSERVING RESPONSES

*Constant attention is required of a speaker.*

Our first point in this chapter is, thus, an obvious but often overlooked one. *You cannot understand your speaking situation or your listeners unless you give them constant attention.* A remote manner interferes with speech relationships. Even when you speak on the telephone you have to remain aware of your listener's presence "out there," at the other end of the line. This kind of awareness is so important to oral communicators that experienced radio and television speakers testify that their communication often deteriorates when there is no physically present audience to "read" and be stimulated by. Experimental evidence, too, indicates that (1) we need human "feedback" if we are to communicate "normally," and (2) we cannot adjust accurately and reasonably to speaking situations unless we "read" our listeners, actually or in imagination (as we do in telephone conversations).

## ADJUSTING TO LISTENERS' PREFERENCES

*A speaker must involve his listeners.*

What effective conversationalists and formal speakers seem to accomplish is to act on the premise that not even their own egos can be well served unless *listeners'* preferences and expectations are accommodated. To do this takes conscious, careful thinking—in advance of and during speaking. But anyone can make the adjustment *if* he will think seriously about what communicating with a particular group of listeners does and does not require of him. Here is an example of one student's efforts in this direction.

A student of landscape architecture whom we shall call Dick Barnes was in a first course in oral communication taught by one of your authors. Barnes was not especially effective orally. He knew it, but he also knew that in his chosen profession an important part of his success would depend on whether

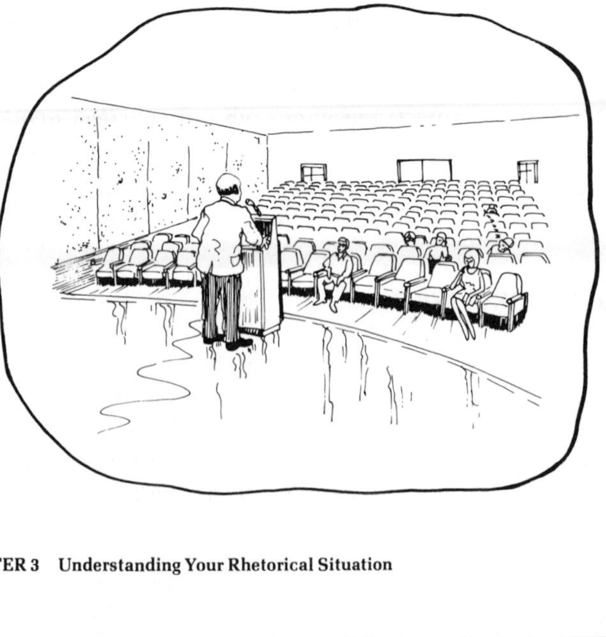

he could communicate abstract and technical concepts of landscape architecture in terms and images that nonspecialist customers could understand and appreciate. There was one other landscape architect in Barnes's class, so Barnes, his instructor, and the class laid out a special plan for Barnes. He would talk regularly about landscape architecture. His fellow architect would check on whether Barnes was "professionally sound," and the class would write down anything that confused or bored them when Dick talked.

Twice Dick tried to explain architectural concepts. Both times his colleague said he was "sound," but his other listeners wrote things like, "I didn't get it" and "You told me more than I wanted to know about that." Dick and his instructor concluded that Dick was not translating his concepts into "images" his listeners could "see." He was not associating his professional ideas with values the listeners could have feelings about. Dick decided to concentrate next time "on the visuals," and his third try worked. He was "sound," and he turned architectural "space values" into seeable, feelable realities. Here is part of what he said:

> Consider the area behind the Dairy Building. It's small, but it's a pleasing area to walk through. You can walk through it and have different experiences each time because of the very different kinds of plantings—shrubbery, flowers, trees. It's an enjoyable place to be. But so is the Mall. It has a canopy. You see it walking through. Half way up, ahead of you, the trees arch together. You are "inside," yet you're out-of-doors. And there at the center of the arch's end you see Pattee Library, with its straight columns. It completes the enclosing of the area. You feel "inside," but you know you're outside and free. These are things a landscape architect means when he says outdoor spaces have "value" or can be given "values." He's saying he tries to put things into outdoor space in such ways that you will say it's interesting to be there or that you like to be there. The value he's talking about is your good feeling; that's what he tries to create with his shapings and plantings.

There was no unmanaged abstraction here. Barnes made "space" and "value" real by transporting his listeners to campus spaces they all knew well enough to picture in their minds. Then he made them feel the "values" he spoke of; through words, he directed their eyes, movements, and feelings—in imagination. That is what the class had been wanting, though they had not been able to tell Dick directly. To solve Barnes's communicative problem had taken careful thinking about how listeners listen and how they assign worth to things they hear. Once Barnes reminded himself that his listeners had to *experience* space through imaginary seeing and feeling, he knew how to define "space values" in meaningful ways. He could thereby direct listeners' thoughts to the intellectual understanding he was trying to create.

When you speak, your goal is always to *direct* thought and feeling. But your directings have to be planned carefully, for listeners do not attend steadily to what speakers offer as the important ideas. Each of us has missed points in a college lecture, heard only half of a newscast item, and mixed up a set of directions because of free-associating thought or daydreaming. Notice the partly pertinent, partly irrelevant thoughts a juror recalls having had as the prosecuting attorney began to speak:

> As he faced us head-on, I noticed how weary he seemed and how arched his eyebrows were behind his glasses. His dogged determination had kept the case moving against the defendants for almost four months; this morning he suffered from laryngitis. I recalled my hostility toward him during the long days of jury selection. Now I listened intently.[1]

No doubt the juror "listened intently," but he was not thinking of the prosecutor's *ideas* in those seconds when he was reflecting on the lawyer's health, eyebrows, apparent weariness, and earlier behavior. But let every speaker take note and remember: this juror was listening as people really do listen. His attention was drifting in and out of the flow of ideas which the speaker was *steadily* creating through words and action.

*A speaker must capture his listeners' attention.*

The important implication of this example is that you dare not assume your listeners can give you unbroken attention. You must plan for and adapt to their tendency to "drift in and out" of attention to what you say. And you must guard against their fascination with details only loosely related to your subject. You will need to make all you say as inviting as possible, and you will need the means for continually gathering your listeners *back:* directing, redirecting, recapturing, and disciplining their wandering minds. In the moments of talk we have quoted, Dick Barnes was doing that expertly; he undoubtedly had better control over his listeners' experiences than the prosecuting attorney had over Mr. Chester's attention.

We have been underscoring two basic facts about speaking: (1) unless you give full and constant attention to the listeners who are in the situation with you, you cannot possibly suit your behavior to the situation; and (2) listening is an erratic business at best, so you must engage in a continuous effort to move listeners' thoughts in directions that make them *prefer* to

[1]Giraud Chester, *The Ninth Juror* (New York: Random House, 1970), p. 104. Mr. Chester, once a teacher of speech and broadcasting and now a broadcasting executive, wrote this interesting book to recount his experience as a juror in a criminal case in New York City.

experience what you are speaking about over anything else. The remainder of this chapter deals with more detailed ways of analyzing speaking situations and listeners' behaviors. Understanding them, you can create communication that will direct the experiences of audiences as your purposes require.

## RHETORICAL SITUATIONS

We have been thinking about speakers' relationships with listeners. Those relationships do not occur in a vacuum. Speakers and listeners are the most important but not the only sources of influence that affect what happens during oral communication.

In our first chapter we discussed rhetorical situations as one base for thinking about speaking to a public. There we noted Lloyd F. Bitzer's contribution to a clearer understanding of the role of the rhetorical situation and drew upon his award winning essay, published in 1968.[2] His conceptualization is so valuable for speakers, we shall draw upon it further and in more detail in the next few pages.

*Different conditions affect the rhetorical situation.*

Let us suppose you are to make a talk. When you speak, specific people will be "out there." They will be in a particular place—in a classroom, in a circle on the grass, in an auditorium, in a small conference room, or some other place. They will be aware of where they are, and they will have some reasons for being there instead of elsewhere. They will be conscious that you are going to try to make them an audience. They will assume that you have reasons for talking to them, but they may or may not be fully aware of what your reasons are. They will probably ready themselves to respond to you (until you begin to bore them), but they will also inevitably respond to all the other forces that conspired to constitute them as your audience in this place and time. They will respond to having been "collected" as an "audience," to their knowledge and feelings about you and everything you represent, to all known objects and persons associated with you, and with the setting into which they have come. They will respond to the other people who make up the "audience," and they will continuously respond to and through their own individual and collective histories. Professor Bitzer's point is that it is wiser to think of communicating within a "set of conditions" like these than merely to think of communicating *to* some people. The people we communicate with, Bitzer rightly insists, are as much conditioned by past and present

[2]Lloyd F. Bitzer, "The Rhetorical Situation," *Philosophy and Rehtoric*, I (January, 1968), pp. 1–14. The essay received the James A. Winans Award for Distinguished Scholarship in Rhetoric and Public Address in 1968.

conditions as we who communicate. What we really do in communication is to create human relationships and try to sustain them *within* a situation that envelops everyone involved.

## Entering a Rhetorical Situation

If you think about speaking in this way, you will think of yourself as entering speaking situations. You will join with other people who, like you, are trying to achieve goals within constraining conditions of time, place, occasion, past history, special expectations, conflicting interpretations of reality, and so on. An audience may or may not think talk is needed in a particular situation. If they do not, you must make them think otherwise, or be silent, or speak to no good effect. On the other hand, if all the forces of the situation have created what Bitzer calls an "exigence"—an urgency or need—which talk can remove or ease, then you can enter the situation with immediate prospects of influencing people.

*Exigences determine a speaker's opportunities and restraints.*

When you conceive of speaking as "entering" situations, key questions ought to arise in your mind even before you begin preparing the ideas that will form a speech. The questions will include these: for whom and for what will this speech situation be "ready"? Do I need to, and can I, adjust the situation or adjust myself to achieve my goals in that situation? What is the exigence or need that I must fill by this speech? What do the forces of the situation invite and what do they discourage? What set of changes "out there" would constitute achievement of my goals?

Asking and answering such questions will tell you whether there are two tasks to be accomplished or one: whether

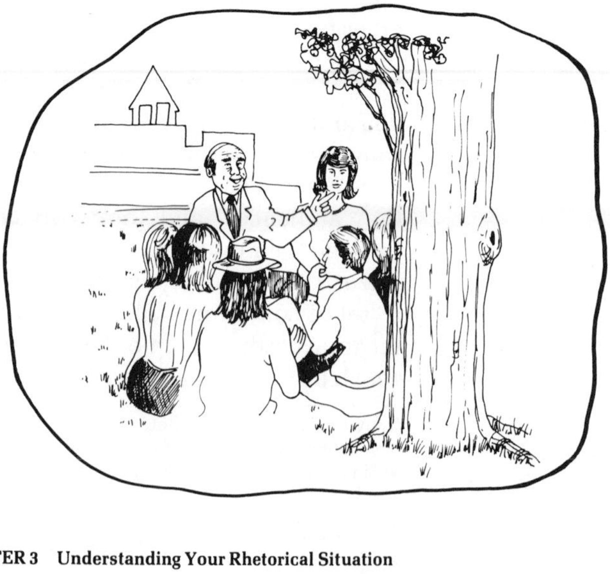

you need to change the situation itself and *then* insert your ideas, or whether you have only to adjust yourself, your ideas, and your goals to exigences and readinesses already existing in the situation.

### Altering Situations

*Some speaking situations can be altered; others cannot.*

In a real sense speaking situations dictate what speakers can do. One of the values of thinking about situations instead of just about people addressed is that you will see which forces "out there" are already working in favor of your goals and which forces you will need to "work around," or oppose, or submit to, or try to change. The fact is that the requirements of some speaking situations can be adjusted in favor of a speaker's personal wishes but others cannot. Two true incidents illustrate the kinds of situations that can and cannot be altered.

*Altering Opinions.* One of your authors recently taught a speech class where there occurred a group discussion in which several students expressed concern about preserving wildlife in the United States. A few days later, there was a series of speeches, several of which dealt with ecology. Class discussion following those speeches produced many sweeping remarks critical of all disturbers of nature. Criticism was showered on various groups from industries to hunters. At this point a biology major decided privately that the climate of opinion was becoming too one-sided and, since wildlife management was one of his interests, he decided to "straighten things out" by giving a talk on the importance of hunting female deer under regulations. He knew, however, that he would speak in a situation in which destruction of wild animals had come to be frowned upon. Moreover, newspapers and broadcasting stations were then carrying news reports attacking hunting. Both the history of the class as an audience and the publicized claims of conservationists had created a situation favorable to another speech on ecology, but a speech endorsing hunting of any kind would have to be worked out with care if it were to have any positive influence.

He began his speech by recalling earlier talk about "management," "protecting the balance," "caring about nature," and the like. Then he said:

> I want you to think some more about "balance." I want you to think about how we are to keep the deer of this state in balance with the space and food we are willing to allow them. I'd like you to think whether you want to protect healthy deer or sick and scrawny ones, whether you want more deer killed on highways, and whether you have any sympathy for the human beings who run the farms of our

> rural areas. Let me tell you about the balancing problems that affect the lives of deer.

He went on to show that natural reproductive processes would cause deer in his state to overpopulate available wild land every two years unless a certain number of does were regularly eliminated. Fewer than the required number had been killed in past years, he said. The present imbalance was justification for extending the annual doe season. Several listeners' reactions were well expressed by one student who said, afterward: "Now you've got me almost embarrassed. I don't hunt; I don't even like the idea. But the way you put it, it seems like I *ought* to take up hunting deer if not enough other people do. Really, I don't feel too comfortable!"

The incident illustrates that where the forces creating a speech situation have only shaped *opinions,* an astute speaker can usually change the restrictions of the situation by taking time to discover what there is in the opinion-making background that can be used to justify *other* directions of thought. The biology major seized upon the ways in which "balance" had been installed in his listeners' minds as a "proper" concept, and he artistically made his thoughts about doe hunting suitable for the situation by linking all of his potentially unacceptable ideas to that agreed-upon, positive value.

*Violating Assignments.* There are times, however, when situational forces prescribe so firmly what speaking must do that they create a virtual "assignment" for whoever speaks. This kind of situation existed in 1971 at a national conference of officers of college and university women's associations. The conference's planning committee invited a well-known newswoman to be the keynote speaker at the conference. They also planned the rest of their program around the problem of how women's associations ought to redefine their functions in a time when student affairs were predominantly coeducational.

We do not know exactly what the planners of the conference told their keynote speaker about their general plans, but the call for the conference and the published titles of workshops made clear what the conference's main theme was to be. Perhaps ill advisedly, the planners scheduled workshops on the theory that the keynote speech would contain ideas that would furnish starting points for later discussions of what college women's associations ought to be doing.

The keynote speaker spoke interestingly about the experiences of professional women, especially journalists. Nothing was said about college women's associations. The conference leaders were upset, and audible murmurs developed during the speech—apparently indicating that listeners were perplexed or losing interest or both. The speech was an excellent one for this speaker to make, but this was not a situation that welcomed it. Whether she knew it or not, the keynote speaker had been given an assignment by previous planning and publicity for the conference. The assignment was "violated," and the audience became uneasy. The conference "got off to a very slow start" according to the planners. Whatever may have been the reasons for the misunderstanding, the incident illustrates that situations can develop in ways that dictate assignments which speakers cannot ignore and still succeed as speakers.

There was an equally illustrative sequel to the above incident. During the next year, one of the disappointed planners was wise enough to invite the *same* newswoman to give the *same* kind of speech to a campus gathering of women students. This time the situation was defined by announcements that there would be a speech on "Women in Professional Life." This time, the speaker was eminently successful, and so was the entire meeting. This time, the assignment of the situation, and the speech *fit*.

Something like what happened at the conference of women's association leaders happens in a classroom when expected patterns of speaking are violated. If a nationally known newswoman cannot alter an assignment from an all-woman audience, it is unlikely a student speaker can easily alter classroom expectations. Not to try to persuade when everyone expects persuasion is rather like making an appeal for funds at someone's birthday party—it must be specially justified if done at all.

From what we have said, these guidelines ought to be drawn. You will be wise to analyze what your speaking situation will invite, allow, and discourage. To do this, you must look behind your listeners—important as they are—to discover what forces have conditioned them and created readinesses and unreadinesses in them. "What speech from *me* can *do* something here?" is a question you ought to ask before and throughout speech preparation. Once you see your situational options, you can turn attention to special adaptations which further analysis of audiences will enable you to make.

### Conceptualizing Auditors as Potential Listeners

You will be wise to think of every group of listeners as an aggregation of *individuals* having *some* tendency to behave as their situation encourages them to behave, but possessing an even greater disposition to retain their individualities. However, you cannot motivate every member of an audience independently from every other, so you must concern yourself chiefly with what your listeners have in common.

*The speaker must know what his listeners have in common.*

This is not as complicated as it is sometimes made to seem. To begin with, one thing you share with any audience is humanity. Your hearers are people. You can reason out many of their probable tendencies by considering how you would think and feel if you were in their places. Furthermore, there are a number of ways in which people function predictably because that is the nature or habit of their species.

## GETTING ATTENTION

*Three factors influence amount of attention.*

Three things seem to govern how human beings attend to anything, including speech: (1) the *character of the stimuli* that impinge upon us influences the character of our attention; (2) the *expectations taught us* by previous experience influence *how* and *when* we attend; and (3) *what we want and need* at the moment influences our attention. Out of these generalizations we can create some "rules of thumb" for adapting to listeners who make up audiences.

When stimuli yield strong sense experience we attend closely. Dick Barnes's talk on "space values" succeeded because of his careful application of this principle. Language which creates pictures in the mind stimulates imaginary sensory experience. Such language is therefore a specially valuable resource through which to secure close attention. Consider the close attention Randy Cohn was certain to secure as she discussed the "repairing of noses" (see p. 238). If reminded by words, a listener can be brought to reexperience and respond to the "blue-grey glint" of a desert sky he once saw or the "zigzag" outline of a flash of lightning. Words that help people "see," "hear," and "feel" in imagination are among the stimuli you need to loose when you want close attention to ideas.

We also expect to find intelligible *relations* among stimuli. It is our nature to search for similarities and differences among things we hear about. We try to connect those likenesses and dissimilarities with what we have experienced before. This is one of the ways we test how the things we hear are likely to affect us; we judge the future by comparing what we are *told* will happen with what we know *has* happened. Accordingly, a speaker who supplies hearers with easy ways of relating what they hear to their other personal experiences increases the prospect of securing close attention.

What people need and want, or what they think they

need and want, directs attention to whatever promises satisfaction for those yearnings. *It is therefore a natural principle of effective speaking that what is talked about ought to be connected as closely as possible with what the listeners want.*

The ways by which speakers can associate ideas with needs and wants are somewhat complex. We shall, therefore, treat them at several points in this and the next three chapters.

## ACHIEVING CHANGE

Giving attention does not necessarily guarantee listeners' views will change, but changing views is the goal of most public speech. We need then to extend our consideration to the bases of changes in opinions and attitudes.

### Gratifying Biological Needs

We can begin with the basic fact that any audience in any situation is composed of beings who are biologically mammals, having bodily and organic needs generally found among mammals. They all want gratification for hunger, for thirst, for breathing oxygen, for sexual drives, for safety, and for physical and mental comfort. But, being human, they also exercise conscious and unconscious preferences in many of these matters. For example, they seek gratification for physical needs but are capable of suppressing some of those needs when they want something else even more. All of us have put off eating in order to meet a friend. Many audiences have endured discomfort because they wanted more to hear a speaker than to be comfortable.

*Helping to gratify biological needs will effect change.*

So, if you want to direct listeners' attention and to change understandings, opinions, and attitudes in some degree, one possibility is to show that you can help your listeners gratify biological needs. Unless they want something else still more, they are likely to listen and to change along the lines you urge.

*Sex.* *Sex* is both a biological and social condition. It makes a difference in listeners' readiness to believe and change. You will need to accommodate what you say to these preferences.

According to most research, women are more persuasible than men, but there is some evidence that this may not be true when the persuader is a woman speaker. It is unsafe to make sweeping generalizations about the social significances of sexual differences, but you can lose nothing by trying to make your speaking inviting for *both* men and women. If you are male, you will be wise to assume that the males in your audience will be harder to persuade than the women, other things being equal. If you are a woman, you ought to expect more difficulties with women than with men. But probably your most important guideline in this connection is that when speaking to mixed audiences you should select supporting and amplifying material that has clear social and personal interest for *both* sexes.

*Age.* Age also seems to affect listeners' attitudes and their readiness to change. There is not much exact research on this matter, but studies confirm the lore of experience: the young are most persuasible and the elderly least so; the young, the middle aged, and the old tend to give closest attention to different aspects of ideas. In general, you will be well advised to follow the implicit guidelines of Aristotle. None of the observations we are about to paraphrase from him has been disproved and many have been confirmed in a variety of ways.

Aristotle tried to address himself, as few modern psychological studies have, to "the proper means of adapting both speech and speaker to a given audience." He sought rhetorical generalizations about the young, "men in their prime," and the elderly. Below is a quick summary of his observations, and if you take the trouble to compare them to the results of public opinion polls which report opinions by age groupings, you will be struck by the modernity of what he said.

In youth "men have strong desires, and whatever they desire they are prone to do. Of the bodily desires the one they let govern them most is the sexual; here they lack self-control. They are shifting and unsteady in their desires. . . ." They are "quick to anger, and apt to give way to it," and they are "fond of honor" but even "fonder of victory." Money means relatively little to them "for they have not yet learned what the want of it means." They are not cynical; rather, they are trustful "for as yet they have not been often deceived." Being quick to hope, and living much in anticipation, "they are easily deceived." Though brave and spirited, they are also shy. Being idealistic, "in their actions they prefer honor to expediency" and are dogmatic. "All their mistakes are on the side of intensity and excess. . . ."

In middle life, Aristotle thought, people "will be neither excessively confident . . . nor yet too timid; they will be both confident and cautious. They will neither trust everyone nor distrust everyone; rather they will judge the case by the facts. Their rule of life will be neither honor alone, nor expediency alone. . . ." They will temper valor with self-control, and they will be neither parsimonious nor prodigal with their possessions. Generally, "all the valuable qualities which youth and age divide between them are joined in the prime of life."

The aged have characteristics opposed to those of the young. Thus "they err by an extreme moderation" and are "positive about nothing" for they have lived long and been disappointed much. They tend to be cynical and "put the worst construction on everything"; they are suspicious, and sometimes small-minded. They "aspire to nothing great or exalted, but crave the mere necessities and comforts of existence." They are constantly apprehensive and "live their lives with too much regard for the expedient and too little for honor." What other people think means little to them, for they "live in memory rather than in anticipation."

Aristotle concluded: "Now the hearer is always receptive when a speech is adapted to his own character and reflects it. Thus we can readily see the proper means of adapting both speech and speaker to a given audience."[3]

In Aristotle's generalizations are useful guidelines for thinking about the varying interests that need to be invoked for listeners of differing ages. You cannot, of course, always gratify the idealism of youth and the caution of age with the same idea or argument. But more often than most speakers realize, ideas are at once idealistic and expedient. For example, the notion of helping a minority group has humanitarian, economic, and security-assuring aspects. Which ones you should stress ought to be determined in part by what you can infer from a study of the age groups that will be represented in your audience.

*Intelligence.* *Intelligence* is another attribute that everyone has to some degree. It ought to be noticed as an aspect of listeners' "conditions" to which you will need to adapt. If your listeners are supposed to have "high intelligence," this means that on the whole they are adept in verbal comprehension, working with numbers, preceiving spatial relations, remembering, reasoning, using words, and perceiving things speedily. Notice that *language skills* are especially important in this group of things conventionally called aspects of "intelligence." A useful generalization is embedded here. You ought to suppose that the higher your listeners' measured intelligence, the better they will be able to understand what you say to them and to interpret and evaluate what you say. If you know there are people of limited intelligence (as it is measured) in an audience, you ought to try to give them special help in understanding what you

[3]From *The Rhetoric of Aristotle*, translated and edited by Lane Cooper, pp. 132–137, bk. II, chaps. 12–14. Copyright 1932, renewed 1960 by Lane Cooper. Reprinted by permission of Prentice-Hall, Inc., Englewood Cliffs, New Jersey.

say—perhaps by demonstrating things instead of just talking about them. In short, an estimate of the "intelligence" of an audience is a cue to how easy or difficult it will be for that audience to respond to the *verbal* parts of your message.

An estimate of "intelligence" is a clue to something else. People who score high on intelligence tests are also quick to see, or think they see, mistakes in what is said. This means that the higher the measured intelligence of your listeners, the more careful you should be to justify and qualify, in words, the things you say. Of course, for an audience of any level of intelligence, getting and maintaining attention is of first importance. If listeners do not find what you say interesting, they will not apply whatever intelligence they have to what you tell them.

You ought to consider one other thing in adapting to the intelligence levels of audiences. Your classroom audiences will not give you much experience in making such adaptations; practice in adapting to different levels of intelligence is best gained outside university settings. College students for the most part have more linguistic ability than most groups. It is outside academic communities that you will find the listeners who truly challenge your ability to adapt to the wide variety of language aptitudes we all confront in our lives outside schools.

### Strength of Attitudes

*Strength of attitudes* is another quality of listeners that you should try to estimate. B. E. Lane and D. O. Sears have made a succinct statement of what you will face in this connection:

> People who differ from you will tend to distort your views. When you differ slightly from your friends, they will think you agree with them. Your enemies will think you disagree with them more than you actually do. Both tendencies will weaken your capacity to influence them in the way you wish to.[4]

*A speaker must know his listeners' attitudes and their degree of strength.*

These observations imply that speakers ought to consider whether their audiences are likely to be friendly, indifferent, or hostile to ideas that need to be presented. If you can discover which kinds of attitudes prevail *strongly*, Lane and Sears' remarks tell you what kinds of misunderstandings to guard against. And do notice that friendly audiences are almost as apt to misunderstand as hostile audiences. People friendly to your ideas will tend to agree with you *but on their own terms*. Sometimes this will fit your purpose, but at other times it will be necessary to make special efforts in order to get friendly listeners to

[4]B. E. Lane and D. O. Sears, *Public Opinion* (Englewood Cliffs: Prentice-Hall, Inc., 1964), p. 51.

see the importance of *new* reasons for thinking as they already do.

Research provides two other guidelines for speakers seeking to change other people's views. First, the more firmly your listeners hold a view, the easier it will be to strengthen that view and make it seem important; but the stronger their views, the less change away from that view you dare ask for in any one communication. Even a hostile listener's views can, perhaps, be changed a little if you proceed cautiously and show respect for attitudes he already holds. But if you ask a hostile or a doubtful listener to make large, immediate changes, you are apt to be rejected. Second, if certain attitudes are held *lightly* by listeners, you are safe in asking for large changes and for full acceptance of new ideas related to these attitudes. The reason is that when attitudes are lightly held, accepting new views is often easier than splitting hairs or disagreeing about a matter that seems minor.

### Rhetorical Qualities for Interest and Change

Certain interesting and change-evoking qualities can be "built into" any speaking. Put differently, any speaking can be *given* attention and change-inducing qualities. There are basic ways in which this can be accomplished.

*Simplification aids persuasion.*

*Simplification.* Talk can always follow the ways an audience is used to thinking. What listeners are used to thinking is easy for them. Ideas developed in those familiar patterns are seen as *simple*—in a complimentary sense. The biology major who spoke on deer hunting remembered that his classmates had "learned" from earlier discussions and speeches to simplify an entire group of ecological complexities into a problem of "maintaining nature's balance." Perceiving this, he was able to make *his* problem seem both simple and significant by developing it as a problem in "balancing" natural forces. By this same strategy of using the familiar, "balancing" way of thinking, he could have talked successfully to his class about fishing, oil depletion, waterways, or farm practices. The listeners' simplification of ecological issues was there to be used; the listeners were ready to apply the "balance" theory to anything having to do with natural forces.

Similar options are open to you in any situation. Find out how your listeners are used to thinking about subjects like your own, and then treat your subject in that same way as far as you can. Even if your listeners have no ways of thinking that are peculiar to them as a group, they are bound to think in simplified ways that are common to their culture. Consider a few of many such simplifications: everything has some price, promises should be kept,[5] wide reading is a mark of intelligence, humanitarian motives are better than economic motives, there can be no effects without causes, precision is a mark of good workmanship, competition keeps prices down, etc.

There are thousands of such everyday formulas by which people in our culture interpret the facts about them. What we are saying is that wherever you can explain an idea or argue for it using these familiar ways of thinking, you will be seen as explaining clearly and, in very many circumstances, as arguing persuasively. The formulas may be unique to a situation, as was the "balance formula" in Dick Barnes's class, or they may be cultural. Whichever kind, if your ideas will not suffer from being put in these forms, the forms offer an avenue to improved attention and willing belief.

## FEATURES OF ATTENTION AND INTEREST

*Nine qualities of speech always enhance attention.*

Because listeners and listening are as we have described them, certain features of speaking always enhance attention and seize listeners' interest. Below is a brief statement of what each of these features is, accompanied by the reason each is likely to secure attention and interest and by quick examples.

| **Feature** | **Basis of Influence** |
| --- | --- |
| 1. *Activity:* actual movement suggested by the idea or by verbal imagery or by activity displayed in speaking. You draw a sweeping curve on the blackboard, or you say, "He *scurried* out of his hiding place." | Noticeable *change* or movement always tends to attract attention; real or imagistic movement creates the sense of change; a speaker's movement *is* change. |
| 2. *Proximity:* showing things as near in time or space to the listener, or as near to one another (actually or figuratively). You draw two shapes close to one another, or you say, "Such a person could be sitting next to you on the bus." | Adjacency is among the simplest relationships to perceive, and adjacency to a listener (real or imagined) implies the listener is or could be directly involved. |

[5]This theme is the basis for the entire first section of Dr. Martin Luther King's famous speech "I Have a Dream," delivered in Washington, D.C., August 28, 1963.

| | |
|---|---|
| 3. *Realism or vividness:* pictorial or other sensory qualities introduced by imagistic language or action or physical illustration. You say, "I was covered with *black, sticky mud,*" or point to where the mud covered you, or you bring some mud and show what it is really like. | Learning through the senses, directly or vicariously, is the basic experience by which knowledge is gained and survival defended. |
| 4. *Familiarity and novelty:* association of ideas with what listeners know, or presentation of what was either unknown or never perceived in the way proposed. You compare governmental budgeting to family budgeting, or the family budget to regulating the international balance of payments. | All humans prize and attend to what they have experienced before; they also enjoy or are curious about experience that is new. |
| 5. *Conflict and suspense:* showing either animate or inanimate things in opposition to one another or in competition with one another, the details or the outcome being in either case uncertain in some degree. You inject the image of a contest between science and the environment, or you say, "This is a *race* between ideas and fear," or you inject a "fight image" or illustration. | Opposition is the most obvious of differences, hence easily perceived. When active clash or competition is present, *change* and the *unknown* are both present to draw human attention. |
| 6. *Vitality:* associating ideas or objects with matters of direct concern to the lives of people—especially the lives of listeners. You relate a financial topic to listeners' own purchasing and saving, or you make listeners see *their* future lives depend on the science-environment contest. | Personal interests and purposes are prime reasons for granting attention; what seems to touch life itself has special significance for all. |
| 7. *Specificity:* presentation of precise detail. You say, "spreading oak" instead of "tree," or you show a model or mock-up instead of just describing, or you give descriptions for which listeners can fill in details, as Dick Barnes did with campus scenes. | The more concrete or specific any concept, the more easily it is acquired by humans—provided the detail does not obscure the nature or meaning of the *whole*. |

| | |
|---|---|
| 8. *Intensity:* the force of any aspect of communication—of voice, movement, or energy of language. Wide variations in intensity levels are possible in sound, physical energy, and vividness or color in language. You increase loudness for emphasis, move to lean toward listeners, or point, or you say with deliberateness, "This next point is the most important one," or you say, "The floor was littered with garbage" instead of "covered with debris," thus getting greater intensity through greater specificity. | Within certain limits too complicated to explain here, the strength of impact of any stimulus tends to vary with the intensity of the stimulus; also, noticeable *changes* in stimuli and *contrasts* between intensities of stimuli draw attention to the *dissimilarities* and to *change*. |
| 9. *Humor:* introduction of exaggeration, incongruity, irony, word play, unexpected turns of thought or phrase. Left-handed people have been discussed as a minority denied civil liberties and "equal rights." You might talk about playing basketball as though the game were warfare, or call football "agitation of a bag of wind." | The nature of response to humor is not fully understood, but the attractions of the *novel* or unexpected and satisfactions derived from safely regaining reality—the *familiar*—after having expectations built up, then reversed, appear to be involved. |

We hope you will see from the lists above that the general qualities for which you must strive in speech are not qualities invented by pedagogues or impractical theorists. Our speech needs these qualities because people attend to some kinds of qualities more readily than to others. Therefore speech must symbolically represent activity, proximity, realism, familiarity and novelty, conflict and suspense, vitality, specificity, intensity, and humor. Those are the features of ideas, behaviors, and things we all attend to most readily.

*Using Features of Interest and Change.* It is all too easy to make a superficial interpretation of what we have just said. Just any adaptation to the interests of listeners will not serve your speech, nor will just any active image or bit of suspensive development. What is needed is to build into your basic speech materials the attention-getting and interest-arousing features that serve both your own meanings and the nature of specific listeners in specific situations. You must calculate your requirements and *choose among* your resources.

Not every idea can be discussed so that it seems near in

time or space; therefore, if that is not possible perhaps the idea can be contrasted with its opposite (conflict) or be shown as directly connected with someone's experience (vitality). Consider what Leonard Bernstein once did with the relatively unexciting concept *recitative*. The excerpt is from one of his many successful television lectures on music.

> Now how does a plot get furthered by the use of music? There are a number of ways—ballet, underscoring, choral devices, etc.—but the most common technique for telling your story musically is the recitative, or *recitativo*, a word which you certainly know as somehow connected with opera, but perhaps are a bit foggy about. What is this recitative, anyway? Let's suppose I am in a musical show whose plot calls on me to inform my wife that chicken has gone up three cents a pound. In an ordinary musical show I would simply say to her, "Chicken is up three cents a pound," and my wife would burst forth then, singing a lament about the high cost of living. But in an opera, I would sing my line, and I would have to resort to the recitative—let's say in the style of Mozart. . . . [Here Bernstein sang, "Susanna. I have something terrible to tell you. I've been talking to the butcher, and he tells me that the price of chicken has gone up three cents a pound. Please don't be too depressed, dear." These lines were sung first in the musical style of Mozart, then of Verdi, then of Wagner. Bernstein resumed the lecture proper with what follows.] But no matter how expressive I get, I am still singing something of less musical importance than the song itself, which my wife will sing immediately afterward. It's the song, or the number, that will get the applause, no matter how heart-breakingly I tell the price of chicken. The function of my recitative is to set up the situation for the song.[6]

In this short passage Mr. Bernstein used every feature of interest listed in the table above except proximity and intensity. In addition, he sang, which was a *variation* of intensity. There is *activity* in the fact that the recitative is shown to be a response; *vividness* in the notion of the price of chicken and in terms like "heart-breakingly"; *familiarity, novelty,* and *humor* in his choice of the price of chicken as a musical subject; *conflict* of a sort is expressed in the contrast between recitatives and the major songs that follow them; the idea of prices invokes *vitality;* there is *specificity* in "three cents" and in the illustrations of styles of recitatives; and, of course, Bernstein's basic *enlivening* device is the *humor* of his entire amplification of a definition. Actually, Bernstein also supplied great activity and intensity by his manner in giving the lecture.

---

[6]Leonard Bernstein, "American Musical Comedy," in his *The Joy of Music* (New York: Simon and Schuster, 1959), pp. 153–157. Copyright © 1954, 1955, 1956, 1957, 1958, 1959 by Leonard Bernstein. Reprinted by permission of Simon and Schuster.

This is an example of building into talk those features that give language force in any speaking situation. One need not be a great musician to do it. Dick Barnes did it. So can you. You have nine basic resources; some can be used in any situation and in dealing with any subject. Activity, proximity, realism, familiarity or novelty, conflict, vitality, specificity, intensity, and humor are for the most part qualities we *give* to our subjects by the *ways* we discuss them. We need to give talk these qualities because our speech situations are *human* situations, and these happen to be the qualities to which human beings most readily attend under all circumstances.

## SUMMARY

This chapter has been about rhetorical situations. Upon completing it you ought to be fully alive to ways in which the *humanness* of every situation for speaking defines (1) what speech *ought* to do here, (2) what speech *might* do here, (3) what speech probably *cannot* do here. We have made these major points. What you can and should do in speaking is always in some degree regulated:

1. By the fact that listeners are bound to be both responsive yet erratic in their attention.
2. By the fact that the place, the time, the conditions of meeting, and even the past histories of listeners and speakers set limits and open opportunities for what can be accomplished.
3. By the fact that what people want and need in their general and personal circumstances regulates what they welcome, tolerate, and reject.
4. By the fact that simplifying in familiar ways is always welcomed.
5. By the fact that talk which has some or all of nine special features of attention and interest is always welcomed.

These are rough generalizations about what "takes hold" and what does not in rhetorical situations. If you will use them in reasoning about what to say in a situation, you are likely to create speech that serves your goals better than impulsive speaking could do.

## EXERCISES

*Written*

**1.** Write a careful description of some specific audience with which you are familiar (fraternal group, political or other club, religious congregation, or other) giving special consideration to the following:

a. Chief biological wants and needs, if any, that affect this audience;
b. Chief social wants and needs, if any, that affect this audience;
c. "Assignments" imposed, if any;
d. Any special characteristics of age, sex, expectation, knowledge that all speakers addressing this audience should take into account. In what ways?

2. You are to prepare a short speech using the central idea: "Television should be (or should not be) used as a major resource in general education." Outline the major points you might make in such a speech if it were to be given to audience *a* below; then outline the major points you might try to make if the speech were for audience *b* below. Justify any differences there may be in the two outlines.
   a. An audience of twenty college students aged seventeen to twenty-two, made up of ten men and ten women, assembled for an informal class on study habits, organized for students whose academic records do not "meet the potentialities indicated by standardized aptitude-test results."
   b. An audience of twenty college students aged nineteen to twenty-two, all cadet teachers in an elementary school attending one of a series of weekly seminars. The seminar topic for this meeting is "Motivation." There are eighteen women and two men in the group.
3. Using the text or a recording of any speech, identify the points at which the speaker seems to have adapted content for the specific purpose of suiting it to one or another of the audience characteristics discussed in this chapter. Identify and evaluate the effectiveness with which he took advantage of special resources in ideas and speech.

*Oral*

1. With four or five classmates, work out through discussion an outlined description of your speech class as a rhetorical situation for the next group of talks to be given in your class. Use the subpoints of Written Exercise 1 above as headings for your descriptive outline. *Optional:* As an exercise in completing a group assignment and in reporting, assign parts of your completed outline to each member of your group and have each report that part of the group's findings to the class.
2. Give an informative speech on one of the following subjects: stereotypes, the psychological process called suggestion, the psychological process called conditioned response, the social (or ethical or other) values of college students today, the expectations of audiences assembled at modern ceremonial occasions, the unique expectations of audiences that have power to determine policy or legislate theories of crowd behavior.

3. Prepare and deliver an oral report explaining how a trial lawyer, preacher, or political speaker seems to have described his audience to himself—judging from the way he composed his speech.
4. Explore some specific aspect of audience research, advertising, market analysis, or the relation of market research to industrial design. Prepare and deliver a talk on your findings. Remember, *you* must now adapt your findings to *your* special speech situation!

# Locating Ideas That Will Communicate

# 4

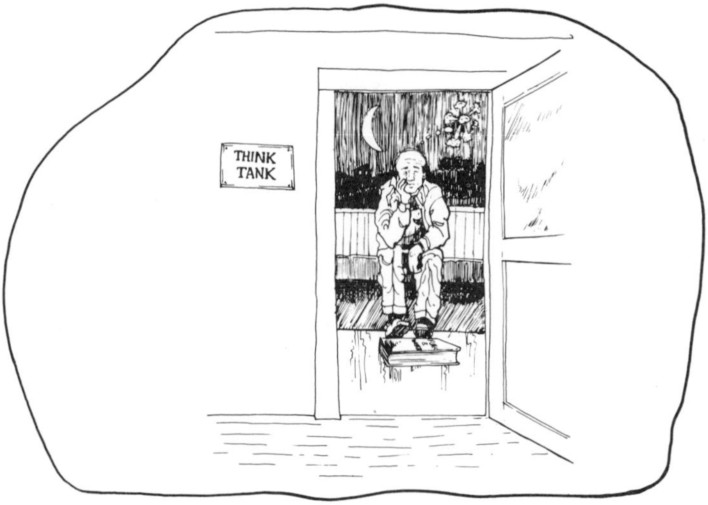


If someone who is not a teacher asks you to say something, the chances are that he or she will give you some direction about what to say. "Tell us about your trip" or "What's that book about?" or "Explain 'Plan X' to us" are typical kinds of invitations to talk. Who has recently asked you, "Will you give us a speech?" When you are in public settings and choose to say something, the situation and your relation to the other people in it usually dictate what needs to be said. It probably would not even occur to you to make an argument for having a skating party to a group of friends trying to figure out whether it is cheaper to live in a dormitory or in a private apartment. But in a speech class things are different. Sometimes, at least, you will be free to choose what to talk about. "Will you give us a speech?" is really the question asked by some assignments. This freedom gives opportunities and creates difficulties. When you are free to choose, finding a subject to talk about may bother you, so we shall focus on that topic in the next paragraphs.

## CHOOSING SUBJECTS

*Four factors dictate the suitability of a subject.*

A good subject for a talk ought to be timely, and it ought to be significant for the listeners. Also, it ought to suit *you* as the person who will do the communicating. And, of course, you should be able to say what is needed in the time allowed.

The points above are four "tests" of a suitable subject for public speech. Your speech subjects should meet these tests, but the tests do not *locate* subjects for you. They only help you to distinguish a promising subject from a poor one. One helpful way to find possible subjects when your mind seems to have gone blank is to try a method called "brainstorming." To do this, you let your mind run freely over all kinds of ideas. You jot down anything at all that is interesting enough to catch your attention even momentarily. In the next paragraph let us show you how the process might work. Ideas put in brackets are ideas that might be talked about; they were jotted down as they came to mind.

*Brainstorming is a helpful technique for locating a subject.*

Just before the author wrote this paragraph he stared at one end of his study for five minutes, jotting down ideas as he looked from one item of furnishings to another. There was a radio-record-player-stereo set [how stereo works, broadcasting, the recording industry, what makes a hit record]. Beside the set was a floor lamp [public utilities and their regulation, the energy shortage, kinds of light bulbs]. In one corner stood a home-size copying machine [photo reproduction processes, the copier industry, copyrights and protection of copyrighted material, photo processes]. On the wall were a clock [how we use our time, daylight saving time, manufacture of clocks, importance of accuracy in timing devices], and a framed, batik reproduction of the author's favorite cartoon [cartoons and comics, hand crafts, use of leisure time]. The book shelf suggested much, but only some got jotted down [the book publishing industry, editing, journalism]. The wall behind the shelf was noticed [the construction industry, architecture]. Twenty-two minutes elapsed between the time the five minutes of staring and quick jotting began and the moment this paragraph was typed out.

Depending on how you count them, the brackets above contain up to twenty-six general topics and specific subjects on which an informed and interested person might make any of several kinds of useful talks. It seems hardly possible that you could not interest yourself and your classmates in one of these topics or some aspect of one. But if you find absolutely no prospect here, try the same kind of brainstorming for ideas wherever you are right now! Look up from this page and jot down discussable ideas suggested by whatever is around you. In fact, you needn't look up at all. Staring at you is paper [manufacturing processes, shortages, prices of paper, kinds of paper, etc.]; there is print [printing processes, the nature of language, book costs]; and this page is numbered [mathematical and statistical processes, lotteries, gambling]. Thus thought can rush on, suggesting interesting things to think and talk about.

Here is another way to discover possible subjects for public speech. Walk about and look at people, animals, machines, plants, buildings, and brainstorm for subjects. Still another way is to play with words. Start with a *class* of things, perhaps *vehicles*. Now, begin naming things that fall into that class: cars, motorcycles, monorail cars, bicycles, trains, airplanes, etc. Have you anything to say about any of these? Try the same method with *clothing, games, inventions, famous authors*. As you run through idea-generating games like these, jot down each often strange, often familiar, idea that pops into your head. This way you get a list of *possible* subjects. When you are through brainstorming, reactivate your critical ways of thinking and sort out the ideas that are genuinely possible for *you*, for the audience you will talk to, and for the kind of situation you will enter. Two or three experiments of the sort we have described are likely to produce more practically possible speech subjects than you can use up in your entire course in speaking.

An idea need not be obviously within your present knowledge to be a promising speech subject. Anything you can and want to learn about is promising. What *is* the relation between copiers and copyrights? What *is* the promise of monorail transportation? How is the competition between miniskirts and pantsuits coming in this year's fashions? A promising subject is one you can learn more about than your listeners already know. If you have that much interest in a topic, there is probably some phase or aspect of it you can treat in an interesting and vital way.

### Mistakes in Choosing Subjects

*A subject should be chosen quickly and researched carefully.*

The two most common mistakes people make in choosing subjects for speaking are: they delay settling on a specific subject, and they view subjects shallowly. A consistent difference between good and poor college speakers is that the good speakers choose subjects carefully but swiftly and stick with them. Poor speakers dawdle and agonize over subjects and shift subjects repeatedly. This is the finding from 1,000 students' diaries written during speech classes. Are poor speakers poor because they procrastinate? We don't know, but making up one's mind promptly and then getting on with the preparation is unquestionably a characteristic behavior of those who finally speak well.

Promising subjects often yield poor talks because they are treated shallowly. Consider euthanasia, abortion, the drug problem, the rhythms of sleep, dreams, capital punishment, patterns of sexual relationship. These areas can yield trite speeches if the speakers simply present other people's treatments. But there are intriguing moral and legal aspects of euthanasia, abortion, capital punishment, and informal sexual relationships. Typical college audiences have not thought these issues out very fully, so you can bring news concerning how abortion raises complex legal questions about when life begins. On the other hand, it is not news to most college audiences that there *are* arguments for and against euthanasia, abortion, capital punishment, drug use, and informal sexual relationships. To rehearse old arguments pro and con on such important topics is to treat them shallowly. The problem for you is to find and talk about aspects of such problems which your listeners have not already read and heard about repeatedly. In the same way, almost anyone who reads popular magazines and newspapers knows there *are* cycles of sleep. To treat that fact extensively is to speak shallowly. But to report new findings about why these cycles occur or what their importance is, to each of us, is to treat a subject freshly.

Our point is that almost any subject can be *made* worth your time and your listeners' time if what you say about it adds something to your listeners' knowledge. But any subject can also be made trivial by discussing what listeners already know. This is why "one-article speeches" are usually trivial. What is said in a single, popular article is usually common knowledge once the article has appeared. Your job is to try to bring some fresh insight or some fuller understanding to your listeners. This is what Randy Cohn tried to do, and she succeeded for the most part. Transplantation of bodily organs is no new subject, but Randy found unfamiliar details to make her talk "news" for her classmates. (See "The Gift of Life," pp. 236–240.)

## DISCOVERING LINES OF THOUGHT

When you have found a subject you think is significant, your next problem will be to discover what you *could* say about it. Then you must decide which parts of that material you *ought* to give your audience in its particular situation. To solve these problems you need a systematic way of working your mind.

*After choosing a subject, the speaker must decide on his main goal.*

The first thing to do is decide what you want your audience to *do* about your subject. Will it be enough if they simply *understand* and are interested in what you tell them? Or do you want to *strengthen or diminish beliefs and attitudes* they already possess? Or do you want the listeners to *accept your advice* concerning your subject? These are the most common objectives you will have. Decide which is your main goal, and you will save time and effort in preparation.

### Getting Understanding

Sometimes you will be content if your listeners simply find what you say interesting and understand you clearly. Speeches to inform are usually of this kind. When you plan to ask for understanding of specific information, the kinds of thoughts and materials you will need are: (1) data about facts or theories to be understood and accepted, and (2) information about the *standards* that are normally used in judging these things to be credible and acceptable. Put differently, if you are going to ask chiefly for understanding, as in informing, you will need ideas and data that define and clarify what you are talking about. You will also need information about how your listeners are supposed to determine whether the data you provide are true or untrue, relevant or irrelevant, significant or insignificant.

*The goal of understanding requires data and interpretation.*

Consider a pair of examples. If you want to explain how oil is brought up from the ocean floor, your listeners will need the facts about the process. They will also need to know how to judge a "good" from a "poor" way of bringing up the oil and, perhaps, of getting the oil from sea to land. Even if you are trying to get listeners to take your advice that one type of fabric is better than another for making a sail or for durable carpeting, you will probably need to explain in order to lay the groundwork for persuasion when that is your main goal. You will need to explain both the nature of the fabrics you discuss *and* how "better" and "poorer" are determined for the purpose you are discussing. These, then, are the two main types of information you need—data about facts or theories, and standards for judging them. These are required to develop a speech in which getting understanding is either your main purpose or any part of your goal.

### Strengthening Beliefs

But there will be times when your listeners will already know and have beliefs about most of what you want to discuss. What then? The goal then shifts. You may want to strengthen or diminish their beliefs. Or you may choose to make the knowledge they already have more firm, more comprehensive, or more detailed. If any of these is your aim in speaking, you will not need to give great attention to basic facts or to standards of judgment. These will be already known. Your main search will be for facts and ideas that can deepen, enrich, correct, or magnify ideas your hearers already have. For example, your goal might be to make your classmates take their right to vote more seriously than they do. You would then need material that shows the *importance* of voting. You would have limited use for information about laws that govern voting, about voting procedures, about the history of legislation on voting, or the like. Or, if you speak to make listeners put less faith than they do in published "odds" on sports like horse racing and professional football, you will need information about how *carefully* (standards) the odds are determined. And you will need data about their proved accuracy. It is unlikely you would need much information about how they are distributed or published or about how much betting goes on.

*The goal of persuasion requires data that conform to accepted beliefs.*

The principle, then, is this: *where you seek to strengthen or diminish existing beliefs, the main task is to connect your subject with virtues, standards, and advantages that your listeners already prize.* Go back again to a speech on the importance of voting. To make this speech effective you need to find ways of associating voting with such virtues as advancing social justice, securing advantages for young people, or accepting responsibilities. You can make the speech effective, too, by finding and using material that associates *not voting* with the spread of injustice and corruption, with disadvantages for young people, and with irresponsibility. In sum, if you want to reinforce or enlarge belief and understanding, preparation ought to begin with a hunt for the virtues and advantages associated with ideas you want to strengthen. If your goal is to diminish beliefs and attitudes, you should begin with a search for ways of connecting them with what your listeners consider the opposites of virtues and what they think of as disadvantages.

### Giving Advice

*The goal of advice giving requires data that point to a positive gain.*

When you want to advise listeners about something like landscaping, health care, investments, or the like, you will usually have to give new information and try to reinforce or diminish beliefs; but these tasks will be incidental to your main purpose: *getting the listeners to choose what you advise.* When this is your main goal, you can once more narrow your field of research and thinking as soon as you recognize your principal task. You will now need ideas that have to do with the *expediency* of choices and actions. If you want people to invest in life insurance, you need to show them what they will *gain* from it. All advising refers to future behaviors, to consequences and practicalities, to costs and rewards. If you advise someone to take a business course, you *must* show that the advantages exceed the disadvantages. Otherwise it is unlikely that your listener will be motivated. People simply do not accept advice unless they can see advantages—either for right now or for the future.

When you plan to advise, then, search first for facts and lines of thought that say something about the advantages and disadvantages of actions and inactions relating to your subject. We emphasize this point because so many speakers collect much material about what the listeners' choices *are* and then forget to develop clear thoughts about *what will happen* if the listeners choose rightly or wrongly. Remembering that advising is advising about the *future* gives you helpful directions for collecting ideas and information that will communicate.

### Choosing Material You Need: A Test Case

To test how practical our advice has been, let us suppose you have decided to talk to your class about the problems of bicycle riders on your campus. You think your student government might be able to set something in motion that would both make bike riding more convenient and protect bicycles from theft. We shall further suppose that your goal in speaking is to arouse enough interest in bicyclists' problems so the class will choose a small delegation to visit the officers of the student government and try to get their cooperation in exploring what can be done about the problems. Now, how shall you work your mind as you begin to prepare this speech?

We have said you should first decide whether you will be primarily seeking understanding, trying to strengthen or diminish beliefs, or giving advice. Your central idea for the talk is likely to be something like this: "When I finish, I want the class to believe that we ought to approach student government officers in hope of starting actions favorable to bicycle riders and owners." Obviously, it is an *action* you want from the class. You will be asking them to take your *advice* and organize a delegation for a specific purpose. So what kinds of ideas and data will you need most? You will need material about the *advantages* of (1) improving things for bicycle rider-owners and (2) approaching officers of student government instead of doing something else. Advantages to whom? To the members of your class. That raises an important further point about kinds of material you will need—there will be both bike owners and nonowners in your audience. You now know where to begin thinking and gathering material. Look for material about *advantages for everyone* that come from helping bicyclists and from actions the student government might conceivably take. You do *not* need much material on bicycling and bicycles *per se*. You do *not* need information about the virtues of bicycling; it is not bicycling you want understood but problems and possible solutions. You do *not* need to discuss standards for telling a good bicycle from a poor one. That people have bicycles of whatever sorts is presupposed by the fact that you think there are problems and reasons to do something about them. In short, seeing that you want advice accepted and that your advice really urges an action lets you concentrate on the kinds of information you will actually use. It saves you time by telling you kinds of material you need *not* seek in preparation.

There is another practical point to be seen in our test case. In order to show that there is, in fact, a "bicycle problem" on campus, you may need to establish special kinds of understanding before you can move on to advise action. That means that some of your preparatory effort must go into (1) securing facts about the *nature* of the problems you will have to explain in order to justify action and (2) securing a clear idea of the size or seriousness of these problems. Accomplishing (2) really amounts to giving information about "standards" according to which listeners ought to decide that the problems deserve action from them. Once more, by taking time to tell yourself what you are actually asking your listeners to believe and *do*, you tell yourself what is most important to concentrate on in speech preparation. That saves time and effort. It also helps you make clear-headed talks because you become clear about your purpose at the beginning of preparation for any speech.

When you know which kinds of material are likely to be of most value to you for a talk, you can begin to work your mind and conduct your research in other standard ways that pay dividends in productiveness and efficiency. The rest of this chapter is devoted to several such helps to rhetorical invention.

### Topical Review and Discovery

*Certain topics dominate all lines of thought and should be considered when preparing a speech.*

For a good many centuries writers on communication have recognized that people talk on a fairly limited number of themes, which recur again and again even as subjects change. Whatever is talked about, the same basic notions appear over and over in discussion. This is not because of laziness; it happens because the kinds of things people are interested in remain much the same from place to place and generation to generation. Consider the broad subject "sociology." What is something one is bound to talk about concerning sociology? One such thing is the *relationships* among people in societies: how they group themselves to form families, to carry on trade, to determine who shall have authority, and so on. But graphic artists are also bound to touch on the topic of *relationships* sooner or later: the relationships of detailed images and forms in particular. If you talk very long about *anything*, this recurring topic of "relationships" is almost sure to come up and to be of some importance.

Most of the things people in a Western culture think about and therefore talk about fall under one or another of the sixteen general terms listed below. No one is likely to treat or touch on all of these "topics" in a short talk, but everyone will develop *some* of these themes in every message. When speaking to general audiences, we seldom develop lines of thought not identified by one of these "topics." Some of the topics listed below concern attributes that things, beings, or events can have; others identify the basic kinds of relationships we see about us and therefore talk about. This is the list.

A. Attributes commonly discussed:
   1. *Existence* or nonexistence of things.
   2. *Degree* or quantity of things, forces, etc.

3. *Spatial* attributes, including adjacency, distribution, place.
4. Attributes of *time*.
5. *Motion* or activity.
6. *Form*, either physical or abstract.
7. *Substance:* physical, abstract, or psychophysical.
8. *Capacity to change,* including predictability.
9. *Potency:* power or energy, including capacity to further or hinder anything.
10. *Desirability* in terms of rewards or punishments.
11. *Feasibility:* workability or practicability.

B. Basic relationships commonly asserted or argued:
   1. *Causality:* the relation of causes to effects, effects to causes, effects to effects, adequacy of causes, etc.
   2. *Correlation:* coexistence or coordination of things, forces, etc.
   3. *Genus-species* relationships.
   4. *Similarity or dissimilarity.*
   5. *Possibility or impossibility.*

Reviewing this list of topics can help you locate ideas for use in *any* speaking situation. Here is an illustration of how you might use the list to discover things you *could* say about future uses of solar energy.

Run down the list asking, "Will I need to say anything about *this* kind of thing?" If so, what? First, try the topic *existence*. Will you need to say anything about the *existence* of solar energy and other sources of energy? If you are to speak to your classmates, they will already know that these kinds of energy exist, but you may need to remind them of what they know—perhaps in introducing your general subject. In addition it will surely be necessary for you to spend some time on what uses of solar energy exist—right now. Thus, just looking at this topic *existence* can tell you some things you might say and some things you must say if you are to make a clear explanation.

Continuing your topical inventory, you can ask next whether information about the *degree* or quantity of anything needs to be talked about. Certainly so. *How much* energy can be captured from the sun's rays and *how much* energy we have from other sources must be commented on. And the *degree* to which solar energy can replace energy from other sources constitutes the main justification for talking about solar energy at all—whether you are an optimist or a pessimist about solar energy. What about space, adjacency, distribution? To us, the topic of *spatial attributes* does not suggest much for a speech on solar energy, so we pass on. What about *time?* Certainly how soon large amounts of solar energy can be harnessed and how soon we shall run out of other sources of energy are items of information you must be ready to give your listeners. The topic *motion* might suggest some kinds of uses to which solar energy can be put. It might also remind you that most information about solar energy treats it as a source of heat but does not emphasize the problems in converting heat to machinery-driving power. This matter could be something you ought to look into to see whether there are problems along this line that will need discussion. *Form* could suggest discussion of what a power plant drawing on the sun's rays might look like, or what *forms* of power can be derived from solar energy. The topic *substance* seems less suggestive, unless that topic, rather than *form*, draws your mind to the different kinds of power that can be derived from the sun.

*Capacity to change* might suggest to you that it would be useful to discuss how easy or difficult it would be to convert from coal, oil, or electricity to solar power. For example, it would probably be easier to shift heating systems to solar power than to convert automobiles. In any case, the topic can suggest that *changes* are involved or implied whenever we take solar energy seriously as a source of power. And *potency*, the capacity to further or hinder anything, suggests once more that how much power we can get from the sun *must* be discussed, and it might suggest that something be said about what factors hinder or help us if we try to make widespread use of solar power.

What solar energy can and cannot do for us is crucial in determining how *desirable* and how *feasible* reliance on solar energy actually is or can be. These topics will become easily discussable when you are fully informed about the *degree* or amount of solar energy that can be harnessed, in what *forms*, and with what *capacity* to meet energy needs that are most serious.

When you turn to common relationships as topics, *genus-species* probably will suggest little that will be needed in your talk. Your listeners probably will not need to have the different sources of energy defined and differentiated, but the other relationships given in our list do suggest useful thoughts concerning the subject we are considering.

You can scarcely avoid having to talk about shortages of other sources of energy as *cause* for our thinking about solar energy as something especially interesting in these times (*effect*). Noticing that the significance of talking about solar energy arises from general knowledge that our other sources of energy are limited ought to remind you that you will need to speak at least briefly about energy shortages—just to interest your listeners in considering what you have to say. And the topic *similarities-dissimilarities* should remind you that it will be useful to contrast the apparently limitless energy emitted by the sun with the obviously limited supplies of the earth's ordinary fuels. *Correlation* as a topic can remind you that so far, at least, it has been necessary to coordinate solar power with other kinds of power in order to ensure constant levels of power and heat. Conceivably you might choose to make this idea of correlation or coordination of energy sources a part of your central idea. For example, a sensible central idea for an informative talk could be: the sun is today a practical source of heat and power if used in conjunction with power from other sources of energy.

Such are the directions along which your thoughts might be guided by reviewing the sixteen topics we have provided. Not every topic in the list will trigger useful thoughts about a given subject, but a "topical review" of the kind we have illustrated can always help you examine your own knowledge of a subject. It will always increase the likelihood that you will touch on truly important themes in a talk. It will give you a quick inventory of what information you already have and what you must still search for.

### Topical Reviews and Research

Francis Bacon is often called the father of modern scientific thought, and it was he who first perceived that topical reviews such as we have illustrated can do more than "help us to shake out the folds of the intellect within [us]." He noticed that similar reviews of standard lists of topics could be of practical use in getting ready to interview someone or even when reading books.[1] His point was that when you want to get information from a specially informed person or from a book, reviewing topics like those we have given can tell you what you especially need to learn. Our example has already shown this at some points. But consider the possibility of running through the list using a question like: will I need to ask the person I am to interview (or the book I am going to read) about the *existence, degree, cause,* etc., of solar energy? With some such question as this you could frame an *agenda* for an interview or for your library research. In Bacon's language you can "know how to question him wisely and to the purpose; and in like manner . . . peruse . . . books and parts of books."[2]

[1]Francis Bacon, *De augmentis scientiarum*, V, p. 3; *Works, IV*, p. 423.
[2]*Ibid.*

*All speeches require some research.*

Reviewing topics does not, of itself, provide information. Reviewing a set of suggestive topics can help you recall things you already know and suggest things you must find out somewhere, but what we might call "routine research" is sooner or later necessary.

Printed sources are, of course, invaluable in the preparatory stage, but beginners too often forget that other people are excellent resources, too. Store managers are usually glad to explain aspects of their businesses. Photographers are happy to talk about photography. Travellers are only too pleased to tell you of the places they have been and the things they have seen. However, using other people as resources usually requires some forethought.

### People as Resources

*Interviews can be a good source of information.*

Public officials, teachers, and other professional men and women are often overlooked as sources of valuable information. Even the busiest people are frequently willing to grant help to students if the students know what they want and are prepared to conduct interviews efficiently. The kind of forethought and consideration that yields valuable knowledge from busy resource persons was illustrated in plans made by four sections of a basic speech course. Academic requirements for degrees had become a topic of discussion in all four sections. Now, a hundred or so students needed specific, authentic infor-

mation. Representatives of the four sections met together, identified the University authorities whose knowledge was most needed, and organized a "Meet the Press" interview session open to all students in the speech course. At the "Meet the Press" session a vice-president of the University and representatives of departments offering required courses were interviewed by the committee that had made the arrangements and by students "from the floor." The administrative and academic representatives were delighted to serve as resource persons in this project because the students had organized a way of exchanging genuinely important information in a fashion that conserved everyone's time.

Sometimes, of course, people who have information others are likely to want make special arrangements for disseminating that information. Congressmen and other officers have staff members specifically assigned to handle requests for information. Many corporations, both public and private, maintain public information departments which you and others can consult. To use such resources you need chiefly a clear idea of what it is you need to know and what kind of organization is most likely to have that information. Then, prearranged and carefully planned interviews and clear, precise letters can open valuable resources to you.

**Firsthand Investigation**

*Acquiring firsthand knowledge helps the speaker.*

Gathering facts and studying situations at firsthand are too often neglected by people preparing to speak publicly. You are fortunate if you have not been subjected to speeches on juvenile delinquency by people who have never visited a youth court or a settlement house. You need not be an ex-convict to speak on prisons or a parent to discuss children; our point is simply that if a speaker neglects firsthand investigation that was readily possible, he cheapens what he does say. The idea was illustrated by a young woman who planned to speak to her speech class on food prices. One point she felt she should know about was whether shoppers paid more attention to price or to convenience when they shopped. With good sense, she decided the best way to get this kind of information was to investigate at firsthand. She equipped herself with a shopping bag "like any other shopper" and stopped a number of shoppers in five supermarkets, asking each whether he or she was in the store because of low prices or the store's convenience. From a few hours of personal investigation she was able to report to her class that in their university town prices were not yet as important to shoppers as the physical convenience of a store's location. Newspaper stories had created the impression that shoppers everywhere were acutely conscious of rising prices, but firsthand investigation proved this was not yet the case in the community where this student planned to talk about food prices.

Notice, too, the unique kinds of information Randy Cohn acquired by firsthand inquiry (see Appendix, pp. 228–229). And for her, as for most speakers who have done firsthand investigations, there emerged the special advantage of being able to speak authoritatively. Whenever you can truly say, "I was there" or "I say this on the authority of personal investigation," you add to the reasons your listeners will have for listening thoughtfully and respectfully.

### First Steps in Library Research

*Library research should be efficiently done.*

The value of reading as research is beyond challenge. What does need discussion, however, is *how* to use libraries when you prepare to speak. Thousands of students and professionals waste hours by using libraries inefficiently and by recording information too casually. The ideal is to find what you need as quickly as possible and record it with such accuracy and thoroughness that you need not return to the source. To do this you need to proceed systematically.

Except when you have a good general knowledge of a subject that interests you or already know exactly what pieces of information you seek, your first move in library research ought to be to read some general survey article or book on the subject you have in mind. If Greek theatre, Greek scientific theories, or Greek politics are subjects that interest you, read some brief, authoritative essay or short book on ancient Greek society. Edith Hamilton's *The Greek Way* is a brief book you could scan quickly. Or an encyclopedia article on Greek art (or science, or politics) might be an equally good starting point. Remember, too, at this point that there are many excellent, specialized encyclopedias. For example, on almost any topic concerning social psychology the *Handbook of Social Psychology*, edited by Gardner Lindzey and Elliot Aronson, will have a good, authoritative essay. Wherever you seek it, you need at the first stage of your investigation (1) a quick overview of the subject so you know its discussable aspects, and (2) leads toward different kinds of detailed information about the subject. Here is how the kind of investigation we are recommending might work on a specific subject.

Suppose you have decided you might like to discuss

something about "modern architecture" in a speech. You might begin by consulting the *Columbia Encyclopedia*, an excellent, handy, one-volume reference work. It would take you no more than five minutes to read thoughtfully the entry under "modern architecture" in this source. From the essay you would learn that "modern architecture" has come into being because a number of new construction materials and some new ideas about buildings have emerged since about 1880. As a result, you would learn, certain types of buildings such as skyscrapers, such building materials as steel and reinforced concrete, and the names of such famous architects as Frank Lloyd Wright, Le Corbusier, and Walter Gropius have all become standard subtopics of discussion where "modern architecture" is considered.

This much information, which you could gather in five minutes of reading, would be enough to tell you that "modern architecture" is too large and perhaps too vague a subject for a short speech but that there are a number of potentially interesting and discussable subtopics related to modern architecture. The same short essay would also give you the titles of three authoritative books on modern building, its history, and some leading architects. And if you looked in the same encyclopedia under "concrete," you would discover the titles of a pair of other books that discuss why the development of reinforced concrete had so much to do with "modern" architectural changes.

The point of our example is this. From a few minutes spent with a good, general source, you can (1) get some notion of the scope of a subject you consider discussing; (2) begin to see how the broad topic can be broken down into smaller subtopics that, themselves, have importance; and (3) begin to accumulate bibliographical leads concerning where to turn next. But any data collecting involves record keeping, too, so we should pause to give attention to efficient note taking.

### Note Taking

Speaker after speaker compounds his difficulties by jotting information on page after page of notebook paper, recording the data in whatever order it turns up in research. If these speakers paused to think how they were going to use the information they recorded, they would start out quite differently.

Whatever information you gather in interviewing people, in reviewing your own thoughts, and in reading will ultimately have to be rewoven into thought units that support your speech purpose and fit the interests and expectations of your listeners. Almost never will the order in which you find ideas be the order in which you will want to present them. Suppose you are going to talk about cancer and think you should identify different types of cancer at some point in the speech you plan. If your notes are jotted down in a notebook in the order in which you found the information, your information about types of cancer will be thoroughly mixed in with other kinds of information—about causes, methods of control, tests for, and so on. On the other hand, if you had recorded all your notes on individual slips of paper or cards, each labeled according to the subject covered by the information on the card, you could in a few moments shuffle the cards marked "Cancer—Kinds" out of your pack of notes, examine what you have, and decide quickly and clearly what to do with this set of information.

*Notes must be well organized to be helpful.*

Your need for a systematic, efficient way of recording information arises as soon as you begin to review your own knowledge about a possible speech subject or read a first, general article like that we have referred to on modern architecture. If, as was the case with Randy Cohn, you know a reasonable amount about your general subject, you will still need some standard, efficient way of recording information as soon as you begin to gather new, specific information.

There are many satisfactory ways of recording information for convenient use during speech composition. This is one:

**Humor—Kinds**

Donald J. Gray, "The Uses of Victorian Laughter," *Victorian Studies*, X (Dec. 1966), 175–176.

". . . nonsense does not end in laughter. And its laughter is the product of devices and habits. . . . The laughter of nonsense is not a surprised recognition of the savagery of nature or the brutality of man. It is rather . . . laughter of release, a happy acceptance of the chance to look at something trivial or profound, pointless or terrifying, without thinking about it."

(Donald J. Gray: Assoc. Prof., English, Indiana University. Specialist on Victorian poetry and humor.)

What you need in any record of information is clear: the record should be complete enough so you needn't make a second trip to the original source; it must give you an accurate representation of what you found; it must allow items of information to be separated, sorted, and compared in any conceivably useful way. As far as we know, only recording individual units of information on individual slips of paper meets the last requirement. So, we say: note separate bits of information on separate note slips and put the complete reference to your source on all slips (or work out some code system for identifying exact sources). It's tedious, but it saves steps! We know from experience the extra steps we have had to take in consequence of sloppy note taking.

### Alternative Stages of Library Research

Sometimes research does not go as smoothly as is suggested by our example of beginning research on modern architecture. Even if you run into troubles, it remains the case that you can do efficient research if you keep your mind on what special resources your library has and how they can be used. To make a real test of what might happen to you in starting research for a speech, one of your authors made the following experiment one evening.

He imagined he wanted to make some sort of speech about *libel*. This was a subject he had just read a news article about and some years before he had read a couple of court cases involving libel. This was the extent of his knowledge as he entered his university library. In his vagueness, he was like many speech students making their first moves toward preparation for classroom speaking.

Inside the library, your author went directly to the reference section and seized the first encyclopedia that met his eye. It was *The Encyclopedia Americana, International Edition.* Under "libel," he found a clear article that discussed libel, defining it, distinguishing it from slander, explaining what constitutes "publishing" a libel, and giving exceptions to general rules about what is and is not libel. So far, so good. The essay was clear and intelligible, but there was a problem. It gave no directions at all about where one ought to look for further, more detailed information about libel! Your author tried again. This time he pulled down the most famed of encyclopedias, the *Encyclopaedia Britannica.* In it there was a longer and much more technical essay. In fact, it was so technical that some of the points were quite beyond your author's understanding. This article concluded with a bibliography telling where to find authoritative histories of libel law in the United States, Great Britain, and Scotland. But it was not the *history* of libel laws that your author was envisioning talking about, so these references were not altogether helpful. Obviously the "encyclopedia route" was not working very well on this subject. Were there other promising alternatives? Yes. Indeed there is at least one alternative in every library; it is called the "card catalogue." When the "encyclopedia route" fails, the next best move is almost always to turn to the catalogue of books held in the library—but you need to use this resource thoughtfully, too.

Pursuing his experiment, your author went to the catalogue of books held in his university's library. There, under the heading "libel," were cards identifying more than fifty full-length books. Their publication dates ranged from 1906 to 1974. Since his idea had been that he might speak about libel *today,* your author arbitrarily decided to ignore any book published before 1950. And since he was still no expert on libel, he also decided to ignore any title that sounded technical or that seemed to imply that the book in question was about a limited aspect of libel. These exclusions, plus a disregard for a few titles that sounded as though the books would be very boring, brought the whole list down to this set of six "most promising titles":

Clark Gavin, *Foul, False, and Infamous: Famous Libel and Slander Cases of History* (1950)
Charles Angoff, *The Book of Libel*(1966)
Paul P. Ashley, *Say It Safely* (1969), 4th edition
Clifton C. Lawhorne, *Defamation and Public Officials: The Evolving Law of Libel* (1971)
George P. Rice, *Law for the Public Speaker* (1958)
Robert H. Phelps, *Libel: Rights, Risks, and Responsibilities* (1966)

Even this short list could stand winnowing since this was the *first stage* of a presumed investigation for a speech. Gavin's and Lawhorne's books sounded as though they might contain useful examples to look up later; for now, they could probably be deferred. Angoff's and Phelps's books sounded good to check out if one were looking for some technicality about libel laws, but it seemed too early for that. Rice's book certainly needed to be looked at because it might be a source of information specially suited to a speech in a speech class, but first your author needed *background* material on libel and libel laws. Ashley's *Say It Safely* seemed the obvious book of the sextet to check out immediately. How could one know this? *The information printed on the catalogue card made clear this book's importance.* The book appeared in its fourth edition in 1969, though it had first appeared in 1956. Obviously a good many people thought this was a book worth buying! Furthermore, the book was published by The University of Washington Press, Seattle. Generally speaking, university presses are careful about their reputations and would be unlikely to publish a carelessly written book. On the other hand, the title was casually phrased, and this suggested it might be a book written for laymen—in which case it would be at your author's level of sophistication.

On the basis of these bits of information—all on the catalogue card—your author asked for *Say It Safely*. His reasoning paid off! The book turned out to be written by an attorney as a "manual for journalists and speakers." Its chapters covered most of the same topics that had been mentioned in the two encyclopedia articles that had been scanned. This fact suggested that the book was reasonably complete in coverage. In addition, the book contained discussions of libelous broadcasts and pictures. This was an unexpected "plus." Best of all, there were careful interpretations of all legal decisions cited, and there were examples of the kinds of statements, pictures, and the like which would be judged libelous. Clearly this was an ideal source to read next if one were working up a speech for a general audience on some aspect of libel.

From start to finish, this entire experiment, including the only partially successful attempts to work from encyclopedias, took only forty minutes. In that time your author scanned two essays, jotted down the main topics usually discussed in connection with the subject of libel, collected a preliminary bibliography of a half-dozen potentially useful books, and found and briefly scanned an excellent book which he could read as his next step in research for the speech he imagined he was preparing.

Our points about using libraries are these. Almost always, proceeding as we have illustrated will cost you less time and give you better results than wandering randomly among indexes to periodicals and card catalogues. On the other hand, when you know *exactly* what you want—what *point* you need information about—it is time to consult a comprehensive index like *The Reader's Guide to Periodical Literature* or *The New York Times Index*. Such indexes to specific articles and news reports are invaluable resources once you know what *specific* information you need; but while your ideas about subjects are still vague, you will work most efficiently by beginning your library research with general articles and books. Large as some libraries' card catalogues are, they, too, can lead you to *general* information if you let the information printed on the cards guide you toward the kinds of materials most important to you *now*.

As any talk takes shape you will find you need a variety

of specific bits of information with which to amplify and support the general ideas you evolve as leading lines of thought in speaking. You are apt to need certain statistics, some authoritative statements, specific dates, facts about topography or design or authorship, and the like. General sources do not usually give you much of this kind of detail. For this class of information you need to explore some of the many collections of classified data and to turn to periodical articles which deal with specific facets of your subject. For factual data of many sorts, especially statistical information, you will do well to consult *The World Almanac* or the *Statistical Abstract of the United States* or some similar source of miscellaneous factual information your library may have. For the essential facts about newsworthy events, consult *Facts on File* or follow up leads you can find in *The New York Times Index*. For events that have occurred since World War II, *Facts on File* is especially helpful since virtually every major event in the world is briefly identified there by date, and an excellent subject-matter index is provided. The specialized encyclopedias we have already mentioned are also good sources of detailed information simply because their articles are specialized. If it is a quotation you are trying to trace, *Bartlett's Quotations* is the standard source with which to begin. And specialized books like Gavin's *Foul, False, and Infamous: Famous Libel and Slander Cases in History* and Jane's *Ships of the World* and *Aircraft of the World* are examples of other sources of special, classified facts readily identifiable from the titles of the works.

*Good library research moves from general to specific sources.*

If your research is to be efficient, it is important that you recognize that one investigates and reads differently on moving from general to specific source materials. When you deal with general materials, you ought to expect to do a good deal of scanning, looking especially for ideas and facts that seem so important you will probably want to follow them up in more detail at a later point. When you hunt for specific data, your reading will be intensive but you will skip over books, articles, and sections of source materials that do not deal with the particular *class* of detailed information you know you need. A good researcher for public speech begins as a general explorer, spying out the "lay of the land" relative to a subject; gradually he becomes a "digger," a searcher first for one set of details and then for another. His first surveys are sweeping; his final inquiries become almost microscopic and highly selective.

When the standard moves in research fail to produce what you need, there is usually another invaluable resource. Most libraries have one or more persons designated "reference librarian." These people are thoroughly familiar with all the resources of your library. They are almost always eager to help you solve research problems, but they have to be asked, and asked clearly, so they can understand precisely what you are looking for. Consult them when the routines we have described do not work; they are experts on aids to research, and they understand better than anyone else what is and is not available in your library.

## HUMANIZING IDEAS

*Research material needs to be sifted, integrated, and organized before using.*

Ideas, facts, examples, and the like are never entirely ready for listeners just as you find them in research. All speech materials have to be specially sifted, integrated, and organized to suit the readiness of your listeners. Two examples should clarify this point.

Some years ago Professor Laura Crowell made a careful study of the ways President Franklin D. Roosevelt and his team of speech writers put together an important address which Roosevelt delivered to the Congress on January 6, 1941. The history of that speech is a good example of how expert speakers convert the raw materials of research into humanized messages that have significant effects on other people.

Roosevelt's speech went through seven different drafts before it was given. At the first step in preparing the speech, Roosevelt composed five pages of material to show his assistants what general lines of thought he wanted to develop. In the next stages of preparation Roosevelt and his staff *added* supporting materials and introduced *new* ideas that had not been in Roosevelt's original thoughts. When most of the needed support and amplification had been included, Roosevelt and his aides went through a stage of shifting ideas from place to place in the speech. Their goal was to get major thoughts into their proper logical and psychological relationships. As they did this, however, they also began to drop out a number of details they had formerly thought they wanted. As a result, what had begun as detailed arguments or explanations were now sometimes reduced to brief statements where it seemed the President's simple assertions would carry enough weight with the audience.

As they worked over the last drafts of the speech, the composers seem to have concentrated on sharpening language. They inserted alliterations, parallelisms, and reconstructed statements to give ideas better emphasis, and they further rearranged the order of minor points to achieve climaxes. In fact, it was only in the fifth, sixth, and seventh versions of the speech that the final shape of what Roosevelt would say began to emerge clearly.

Professor Crowell makes the important point that most of all this work in composing Roosevelt's speech aimed at more perfectly *adapting* Roosevelt's personal ideas to the ideas and feelings Roosevelt and his aides believed already existed "out there" in the audience to be addressed. Crowell concludes:

> Considering that the first wording of the ideas was done by writers with long training on scores of earlier addresses and thus the first sentences embodied much of the style desired, considering that each sentence, each word, underwent severe scrutiny not only in itself but in the light of changes made elsewhere in the address, one begins to understand the power of the final draft.[3]

Planning and humanizing of the kind Roosevelt and his staff carried out need to be, and can be, carried out by student speakers. What follows is a true narrative.

Bob Barth was one of a class of fifteen students, all but four of whom were college freshmen. Nine were women and six were men. In conference with his instructor, Barth revealed that he would like to explain the operation of jet aircraft engines in his next speech but, he said, this probably would be unwise since only two of the fourteen students who would be his audience had even an elementary knowledge of mechanical and physical principles. Barth's judgment on his audience was exactly right; most knew nothing and seemed to care nothing for the world of physics and aeronautical engineering. Nonetheless, Barth's instructor contended that this was an excellent opportunity for Barth to experiment with what careful selection of ideas could accomplish with a difficult audience. Barth reluctantly agreed to do what he could and set doggedly to work designing a speech that assumed little interest and no mechanical knowledge on the part of his hearers.

On the day of his speech Barth began by saying:

> I am going to talk to you today about jet engines. I suspect you think you aren't interested. Probably what's in your minds now is something like this.

Here Barth uncovered a rough but clear drawing of a jet engine "pod" covered with such words as "dangerous machine," "complicated," "for mechanics only," "expensive." He continued:

> The fact is that in principle at least jets aren't complicated. They're rather simple. If you've ever blown up a toy balloon and then let it

[3]Laura Crowell, "The Building of the 'Four Freedoms' Speech," *Speech Monographs*, XXII (November, 1955), pp. 266–283.

> out of your hands to watch it shoot through the air as the wind escaped, you not only know something about jet propulsion, you've used it. Let's begin right there—with the air escaping out of the balloon.

In this vein Barth covered simply and accurately the elemental facts about the construction and operation of two types of jet engines. The language of the speech was simple and the examples were always from everyday life. No chalkboard was available, so Barth had prepared some unpretentious, freehand, crayon drawings on cardboard sheets which he could use to help him communicate things that were hard to put into words. There were few marks of special artistry in the speech—just artful simplicity and sympathy for the listeners' attitudes and problems. When Barth finished his talk there was a ripple of applause—the first applause heard in that speech classroom. At the end of the hour, two young women who had been in the audience exchanged observations as they walked from the room. "I learned more today than I do in most class periods," said one. Her companion replied, "Yes. And imagine! I even thought I understood that engine!"

What happened? A speaker accepted his audience as he found it, *adjusted* his own knowledge and thoughts to the listeners' limitations and needs, and gave the hearers as much information as their little knowledge, his inventiveness and art, and the time would allow. Without fanfare Barth gave his listeners two always alluring reasons for paying attention: I can help you understand what has so far seemed mysterious to you, and you will find the whole experience of understanding much easier than you expect. Scarcely any subject is unsuited for discussion when speaker and audience approach it in this spirit.

In all public speech the crucial task is to fit subject and ideas to the particular group of human beings who will be addressed. Roosevelt's extensive revisions and Barth's expert simplifications show that this *can* be done—whether you are a college freshman or a President. You will always have secured your raw materials for speaking from a variety of sources; then, your job becomes one of weaving those materials into a *special* message from *you* to the living, breathing, uncertain *people* who will listen to you. The basic way to do this is to show your listeners how *they* can use or profit from what you are telling them. A successful, humanized public speech is not an essay addressed to just anyone, nor is it a bag of thoughts and feelings to be "unloaded." It is an invitation to listeners to *gain* from understanding what you have come to understand and feel as you have prepared to speak.

## SUMMARY

This chapter has been about ways speakers need to work their minds when they enter the first stages of preparing for public speech. If you have understood us, you understand why and how it is that:

1. The technique called brainstorming can stir up from your mind interesting and discussable subjects about which you could talk informingly and interestingly to an audience.
2. By clearly making up your mind whether you want your listeners (a) to understand and accept something, (b) to believe something more or less firmly, or (c) to accept your advice about something, you narrow the range of your major efforts in preparatory thinking and research.
3. Reviewing the attributes and relationships listed on pp. 71–72 can help you to recover useful information that might otherwise lie hidden in the recesses of your mind. This kind of topical review can also help you in planning how to interview other people and how to read when you do library research for a speech.
4. It is a wise tactic in reading for a speech first to locate general and, only afterward, specific material that is relevant to your purpose as a speaker.

In the final section of the chapter we offered you two examples of how careful speakers revised and adjusted material they had collected so that what they finally *said* would be true to the facts and also true to the needs and interests of the people who would be their listeners. From these examples we hope you have gained a practical understanding of what expert and student speakers really *do* with their research findings in order to make the ideas *humanly* interesting for specific audiences.

The examples with which we concluded this chapter do not identify the specific questions speakers have to ask themselves as they sort out the information they have collected. These are questions like: When have I *enough* material on a point? How do I distinguish "strong" from "weak" material in a speech? How do you "prove" something to a listener? These are the major questions we shall try to answer for you in the next chapter.

## EXERCISES

*Written*

1. Assume you are to speak to a classmate, or to your entire class, in favor of majoring in the academic subject that interests you most.

Identify three lines of thought (topics) that it would be useful to discuss with the audience you have decided on. Identify three other lines of thought that are relevant to your subject but which you would *not* choose to discuss with the listeners you have in mind. Explain the grounds on which you include and exclude each line of thought you cite.

2. Assume you are to give a classroom speech on: "It is important (or is not important) that college-aged voters vote regularly in local and national elections." Which of the sixteen lines of thought listed in this chapter suggest the most promising lines of research for this speech? Explain why the remaining "cues" are not potentially useful as guides to promising information for this speech.
3. Identify the lines of thought (topics) used in some brief, familiar speech such as Lincoln's "Gettysburg Address," Shakespeare's version of Mark Antony's speech over the body of Caesar in *Julius Caesar*, Dr. Martin Luther King's "I Have a Dream" address, or some other. Defend or criticize the speaker's choice of these lines of thought. Were there other topics he might as wisely have chosen? If so, illustrate how one of them might have been incorporated into the speech.

*Oral*

1. Give a short speech in which you explain two different ways a proverb or a maxim might be interpreted. Or choose a specific process and present two different ways that process might be effectively explained to an audience.
2. Give a brief report on a speech or editorial you have heard or read and in which you believe the creator made exceptionally inventive use of the lines of thought available to him—or failed to take advantage of lines of thought open to him.
3. Form a committee with three or four of your colleagues. Compose an outline or sketch of a speech, editorial, or other practical message intended to accomplish a specific purpose with an audience your committee imagines and describes. When the committee has settled on purpose and audience, use the cuing terms in this chapter to construct a committee's list of *all* the things it might make sense to include in the message. Then cut this list to the topics that *ought* to be covered, and prepare the committee's sketch or outline of the whole message.
4. To intensify your awareness of the many ways most subjects can be treated in speech, divide your class into groups of three; assign a *noun* to each group (trees, girl, car, Eskimo, etc.); have each group member choose a "cue" from pages 71–72 and then prepare and give a two-minute talk on the assigned subject, using chiefly lines of thought suggested by the chosen cue word. You should discover that there are more interesting things to be said about simple subjects than you supposed.

# Invention: General Tactics

# 5

When you have collected material for a speech, there remain further tasks of rhetorical invention. *"Invention" in speaking is discovering communicable ideas and their logical and psychological aspects.* It is with these "logical and psychological aspects" of discovered ideas that we want to deal in this and the next chapter.

*The speaker must consider the logical and psychological aspects of his subject.*

As you saw in the examples of Franklin Roosevelt and Bob Barth, at the end of Chapter Four, when a speaker knows what he or she *can* say about a subject, there comes the task of selecting what is "just right" to say in the situation the speaker will enter. The problems here are tactical. You probably know more than you need to say and there will be more than one way of treating your material. The issue is: what are your *best* moves, or tactics, for fitting your material and methods into a speech *you* can make effectively in your particular rhetorical situation? Normally you will need to begin this phase of preparation by reviewing the goal and purpose you originally set for yourself.

## REVIEWING PURPOSES AND GOALS

You had a purpose and some overall goal you hoped to accomplish when you set out to collect supporting material for the speech you plan. But you are always free to change your plans. That may seem too obvious to say, but have you never made a plan for something and then felt committed to it even after second thoughts told you it was not a very good idea? This is a kind of rigid thinking you ought to avoid in planning for public speech.

Not long ago a student in one of our classes planned a report on the "secrets" of Billy Graham's success as an evangelistic preacher. He was satisfied at the outset of his preparation that the "secrets" would be found in the ways in which Graham composed and preached sermons. But after he had done considerable reading about how Graham's "Crusades" are planned, he came to the conclusion that the "secret" was actually in the detailed planning that comes before the Reverend Graham even appears in a city to preach. Obviously the purpose of this student's report had to be changed and his goal in making the report changed also. His original subject sentence, "The qualities of Graham's sermons show us sources of his success," had to be changed to, "The careful planning of Graham's 'Crusades' makes his successes possible." His goal shifted from making listeners see how Graham's sermons work to making them see the significance of detailed, preliminary planning. The point of this example and the general point we want to make is that when you know a subject well, you may prefer to or may have to make a speech somewhat different from the one you foresaw when you began preparation. That is not always the case, but if it is, there is nothing wrong with changing your purpose and goal as preparation progresses.

*After research, the speaker must review his subject sentence.*

Whether you shift purposes or not, you must in any case have a very clear idea of exactly what you want to do before you begin to "flesh out" your speech. For this reason alone it is intelligent to review your purpose when research is completed. Review to see whether your subject sentence still says clearly (1) what your goal is in talking about this subject, and (2) what deserves to be included and excluded as you develop your talk. Making sure you have such a clear statement is a very practical matter. All experiments that have tested what happens when speakers tell their listeners their purposes show that stating a clear purpose helps listeners to understand and retain what they are told.[1] You should, then, tell your audience exactly

[1]Among studies that have shown this effect are Donald L. Thistlethwaite, Henry deHaan, and Joseph Kamenetzky, "The Effect of 'Directive' and 'Non-Directive' Communication Procedures on Attitudes," *Journal of Abnormal and Social Psy-*

what your purpose is, unless doing so will introduce special disadvantages as it might when you seek to persuade a hostile audience. But how can you tell listeners what you are trying to do, or even *know* what you are trying to do, unless you are sure nothing you have found in research gives you reason to change purposes and goals? This is exactly the point at which Randy Cohn seems to have slipped up. When she submitted her choice of subject paper, she said her subject sentence was, "I am here to give you the chance of a lifetime, a chance to help mankind, a chance to give of yourself, a chance to give the greatest gift of all—the gift of life, by simply signing your name." (See p. 230, Appendix.) That was not a very precise subject sentence in the first place. When she investigated her subject, she discovered that transplantation of organs has a long and unusual history. She became fascinated with this history, as her diary shows. The subject sentence (central idea) on her final outline was nearly the same as her original one, but *it does not even suggest that she would talk about the history that actually took so much of her time.* Had she reviewed her goal and subject sentence more carefully after research, her speech might have been much better balanced—*or* she might have given a somewhat different kind of speech. In any case, Randy did not recheck her plans closely enough and in consequence gave herself too little time to persuade the audience to sign organ-donors' cards.

When you are sure your purpose is clear and is precisely as you want it, you are ready to sift your collected material to find those ideas and pieces of information which will accomplish precisely what you are aiming at. This is first of all a matter of finding "enough" reasons to make your listeners believe you. In the rest of this chapter we shall suggest how you can estimate what is "enough" and what is "right" for your task.

## PROOFS

What people call *reasons* may or may not be the result of close reason*ing*. We all decide what is "sufficient" and what seems "good" to us by exercising close reasoning at some times and by responding on the basis of our habits at other times. But however we arrive at a conclusion, we tend to demand the following things when we listen to speakers who seek to influence our beliefs:

---

*chology*, LI (July, 1955), pp. 107–118; Donald K. Darnell, "The Relation between Sentence Order and Comprehension," *Speech Monographs*, XXX (June, 1963), pp. 97–100; Ernest Thompson, "Some Effects of Message Structure on Listeners' Comprehension," *ibid.*, XXXIV (March, 1967), pp. 51–57.

*Three demands are made on the speaker.*

1. We demand that either what the speaker says or something in our own experience shall connect what we are asked to believe with our own personal interests. For example, before we buy a jacket we require that either a salesperson or our own thoughts shall tell us that this jacket would be pleasantly warm or look well on us or otherwise give us some *satisfaction.*
2. We demand that either what the speaker says or something in our own experience shall make the choice we are to make seem *rational.* Whatever makes us think a jacket would be warm or look well has to seem *reasonable* as well as gratifying. A famous psychologist has said that nothing we do ever seems illogical to us at the moment we do it. It may seem illogical to other people or even to us, at a later moment, but in the instant we act or believe what we hear we have to believe there's a "good" reason for acting or believing.
3. We demand that a speaker and his sources and sponsors seem to *deserve our confidence,* at least on the subject being talked about. Several experiments have shown that an audience of college students is likely to believe an ex-convict more than a college student if both make statements about prison conditions. The preference is natural. Whatever else, the ex-convict knows about prisons at firsthand, so unless the listeners have reasons for thinking he is dishonest about his subject, they will put more confidence in what he says than in what is said by someone who has only read about prisons.

If you examine your own listening, you will discover that you are always making these three interrelated kinds of demands on those you hear.

Suppose someone is talking to you about an engineering curriculum. Certain questions constantly pop into your mind. We could phrase them this way: Why should *I* care about the engineering curriculum? Why bring this up *now*? Why should I believe the curriculum *is as you say it is*? Why is what you urge on me *better* or *truer* than an alternative? Why should I listen to *you* on this matter?

Whoever talks about engineering curricula can expect these questions to arise again and again in any listener's mind. And if we substitute another subject, we shall find listeners raising precisely the same questions. They are commonplace, recurring questions asked by listeners of any speech on any subject.

Notice that some of these questions ask whether the listener's personal interests are going to be satisfied (Why should *I* care? Why bring this up *now*?); some ask for rational justifications (Why should I believe things *are as you say they are*? Why is what you urge on me *better* or *truer* than an alternative?); and another asks about the speaker's qualifications (Why should I listen to *you* on this matter?). If you see to it that these five questions are satisfactorily answered either by what you say and do or by something your listeners are already aware of, your speech will have the personal-interest, rational, and source justifications that audiences demand as the price of shifting their attitudes and beliefs. So, our immediate problem becomes: How do these questions get answered through speech?

### Developing Personal-Interest Justifications

*A speaker's ideas must appeal to listeners' personal interests.*

The chief ways you can show listeners that their own interests and preferences justify what you say can be seen in a brief excerpt from an actual speech. Below are a few statements made by Dr. Daniel J. Boorstin, historian and Director of the National Museum of History and Technology in Washington, D.C. Dr. Boorstin was addressing the Associated Press Managing Editors' Association on "Dissent, Dissension, and the News." He wanted his listeners to differentiate between "debate" and "dissent." He apparently wanted them to approve of "debate" but to disapprove of "dissent." Look, now, at how Boorstin worked with his hearers' attitudes in a *patterned* way so that what he said would turn their thoughts in the direction of the responses he wanted: approve "debate," disapprove "dissent." We have broken the passage into individual thought units and opposite each identified the kind of justifying response Dr. Boorstin apparently was working for.

| **Boorstin's Remarks** | **Responses Apparently Wanted** |
|---|---|
| A debate is an orderly exploration . . . | *Order* and *exploring* are "good." *Debate* has these qualities. |
| of a common problem that presupposes the debaters are worried by the same question. | *Common interests* and *agreement* make for *order—debaters* have "good" goals. |
| It brings to life new facts . . . | *Facts* and *newness* are also "good"; *debate* has that "goodness" too. |
| and new arguments which make possible a better solution. | *Newness* and *better solutions* are "good," so *debate* has further merit. |
| But dissension means discord. | *Discord* is "bad"; *dissension* has this quality. |

| | |
|---|---|
| As the dictionary tells us, dissension is marked by a break in friendly relations. | *Breaking friendship* is a mark of *discord; dissension* has this "bad" quality too. |
| It is an expression not of common concern . . . | *Dissension* denies the "good" of *common interest,* further rendering it "bad." |
| but of hostile feelings. | *Hostility* is the opposite of *agreement,* one of the "goods" *debate* develops; another way *dissension* is "bad." |
| And this distinction is crucial.[2] | [No particular attitude is aroused here. Dr. Boorstin missed an opportunity to fix the pattern firmly with something like: "Debate is productive; dissension is discordant, unfriendly, and unproductive."] |

Dr. Boorstin did not engage in formal reasoning, but he did cite an authority: "the dictionary." He said nothing directly to show that he was qualified to say what he did; perhaps his reputation as a distinguished historian made it unnecessary for him to qualify himself further. What he did do was justify his thought that "debate" is desirable and "dissent" undesirable by trying to activate a series of favorable and unfavorable attitudes which the listeners presumably already had within them. If he convinced his hearers, he did so by rousing and directing their predispositions and self-interests.

This is the kind of "proving" you must learn to use whenever the strongest support for what you want accepted lies within your listeners rather than in the data outside them. Let us suppose you want to have your classmates accept the proposition that students learn better under skillful than under careless teachers. It would be silly for you to try to "prove" this point by offering statistics from educational research and quotations from authorities. As students, your listeners will already have within themselves the most powerful proofs you can find. Experience will have taught them that disorganized lectures and assignments make it hard to learn; that not allowing class discussion restricts learning; that the best showmen are not always the best teachers. These beliefs and attitudes are the strongest "proofs" available to you for "proving" that skill in teaching and efficient learning go together. What you need to do is awaken

[2]The complete text of this speech appears in Wil A. Linkugel, R. R. Allen, and Richard L. Johannesen, *Contemporary American Speeches,* 2nd ed. (Belmont: Wadsworth Publishing Company, Inc., 1969), pp. 203–211. The excerpt quoted appears on p. 205 as "paragraph" nine.

the listeners' memories and experiences in an organized, systematic way that will support your main idea. Your method of proving or supporting in this case is to use the feelings and self-interests of listeners as "proofs." Your task in invention will be to find examples, definitions, comparisons, etc., that will call up the right memories in the right sequence to *make* your listeners come to their own conclusions in favor of your proposition. Your best tactics will be those Dr. Boorstin used. Try to *direct* listeners toward specific judgments and reactions, as Boorstin did.

The biology major, whose talk on hunting female deer was described in Chapter Three, and Bob Barth, whose speech on jet propulsion was cited in Chapter Four, showed how effectively ordinary, thoughtful use of listeners' predispositions can bring audiences to supply their own "sufficient" proofs in support of a speaker's idea. It is important to notice, however, that Boorstin, the biology major, and Bob Barth were not content just to invite listeners to reassert what they already believed; each speaker brought his audience to *new* beliefs because each connected existing beliefs and interests with *new* information. By connecting the old and the new by means of words, each speaker led or directed his hearers' thoughts from familiar experiences to conclusions that had not previously existed in their minds. That is the full, artful use of existing beliefs and interests as proofs in speaking.

### Developing Rational Justifications

*A speaker's ideas must be rational.*

Sometimes "Why should *I* care?" and "Why bring that up *now?*" cannot be answered just by arousing self-interests and prior beliefs and memories of past experiences. When people are doubters, for instance, their basic questions become, "Why should I believe things *are as you say they are?*" and "Why is what you offer *better* or *truer* than some alternative?" These are questions you will have to take care of whenever your listeners have beliefs, attitudes, and interests that conflict with or otherwise fail to support the ideas you offer. Then, you must justify your ideas by showing that they are rational even though they are new or are doubted by your audience.

It is not easy to say what a rational ground for accepting ideas is. Presumably what is "rational" is something that "makes sense" or "adds up." But what makes sense about the things we discuss is almost never universally agreed upon. That is why we *talk* so much about things like politics, religion, patterns of sexual relations, and the like. If someone claims, "The Democratic Party is the party of the working people," is that a

rational statement? Reasons and evidence could be given for the statement and also against it. It could even be argued that the statement is rather silly in itself because working people have such a variety of interests no one party could be for them all and still be a party. There are reasons to doubt and reasons to believe statements of this kind or advice like "A couple shouldn't divorce if they have children." We talk about such matters just because they are debatable. And because people can rationally differ, a very important task in speaking is to give reasons that your listeners will find rational on *their* terms. When you speak to resolve or remove doubts, it does no good to try to prove the doubters "wrong." This will only make them defensive. They will think you are the one who is not "rational." Your job is to find the materials with which you can show them that you are "right" according to *their* definitions of what is rational.

How different views can be about what is reasonable was illustrated in 1971 in a Supreme Court decision. The Court decided a case in which the federal government sought to prevent *The New York Times* and the *Washington Post* from publishing excerpts from what came to be called "The Pentagon Papers." The Court voted against the government's case. The vote was decisive, but *not one Justice agreed fully with any other Justice on the proper reasons* for voting on one side or the other. The Justices issued six different "rational justifications" for the majority's decision and three different sets of reasons for voting with the minority. Why? Because the Justices, like all of us, applied their *own* standards for determining what was "reasonable" about the facts and the laws. The facts and the laws were the same, but there were nine different, "reasoned" interpretations of them. Such dramatic differences of opinion about what is "reasonable" are not common, but what is "reasonable" is always decided by *individuals.* "Reason is in the eye of the beholder." Reason is not regulated by universal laws and rules. This means that if you need to "prove" that an idea is "reasonable," you must prove it with material that is "rational" *according to your listeners' standards.*

How, then, does "rational proof" work in ordinary talk? Let us look at an example from what a number of people have called a very "rational" talk made by a college student. The speaker's title was "What Can We Prove about God?" His central idea was that it is impossible either to prove or disprove in a scientific way that God exists. In the excerpt below Mr. Leon Zellner was refuting a familiar type of argument on behalf of the claim that God must exist. Mr. Zellner, a college junior, said:

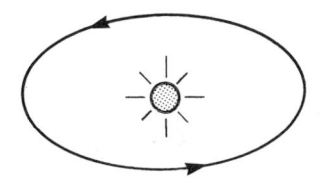

> People who use this type of reasoning about God generally choose some complex kind of natural mechanism and prove—or at least they assume they prove—that the mechanism must have been planned. Thereby, they infer the existence of a Planner. . . . I'll deal [in refuting the argument] primarily with the solar system because we know that better. The followers of this train of thought, of which Sir Isaac Newton was one, say that because the earth and the sun and all the other planets have specific masses and specific velocities, they follow specific courses. They also argue that these courses could not possibly have been selected through the forces of chance. They say these particular orbits were predesigned by some super-being which they call God.
>
> Let me illustrate. Suppose, for example, that this line
>
> 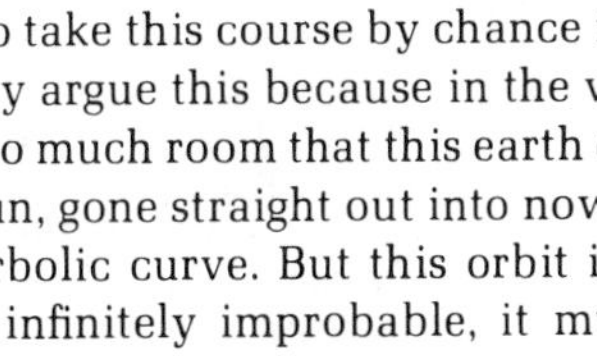
>
> represents the orbit of the earth around the sun. These people argue that for the earth to take this course by chance is infinitely improbable. Basically, they argue this because in the vastness of what we call space, there's so much room that this earth could as easily have spiraled into the sun, gone straight out into nowhere, or followed a parabolic or hyperbolic curve. But this orbit is the path it chose. Since the path is infinitely improbable, it must have been predesigned. That's the argument.

> Now, suppose the earth, rather than following its orbital path, had instead followed this one:
>
> 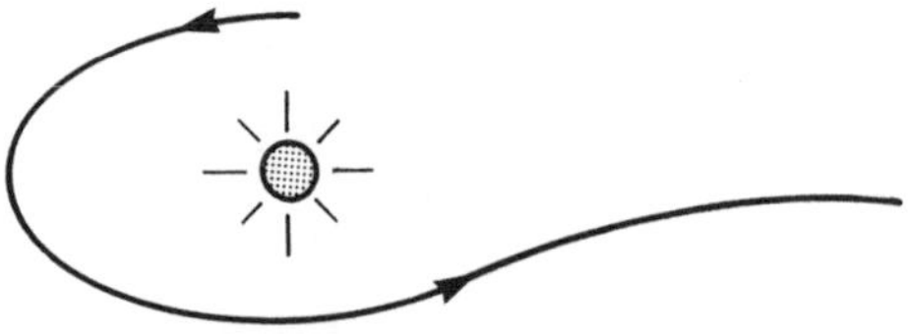
>
> What are the chances that the second path might have been taken? They are equally infinitely improbable. Therefore, the arguers are actually not proving anything, since they are saying, in fact, that all possible courses are infinitely improbable. They aren't proving anything by saying just one of them was chosen. The probabilities for any one path are equal.
>
> . . . No matter what happens in nature, it is infinitely improbable. This is to say, if we try to figure out the probabilities for the fact that it's now snowing here at this moment, it can be proved that it's infinitely improbable that it would snow here today. It is necessary for a whole complex chain of events to occur before it can snow in State College. If the earth weren't rotating at its particular speed, we wouldn't be here with the snow. If the earth were not revolving around the sun as it is, perhaps the climate would be warmer and it would be impossible for it to snow here. If the masses of air had any other set of molecules than they have at this instant, it would be impossible for it to snow. This kind of argument can be applied to anything in nature. Take the existence of a flower in a particular spot. There are an infinite number of places where that flower could grow. So, for a flower that you don't plant but which just happens to grow, it is infinitely improbable that that flower should grow where it does.[3]

The talk continued, pointing out the fallacy of the argument Zellner was criticizing and concluding: "You cannot explain, just by the complexity of a situation, that the complex had to be planned by some all-knowing mind," but neither can you ever demonstrate that it was not.

Zellner's listeners found his talk impressively "logical." So have others who have read it. This kind of response shows that Zellner used methods people think of as rational. So what is it that he really did? To put it briefly, he made his views seem

[3]Excerpted from a talk delivered by Leon R. Zellner to a class in "Effective Speech" at The Pennsylvania State University. The talk was in response to an assignment: address the class on "your personal view" of any issue, set of facts, or other matter of concern to you. A complete text of the speech, with introduction and some critical analysis, appears in Carroll C. Arnold, *Criticism of Oral Rhetoric* (Columbus: Charles E. Merrill Publishing Co., 1974), pp. 335–340 and *passim*. Printed by permission of Leon R. Zellner.

more *probable* than any other views the listeners and readers happened to know about. That is essentially what it is to justify anything rationally. You give evidence and reasoning that make more sense than any other evidence and reasoning your listeners can think of.

We can diagram what Zellner did if we use a method devised by the English logician, Stephen E. Toulmin.[4] In Professor Toulmin's way of thinking about practical reasoning, people give some—and sometimes all— of six kinds of material. At most, they express elements of reasoning that Toulmin calls *data, warrants, backing for warrants, claims, qualifications of claims,* and *conditions of rebuttal* that make "qualifications" seem necessary.

A simple example will show how Toulmin would analyze a practical argument. Suppose someone says the following to you: Bet on the horse, Mary's Leg. She has a good chance to win. The best jockey in the race is riding her and she comes from a line of very fast horses. Rider and breeding are the things that really count in horse racing. Of course, Mary's Leg isn't much of a mudder, so if it rains, don't bet.

We could diagram this argument—the like of which you can hear at a race track almost any day—as in Figure 3.

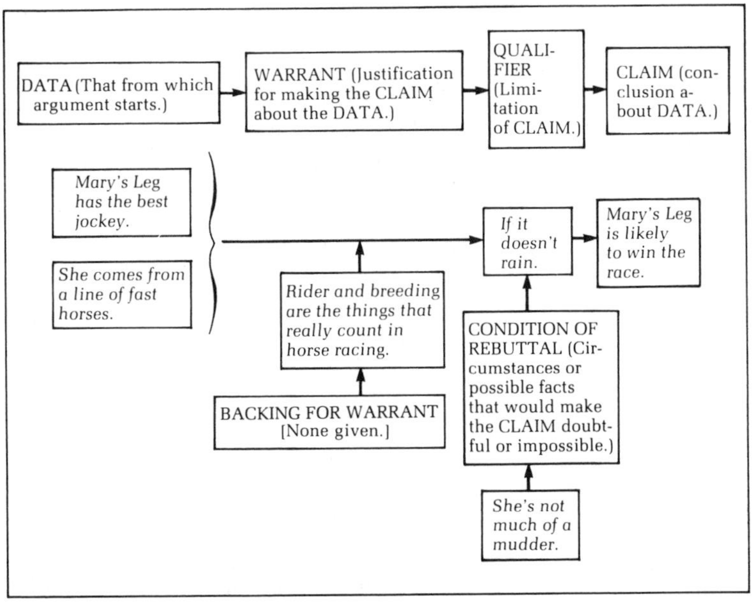


**FIGURE 3.**

[4]Stephen E. Toulmin, *The Uses of Argument* (Cambridge, England: Cambridge University Press, 1958). See especially Chapter 3, "The Layout of Arguments."

From Figure 3, we can see certain things about the argument and the points at which its rationality might be either applauded or questioned. Only two facts *(data)* were given. Is that enough to know about a horse in a race? Whether it is or not depends on the person responding to the advice to bet on Mary's Leg. Whether he bets also hinges on whether he believes that "Rider and breeding are the things that really count in horse racing." This *warrant* is *not* given any *backing*. If the listener believes the *warrant* anyway, the *data* become *reasons* for believing and betting. But the arguer does not ask us to believe Mary's Leg will *certainly* win. She has a fault: she doesn't run well in mud. So, the conclusion we are asked to draw from the *data* is a qualified one. If it doesn't rain, we are told we should believe Mary's Leg is likely to win.

Using this description of how arguments can work and what their parts are, let's look first at the argument which Leon Zellner presented and then refuted in his speech. That first argument is shaped like that in Figure 4.

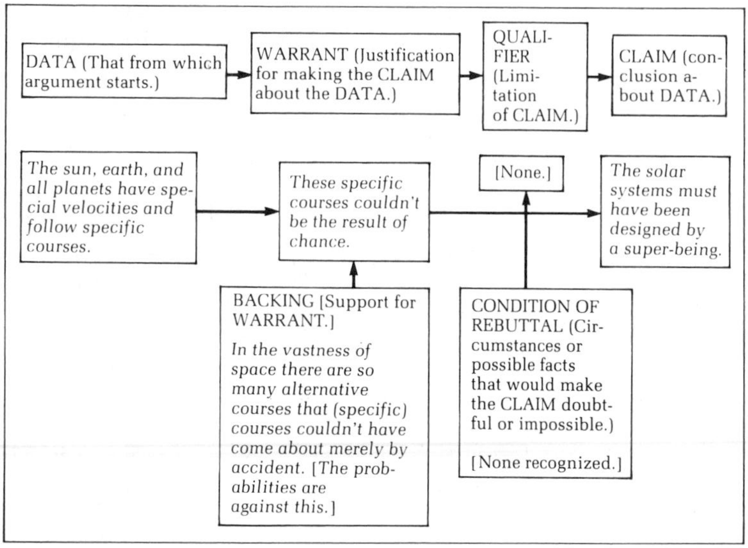


**FIGURE 4.**

In what are printed as the first two paragraphs of our excerpt (p. 97), Zellner restated a familiar philosophical-theological argument. The argument has been made again and again in efforts to prove that an all-supervising God must exist. At the end of the second paragraph a listener will be impressed or unimpressed with the argument as Zellner explained it, depending on whether the argument's *completely unqualified claim* seems reasonable now that he has heard the *data, warrant,* and *backing for warrant* which Zellner gave. But Figure 4 shows us exactly where doubt could most easily occur: *must* design by a super-being follow from the rest of the argument? Is that the only, and the necessary, conclusion? Here's the weakest spot in the whole argument—no possible *condition of rebuttal* or *qualifier* is recognized. A person would seem reasonable to explore this spot further. That is exactly what Zellner did, and by doing so he made himself seem reasonable and his proofs seem reasonable.

In what is printed as the third and fourth paragraphs of the excerpt, Zellner asserts his own conclusion or *claim:* "The arguers are actually not proving anything." Next, he offers these supports for his *claim:*

1. The probabilities for any one path are equal.
2. No matter what happens in nature, it is infinitely improbable. For example:
   a. it is improbable that it should snow here, now;
   b. it is improbable that any wild flower should grow where it does grow.

In effect, Zellner is saying, "The available *data* do not allow any conclusion, so neither the original argument nor its opposite is 'proof' in any logical sense." This contention depends for credibility on Zellner's assertion that there is just as much logical probability that the earth should *by chance* have followed the orbit

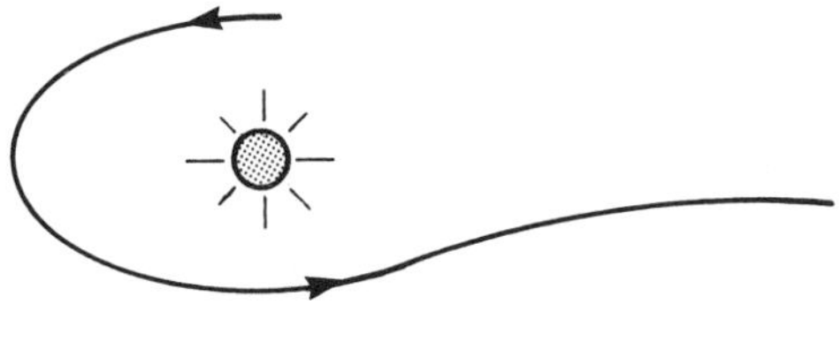

as there is logical probability that it should by *chance* have followed the path

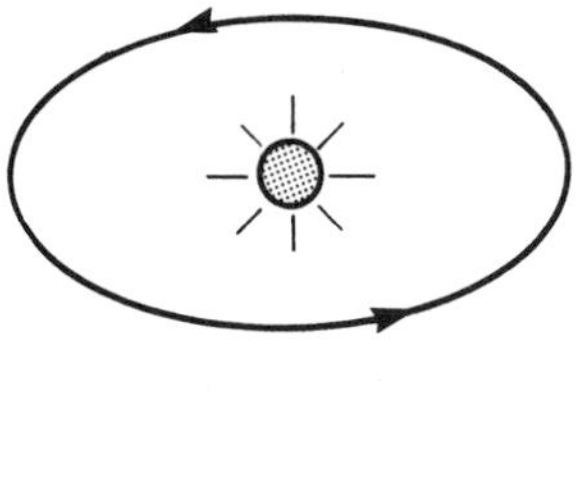

Through his other examples (snow and the flower), he is alleging that any natural event is *logically* improbable. If that is so, we cannot infer from such events whether they are or are not parts of a grand, supernaturally determined design. He denies the *warrant*.

The rhetorical goal of all Zellner's reasoning was to make his listeners accept *his* final *claim:* you cannot prove or disprove God's existence by scientifically logical methods. How do we respond to such reasoning? Do you believe his final *claim*? Your answer will depend partly on how clearly you understand his contention that any specific course of sun, earth, or other planets is as improbable, but no more improbable than, the courses the planets actually follow. This is his attack on the original *warrant*. Whether you believe Zellner will also depend on what you think of his examples of the improbability of a snowfall in a particular place and of a flower's growth in a particular place. Are these fair analogies to the planets' courses? Are they true examples of "probabilities" in nature? If you think they are, you will probably accept Zellner's denial of the original argument's *warrant*. If you challenge the examples, you are likely to disagree with Zellner's conclusion.

Now, we can see how people respond to reasoning generally. Whether you "buy" any argument depends on (1) whether the parts of an argument conform to what *you* are inclined to believe or are used to thinking, and (2) whether you can put the parts of the argument together in your own head in a way that makes them sufficient to satisfy *your* sense of what is *probably* so. It is actually *your* beliefs and *your* standards of reasoning that determine whether you say "Yes" or "No" to Mr. Zellner. *What is "reasonable" or "rational" in rhetorical speech depends on what the listeners grasp, identify as elements of reasoning, and define as sufficient.* Zellner was clear enough and "logical" enough to satisfy the class and instructors who listened to him. That does not prove he was right. The fact is that the argument Zellner attacked and the argument he used in his attack have *both* been called "strong" by thousands of people over several centuries.

All you can do in proving an idea rational is what Mr. Zellner did admirably. You can locate the particular patterns of thought which your listeners are most used to. You put them together into arguments which your listeners will find "more reasonable" than anything else they know of. Zellner found these kinds of argument for *his* listeners. It does not matter that there are other people who would say Zellner's proof was faulty. Those people were not in Zellner's audience. Beside this is the fact that the way Zellner chose to argue has a generally good reputation in a centuries-long debate over whether the universe was planned. His argument was "reputable," another good test of what is rational.

Speakers sometimes make the mistake of giving only the rational justifications that their *own* minds find accurate, understandable, reasonable, and sufficient. If the real audience is apt to apply more exacting standards of justification than the speaker applies to his material, the speaker errs. On the other hand, you can bore listeners by giving them more rational justifications than they care for. You can avoid both kinds of mistakes if you ask yourself: (1) is my proof sound enough so that *I* believe it, for myself, and (2) how much *more* or *less* explanation and support do I need to satisfy my particular audience in the rhetorical situation in which we shall meet? It seemed to his audience that Mr. Zellner both believed what he was saying, for himself, and that he gave *enough* reasons for the audience to believe him—at least for the time being.

No one can tell you how to build just the right rational justifications into any particular speech. In the logic of public communication, "One man's meat is another's poison." As you develop each speech, you must ask at each stage what *your* listeners will probably demand as reason and evidence. Then draw from information you have collected (or from new information) whatever is necessary to make your views rational in the judgment of those listeners.

### The Speaker as a Justification for Ideas

*The speaker must arouse confidence in himself.*

How much rational support for ideas is necessary often varies with who presents the ideas. "Why should I listen to *you* on this matter?" is a question always present in the thoughts of audiences. The importance of meeting the question was pointedly stated by Aristotle:

> The character of the speaker is a cause of persuasion when the speech is so uttered as to make him worthy of belief; for as a rule we trust men of probity more, and more quickly, about things in general, while on points outside the realm of exact knowledge, where opinion is divided, we trust them absolutely. This trust, however, should be created by the speech itself, and not left to depend upon an antecedent impression that the speaker is this or that kind of man. It is not true, as some writers on the art maintain, that the probity of the speaker contributes nothing to his persuasiveness; on the contrary, we might almost affirm that his character is the most potent of all the means of persuasion.[5]

[5]From *The Rhetoric of Aristotle,* translated and edited by Lane Cooper, pp. 8–9, bk. 1, chap. 2. Copyright 1932, renewed 1960 by Lane Cooper. Reprinted by permission of Prentice-Hall, Inc., Englewood Cliffs, New Jersey.

Modern scientists have devoted much study to this kind of "personal proof." On the whole their findings indicate that listeners look for a specific pair of attributes in speakers. These Aristotle called "intelligence" and "character"; investigators of the past twenty years have variously called them "competence and trustworthiness," "expertness and trustworthiness," and "authoritativeness and good character."[6]

Everything you reveal through your speaking can play a part in maintaining, strengthening, or weakening listeners' confidence in what you say to them. Showing them your knowledge, analytical power, organizational ability, verbal skill, apparent interest in them, and your understanding of the speaking situation will be at least as important as justifications based on self-interest and rationality. To see how you can build claims to intelligence and trustworthiness into speech, consider first how a public figure did it. Probably no one in modern American history has been more obviously concerned to prove his credibility and fairness than Theodore Roosevelt, so we take him as our first example.

On April 5, 1906, Roosevelt pleaded for moderation and balance in the journalism of the "muck-rakers," some of whom had been carried far from fact by their zeal to expose corruption. In his famous speech, "The Man with the Muck-Rake," Roosevelt said:

> It is because I feel that there should be no rest in the endless war against the forces of evil that I ask that the war be conducted with sanity as well as with resolution.
>
> The men with the muck-rakes are often indispensable to the well-being of society; but only if they know when to stop raking muck, and to look upward to the celestial crown above them, to the crown of worthy endeavor. There are beautiful things above and round about them; and if they gradually grow to feel that the whole world is nothing but muck, their power of usefulness is gone.[7]

Here Roosevelt earns some personal credit by speaking moderately. He concedes what he needs to—that exposing "muck" and corruption often does good. Because he concedes this, his criticism of muck-rakers seems fairer. Roosevelt also claims he is trustworthy by taking care to define his position exactly. By doing this he implies that his is a sane and sensible position. Then he claims the journalists ought to share his posi-

---

[6]For a good summary of modern research on *ethos* see Gary Cronkhite, *Persuasion: Speech and Behavioral Change* (Indianapolis: The Bobbs-Merrill Company, 1969), pp. 172–178.

[7]From "The Man with the Muck-Rake." A full text with Introduction and some critical analysis appears in Carroll C. Arnold, *Criticism of Oral Rhetoric*, pp. 288–297 and *passim*.

tion. Finally in the last sentence, he declares that an immoderate view is both mistaken and makes journalism useless. In these ways he claims credit for himself directly and also indirectly. Furthermore, he borrowed his muck-rake metaphor from John Bunyan's *The Pilgrim's Progress.* That famous book is an allegory which most educated listeners would understand in 1906. The whole book insists strongly that to concentrate on material things is not only mistaken but sinful. By the simple act of borrowing the "man with the muck-rake" idea, Roosevelt casts doubt on the intelligence and trustworthiness of the people he is criticizing.

These are representative ways by which speakers enhance their own images and so invoke *themselves* as "proofs" of their positions. There are also more obvious but no less important ways of enhancing speakers' authority. The late Ralph Zimmerman, when an undergraduate at Wisconsin State College, Eau Claire, Wisconsin, impressively invoked his authority in a speech entitled "Mingled Blood." His opening words were:

> I am a hemophiliac. To many of you, that word signifies little or nothing. A few may pause a moment and then remember that it has something to do with bleeding. Probably none of you can appreciate the gigantic impact of what those words mean to me.

At a later point Zimmerman tellingly used his own disabilities as proofs in explaining the disease:

> If internal bleeding into a muscle or joint goes unchecked repeatedly, muscle contraction and bone deformity inevitably result. My crooked left arm, the built-up heel on my right shoe, and the full-length brace on my left leg offer mute but undeniable testimony to that fact. Vocal evidence you hear; weak tongue muscles are likely to produce defective L and R sounds.[8]

Mr. Zimmerman's subject matter was exceptional but his method was not. He offers the familiar proof: "Believe me because I have experienced what I speak of." That every listener could hear his weakly formed "r" and "l" sounds was more dramatic evidence that he had really "been there." But you could display a piece of coal you had personally picked up in a mine and by doing so establish that you are specially qualified by experience to speak about coal or mining.

You have not the initial *ethos* of a Theodore Roosevelt nor, we hope, the dramatic physical disabilities of a Zimmerman, but the methods we have illustrated from their speaking

[8]Copyright by the Interstate Oratorical Association. For a full text of this speech see Linkugel, Allen, and Johannesen, *Contemporary American Speeches,* pp. 199–203.

are open to you. As you build your speeches you can concede what needs to be conceded as Roosevelt did; you can choose ideas that clearly avoid extremes which your specific listeners would reject; you can arrange your material so that your talk will contrast the good sense of what you say with the lesser wisdom of opposing views. You can also put in allusions and other references that associate you with what is intelligent, candid, and in your listeners' special interests. If you have done first-hand investigation on your subject, or if you speak from your past experience, "I have seen it" or "I have been there" or even "I read it carefully" are claims to respectful hearing which you can build into your speeches as efficiently as Ralph Zimmerman.

Consider how effectively several of these tactics were used by Robert Dike in a classroom talk given in the Spring of 1971 at the University of Delaware:

> As a resident of this state I'm not against normal industrial and population growth, but I am against this dam as a means to supply water for this anticipated growth. There are two basic reasons behind my opposition. The first is conservation; the second, for want of a better title, I've called "governmental injustice."
>
> Believe it or not, the White Lake Creek is the last clean stream in this small state of Delaware. If you ever go up into the area of the Creek, what you'll find is a quiet, scenic, very beautiful forest. I was there recently and, believe me, it is, indeed, beautiful. There are over 30 varieties of wildlife present—ranging from deer and foxes to the rare flying squirrel. And some 143 species of birds and 20 different types of reptiles and amphibians. Plant life is just as richly abundant—more than 250 species—43 kinds of trees and well over 200 varieties of wildflowers.
>
> No one can doubt that this region is one of Nature's unique havens, but what will happen to this untouched beauty if the dam is built?[9]

Mr. Dike had earlier given his listeners the plans for a new dam. Having now announced his opposition and previewed his reasons, he was moving into a "conservation argument": water impounded by the dam would destroy the White Lake Creek area. At this point he took special steps to establish himself as worth listening to. He revealed his personal acquaintance with the area. He proved that he knew his subject intimately because he was able to give very precise statistics and a remarkably full inventory of the natural phenomena in the area. Surely his listeners must have felt he had intelligence and competency on this subject since he took such pains to

[9]This excerpt is from a recording of Mr. Dike's speech provided by Dr. Patricia Schmidt, formerly Instructor in Speech, University of Delaware, Newark, Delaware, by permission of Robert Dike.

show that his knowledge was firsthand and complete. The same opportunities for establishing yourself as a credible source are open to you.

Other methods of providing source justification can be illustrated briefly. Franklin Roosevelt's famous salutation, "My friends—" or his "you and I know" or any speaker's use of the pronouns, "we," "us," "our" instead of "I," "me," "my" exemplify small expressions of goodwill and friendly identification with an audience. They are open to anyone's use. Simply to use cogent arguments as Zellner did or to cite the best rather than a second-best authority hints that you have intelligence and knowledge. A dispassionate recital of arguments for or against the position you are taking can suggest: "He's keeping his feelings under control and so is more to be relied on." Demeanor, too, leads to source justification. Listeners prize conversational directness, general pleasantness, and unselfconscious action, voice, and diction because they interpret these behaviors as signs that nothing is diverting the speaker's attention from his business with us, his hearers.

As Aristotle was first to say, it is not just reputation but everything a speaker does that gives his message credibility. If you analyze your speaking situation thoroughly, you will know what qualities you must display if you are to make yourself a justification for what you say.

Beginners sometimes tend to see this need to adapt themselves to listeners' perceptions as an invasion of their own private rights to be themselves. It is not. All listeners ask is that you be yourself in ways *they* understand as intelligent and trustworthy. They ask to be *shown* that you have good sense and

integrity. If you will show them that, on your terms, they will let you try to change them; otherwise they will not. What is required of you as a public speaker is that you set up conditions of *mutual* respect between yourself and others. It is worth remembering that if a speaker consistently abandons his own judgment in hopes of winning listeners' regard, he will eventually be tagged as unintelligent and untrustworthy because he will seem unpredictable and lacking in a clear, fixed view of things. What he says eventually comes to be called a "line" and he a "con artist."

Establishing yourself as justification for what you say is usually a matter of showing that you have brains, integrity, and trustworthy intentions toward those with whom you speak. Then there can be mutual respect between you and your listeners, and that is what "proves" in public speech.

### Combining Proofs

*Combining the three proofs helps ensure a successful speech.*

What does speech sound like when a speaker defends his ideas by combining the three kinds of justification we have discussed? Here is an example taken from a broadcast in New York City in 1969. During the election campaign for Mayor of New York City which took place during that year, station WNEW-TV brought together the three leading candidates for a discussion program titled "Law and Order."[10] Mayor John V. Lindsay appeared as the candidate running for re-election. One of his opponents said that Lindsay's administration did not adequately help police to enforce the laws. Lindsay responded with the remarks quoted below. Obviously he was addressing the voters listening, not the opponent who had made the charge. Said Mayor Lindsay:

> The fight against crime requires an effective attack against all crime, and you have to bring together all the agencies of government in order to do it correctly. Since I've been Mayor, we've started the Mayor's Council on the Coordination of Criminal Justice. It's a pioneering thing. It's started over 30 different projects in the city of New York. For example, we found that 50 percent of police time was wasted in the traffic court. We put an end to that with our traffic alert system. Nothing is more frustrating to a police officer than to be sitting on a bench in a courtroom. That is ended, saving eight thousand police tours a year.
>
> Another example. In the Bronx, at night, an officer who makes an arrest used to have to travel all the way to Manhattan

[10]"The David Susskind Show," broadcast on WNEW-TV, October 26, 1969, 11:00 P.M., Eastern time.

> with that person who was arrested in order to go to arraignment procedures. That's been ended. We now have instant, on-the-spot arraignment procedures. This has put all the policemen in the Bronx who make arrests back out on patrol immediately, saving, again, thousands of hours of police time. This is the kind of thing that is important in fighting crime. Forty-three percent increase in arrests in the Bronx alone! This is not handcuffing police. This is not failing—this is not failing to support police. This is the *right* kind of police approach with that kind of reorganization that's important.

Mayor Lindsay then went on for about two more minutes giving other examples of how his administration had improved law enforcement.

In the brief passage we have quoted Mayor Lindsay used as "proofs" the personal interests of his listeners, facts and reasoning, and claims about his own intelligent and trustworthy concern for efficiency and for the safety of citizens. The listeners' interests in safety (especially in the Bronx) were drawn upon to support the importance of what had been done. The specific instances and statistics functioned as *data* supporting an unstated *claim:* "We are doing things well and right." Lindsay claimed and implied that he knew better than others *how* to fight crime, and that he was getting practical results. Yet the unit of talk was a *single* passage that reminded listeners that Lindsay was directly refuting the criticisms of his opponent.

All three kinds of justification operated together in these 240 words of talk which took only seventy-five seconds to utter. But it is important for you to see that these kinds of justification supported each other, combining to make the whole unit of thought still more credible. The examples "prove" Lindsay had acted. If the listeners like "pioneering" ventures and if they are eager to have as many policemen on the streets as possible, their feelings and desires will rise to endorse further the facts Lindsay has given. And Lindsay asserts that *he* understands how crime is best attacked and that his "correct" ways have ended undesirable practices and improved police work. These are all claims that Lindsay's way of doing things is the intelligent, dependable way of acting. If it is, that makes the examples given still stronger. Each kind of justification reinforces the other. The examples make Lindsay more believable; the claims about the "right way" make the instances more impressive. The improvements in safety and efficiency are supposed to arouse favorable feelings toward what Lindsay has done.

An important task in building a speech from materials you have collected is to choose and place your information, expressions of attitude, and appeals to your listeners' interests in ways that make these proofs *combine* in supporting the central idea or subpoint you want believed at any moment. Lindsay's remarks are a model of one way of uniting all three kinds of proof as justifications in speaking.

## SUMMARY

In this chapter we have been considering what it really is to "prove" something in public speech. Proving is very different in speaking from what it is in geometry or formal logic or even in the technical parts of legal pleading. In speaking to all but the most specialized public groups you do not really do the proving at all. You direct the *listeners'* feelings, attitudes, and thoughts in ways that lead them to prove things *to themselves*. If you have understood the major sections of this chapter and the concluding section on "Combining Proofs," you understand why it is that:

1. When your basic research for speech is completed, it is important that you re-examine your overall plan to see whether your original subject sentence and your goals in speaking still express what you want to attempt.
2. You must arouse listeners' personal interests and personal experiences in order to make them able and willing to understand and believe what you tell them.
3. There is no set of formal rules by which you can discover what to tell listeners in order to make your ideas seem reasonable. Only analyzing your audience's probable expectations and their knowledge of your subject can tell you what *they* will find sufficient and therefore rational.
4. *You*—your apparent worth, good sense, and interest in your listeners' well being—are inevitably a part of the proof or disproof of anything you say.
5. The fullest proof you can build into each speech (a) shows the listeners that their beliefs and interests are part of the reasons they should believe you, (b) makes clear how and why anything you claim is justified by information and sensible (for your hearers) ways of drawing conclusions from that information, and (c) unpretentiously makes your own character, intelligence, and attitudes toward listeners authority for what you say.

There are no yardsticks or weighing scales by which anyone can tell exactly what proofs and how much proving will be needed in each and every speech. What is needed and how it is to be supplied must be specially thought out for each rhetorical situation. But we do know the questions all listeners want answered. As we gave them to you at the beginning of this chapter they were: Why should *I* care about it (your subject or point)? Why bring it up *now*? Why should I believe what you say *is as you say it is*? Why is what you urge on me *better* or *truer* than an alternative? Why should I listen to *you* on this matter?

If you choose from your research materials and create from your own mind the thoughts which you believe will answer *all* of these questions for most of your listeners *throughout* your talk, your success will be far surer than Mary's Leg's.

## EXERCISES

*Written*

1. Before beginning other preparation for your next speech, write out a "Choice of Subject" paper containing the following information: (a) an exact statement of your proposed speech subject; (b) an exact statement of your specific purpose; (c) a brief essay explaining why your subject and purpose are timely, significant for you and your audience, amenable to oral presentation, and manageable in the time available. Present this to your instructor for evaluation or have two or three classmates read it over and tell you whether they understand exactly what it is you plan and whether it seems a wise plan for the audience you will meet.
2. Choose an excerpt from a speech and analyze the ways proof by personal-interest, claims to rationality, and self-justification are used to win listeners' agreement. Write a short essay in the manner of ours on Mayor Lindsay explaining what you found.
3. Write a short essay in which you analyze the kinds of proof found in an advertisement in print, on radio, or on television. As part of your essay indicate what an audience would have to feel or believe in order to accept these proofs.

*Oral*

1. With a group of four or five classmates assign each member of the group the task of using one of the three ways of building proof (p. 92) in a one-minute talk about some aspect of a topic your group has chosen. Following each presentation discuss how the one-minute talk could have been made stronger by using additional kinds of justification for what was said. Consider also whether the speaker used his or her assigned kind of justification as well as possible.

2. Using a group like that suggested in Exercise 1 above, choose a subject for an imaginary speech to be given in a situation you have imaginatively worked out. In group discussion, phrase the ideal central idea for the imaginary speech, agree on what main points ought to be made about it, and what kinds of proof would be especially important in developing each point.
3. Prepare and present a short speech on some aspect of a subject you know your classmates disagree about. Try to build enough rational justification into your speech to satisfy a skeptical listener. After the speech, invite a listener who agrees with you and one who still disagrees with you to evaluate how well you proved your point. Conduct a class discussion of their evaluations of your proof.
4. Present an oral report on an advertisement or advertising campaign. Discuss the ways in which personal-interest, rational, and source justification are used in this advertising.

# 6

# Invention: Clarifying and Reinforcing Ideas

If you will turn to the Appendix of this book and read Randy Cohn's comments under "Content and Organization—Teacher," you will find Randy and her instructor had a slight difference of opinion concerning the persuasive and appealing values of historical information used in her speech "The Gift of Life." In his critique of the speech, the instructor had asked, "Is the historical background helping to persuade your audience?" (See p. 243.) Randy responded in her after-the-speech evaluation of what she had done:

> I placed this in this speech for a few reasons. First, to break up the monotony of my plea; second, to compare past knowledge to future and present advances to make it more poignant; and lastly to give it [the speech as a whole] an uplifting, novel quality—more variety.

Randy's defense of including anecdotes, comparisons, and contrasts does not answer her instructor's question about the *persuasive* impact of these materials, but it does admirably point out what some kinds of speech materials can do *beyond* proving or supporting persuasive efforts. They can "break up the monotony" of single-minded talk; they can make what is said about a topic "poignant" (especially interesting and appealing); and they can make talk interesting by introducing variety and novelty. There are, in fact, about nine common tactics you can use in a speech for these purposes.

The tactics of clarifying and reinforcing ideas which we are about to discuss sometimes simply *support* points you make in talking. Sometimes the same kinds of materials allow you to make ideas vivid and especially interesting without adding much further proof. And at other times you can both support *and* clarify or arouse interest by using these sorts of materials. It is important to know what you need to get out of such tactics as telling anecdotes and comparing, as Randy Cohn's experience shows. She was quite right that she made her subject seem more important and interesting by introducing historical anecdotes and making comparisons and contrasts. But her instructor was right too in suggesting that she neglected to ensure that these materials would make listeners more likely to sign cards promising to donate their bodily organs after death. The probability is that Randy's tactics roused interest as she intended but added little to listeners' self-interest in giving their own bodily organs.

*Nine tactics strengthen the content of a speech.*

There are at least nine clarifying and reinforcing tactics you can use to strengthen the basic content of a speech. They are: (1) introducing anecdotes, (2) comparing and contrasting, (3) defining, (4) describing, (5) exemplifying, (6) quoting, (7) repeating and restating, (8) quantifying, and (9) introducing audio-visual aids. Each gives you some possibility of increasing the proof for ideas and each gives the opportunity to clarify and arouse interest. What each can do for you depends on how you use it, so we shall emphasize your choices in the next paragraphs.

## INTRODUCING ANECDOTES

An anecdote is usually a brief narrative illustrating another idea with which it is connected. To clarify or emphasize the damage a storm can produce, you might tell of a family's experience in a tornado. Fables, parables, imagined episodes, or real incidents are all forms of anecdotal amplification. If well chosen, well told, and well applied, they can add special interest to what is spoken because of their narrative, dramatizing form, and they can function as proofs of what you say if you make them seem realistic examples. The "black-leg legend" Randy Cohn told in her speech (pp. 238–239) made her talk on transplantation of organs more interesting, but she did not directly apply the anecdote as proof of anything. On the other hand, she could have concluded the narrative by referring back to the point she had made in paragraph 3: transplantation did not begin with today's headlines or the donor program (p. 237). Had she done that, the anecdote would have functioned as material that aroused interest and also added support to a main idea of the speech. Would she have been wiser to do this than to conclude paragaph 7 as she did (p. 239)?

*Anecdotes must be short, relevant, and in some cases realistic.*

The chief things you need to keep in mind when you use anecdotes in talks are that they ought to be kept short and sharply relevant to the points you intend them to clarify, and if they are also to serve as proof, then they must be realistic, not fanciful or unrepresentative in the listeners' views. If they are economically and vividly told, anecdotes can set events before hearers. The listeners can "live" in the stories as live observers of the things told about. If the events recounted are closely connected with a claim you are making, the listeners can associate their own interest and experiences with occurrences in your story and then the anecdote can seem a justification for what it also clarifies or vivifies. You can, in short, illustrate something or illustrate *and* support it by telling a brief, appropriate story.

## COMPARING AND CONTRASTING

Comparisons and contrasts can also be used either to clarify or to clarify and support ideas. We have many ways of comparing and contrasting. Metaphors and similes are very brief comparisons; antitheses are concise contrasts. But you can also make comparisons between extensive anecdotes, whole arguments, descriptions, sets of statistics, or almost any other elements in a speech. Comparisons and contrasts work well, largely because comparing or contrasting the new with the old is the way by which we have acquired most of our concepts. These methods are basic in our learning processes. Furthermore, conflict and similarity seem fundamentally interesting to people. So you can scarcely find a more common but useful tactic for clarifying a thought than comparing it or contrasting it with something you know your listeners are familiar with.

*Comparisons must be exact if they are to be used as proof.*

Sometimes you will want to prove something by comparing or contrasting. Then you will need to emphasize the *literal* likenesses and dissimilarities between compared or contrasted items. You need not be so careful about this if you compare or contrast merely to vivify a thought. Notice how the author and speaker C. S. Lewis took care to specify how far he was comparing arithmetic and morals in a speech he once gave on the British Broadcasting Corporation's system:

> To be sure, perfect arithmetic is "an ideal"; you will certainly make some mistakes in some calculations. But there is nothing very fine about trying to be quite accurate at each step in each sum. It would be idiotic not to try; for every mistake is going to cause you trouble later on. In the same way every moral failure is going to cause trouble, probably to others and certainly to yourself.[1]

The points of comparison from which Lewis argues are that in arithmetic it is idiotic not to try to be correct even though you know you will make some mistakes, the reason being that each mistake will trouble you in later calculations; in morals *these* matters are the same, he claims, therefore you ought to *try* to be correct in morals. Whether you think his argument a strong one or not depends on whether (1) you think trouble later on is the reason people strive for accuracy in arithmetic and (2) you think problems in morals are enough like problems in arithmetic to *justify* applying the guideline of arithmetic to morals. Lewis has been careful not to let his comparison seem too sweeping, for arithmetic and morals certainly differ vastly in other respects even if they are alike in the reason we try to be accurate in each kind of effort.

When a young Mexican-American said, "Chicanos average 3.9 years less education than Anglo or white Americans—1.6 years less than Blacks," he wanted the contrasts to stand out sharply as dramatic and justificatory.[2] Had Mr. Ponce said only "Chicanos average about four years less education than Anglo or white Americans," the proving force of his contrast would have been weaker because the facts cited were too general to argue strongly.

*Imaginary comparisons can be used for dramatic emphasis.*

You need not be equally careful about making comparisons and contrasts exact if you use them to make a thought vivid without pretending to support contentions. In his famous "Atlanta Exposition Speech," Booker T. Washington said, "No race can prosper till it learns that there is as much dignity in tilling a field as in writing a poem." His comparison was rather far-fetched (tilling a field—writing a poem), but that did not detract because he was seeking dramatic emphasis only. He was not

[1]C. S. Lewis, "The Three Parts of Morality," a speech published in Lewis's *Mere Christianity* (London: The Macmillan Company, 1955). A complete text is also available in C. C. Arnold, D. Ehninger, and J. C. Gerber, *Speaker's Resource Book* (Chicago: Scott, Foresman Inc., 1966), pp. 175–177.

[2]Felipe V. Ponce, Jr., "La Causa," a classroom speech delivered at Indiana University in March, 1971. For a complete text, see Wil A. Linkugel, R. R. Allen, and Richard L. Johannesen, *Contemporary American Speeches*, 3rd ed. (Belmont: Wadsworth Publishing Co., Inc., 1972), pp. 66–70.

trying to prove anything by the comparison. Had he wanted to prove by comparison, he might have said, ". . . as much dignity in tilling a field as in designing a building," emphasizing that all practical occupations contribute to prosperity. In fact, Mr. Washington had argued for his point in other ways. Now, he could afford to clinch his point dramatically by introducing a strikingly unusual comparison between occupations so different they scarcely compared at all.

## DEFINING

*There are eight ways to define.*

Defining is one of our most common ways of explaining things. We define in several ways: (1) by classifying ideas; (2) by differentiating certain ideas from other ideas that belong to the same class; (3) by exemplifying ideas; (4) by explaining an idea through referring to the circumstances in which it commonly occurs; (5) by using the origin of a name to explain what the name actually means (etymology); (6) by explaining what an idea or thing is *not;* (7) by describing or explaining ideas or things from some special point of view (as in explaining a musical note as if we could *see* it as a set of sound waves); (8) by giving the functions of the thing or idea being explained (as when a child defines an automobile as a thing to ride in).

Definitions are exceedingly important in clarifying ideas, but the most formal kinds of definitions tend to be overused in public speaking. You ought to prefer definitions that compare, contrast, or exemplify what you are talking about. Dictionary definitions that classify things and define them by referring to the origins of their names are usually remote from listeners' ordinary experiences and so can be more confusing than clarifying. If you do need to classify things in order to explain them, it is a good idea to present such definitions *after* you have explained by exemplifying, comparing, contrasting, etc. Then, the definition that classifies will sum up what went before. Here is an illustration of defining in this way:

*A good technique is to use a definition as a summary.*

> To understand what a mastodon was, think of an elephant. [Comparison.] Now, imagine your elephant's face is longer than any you ever saw on a real elephant. [Contrast.] If you like, give your elephant four tusks instead of two, for some mastodons had four tusks. Picture his hair as exceedingly coarse and longer than you have ever seen on a circus elephant. [Further detail by example and contrast.] Mastodons are extinct, of course, but they were elephant-like mammals who browsed for their food as elephants do today, and they varied in size from four and a half feet high to the size of the largest elephants of our time. [Functions described, details from the

> point of view of *seeing* provided, and comparison made.] A mastodon, then, was any of several species of large, extinct, elephant-like, forest-dwelling mammals. [Explanation concludes with a formal, classifying definition that sums up previously given details.]

Too often for listeners' easy understanding we hear definitional explanations that are structured in precisely the opposite way. They begin with abstract, classifying definitions like this:

> A mastodon was any of several species of large, extinct, elephant-like, forest-dwelling mammals. They ranged in size from four and a half to fifteen feet high at the shoulder and had somewhat longer heads and coarser hair than most modern elephants.

Here, the attempt at clarifying immediately confronts a listener with the most compact, difficult to understand kind of explanation. If the listener survives the packed details of the classifying definition, he is then given a few details that contrast mastodons' and elephants' features.

Our first illustration of clarifying by means of defining is the easier to understand, hence the better. It illustrates the tactic you ought to adopt when you need to clarify by defining.

Another kind of defining that is popular with speakers but usually not as clarifying or as interesting as they hope is etymological definition—defining by explaining the origins of the names for things. It is not very helpful to most listeners to know that the English word *define* comes from the Latin *definire*, meaning "to limit." It would probably be even less informative to your listeners to tell them that *mastodon* comes from Greek terms meaning *mast-like tooth*. These kinds of definitions can be found in most dictionaries, but if you remember what we said on pp. 9–10 about the importance of keeping communicative "signals" within the areas of speakers' and listeners' *shared* experiences, you will quickly see that most etymological definitions are likely to prove more puzzling to listeners than enlightening. However, occasionally the original meaning of a term does offer the best and clearest way of explaining what you mean. An example is the legal term *habeas corpus*. In Latin the term means, literally, "You may have the body." To point this out may be a quicker, easier way of explaining what a "writ of habeas corpus" is than saying, "This is a writ requiring that a person be brought, usually from prison, before a judge or court." And if for some reason you must mention *maize*, it will no doubt be clarifying to tell your listeners that this is simply a version of a Spanish word which means the same as our word *corn*. Our point is not that you should always avoid telling listeners about the origins of terms you use; we are only saying that you ought to consider whether doing this will help or hinder understanding. Too often speakers use this sort of definition because they want to be impressive rather than because they are striving to be as clear and interesting as possible.

A final point needs to be made about definitions. If you can get your listeners to accept a definition—an interpretation—you exclude from their minds other, competing definitions or interpretations. In a speech at Morgan State College in Baltimore, Stokely Carmichael applied this point to race relations when he said:

> You see, you define to contain. That's all you do. I define this as yellow. It means that this is yellow. That is not yellow. So . . . when I speak of yellow you know what I am talking about. . . . And so for white people to be allowed to define us by calling us Negroes, which means apathetic, lazy, stupid, and all those other things, is for us to accept those definitions. *We* must define what we are and move from our definitions and tell them to recognize what we say we are.[3]

Mr. Carmichael was quite right about the way definitions *argue*. If you can get your clarification by defining accepted, you have in a sense "proved" that your interpretation of any idea, thing, or person is preferable to any other.

## DESCRIBING

Describing is a tactic you will be wise to use when you want listeners to understand how the physical features of anything relate to one another. If you can make these features vivid and their relations to one another suggestive of something your listeners like or dislike, your descriptions can also prove by evoking the hearers' self-interests. A freshman student at the University of Indiana achieved clarity and also aroused a good deal of self-interested concern from his listeners when he opened a speech with these words:

> The strangler struck in Donora, Pennsylvania, in October of 1948. A thick fog billowed through the streets enveloping everything in thick sheets of dirty moisture and a greasy black coating. As Tuesday faded into Saturday the fumes from the big steel mills shrouded the outlines of the landscape. One could barely see across the narrow streets. Traffic stopped. Men lost their way returning

[3]Stokely Carmichael, "Speech at Morgan State College," delivered January 16, 1967. The text was originally distributed by the Student Nonviolent Coordinating Committee of which Carmichael was then Chairman. Full texts may be found in a number of sources including a text with introduction and partial analysis in Carroll C. Arnold, *Criticism of Oral Rhetoric* (Columbus: Charles E. Merrill Publishing Co., 1974), pp. 341–355.

> from the mills. Walking through the streets, even for a few moments, caused eyes to water and burn. The thick fumes grabbed at the throat and created a choking sensation. The air acquired a sickening bitter-sweet smell, nearly a taste. Death was in the air.[4]

Mr. Schalliol's vivid description of the air conditions in Donora pictorialized what actually happened in 1948. The oppressive, threatening physical features of the city clarified and also dramatized the nature of air pollution, Mr. Schalliol's speech subject. More than this, the description formed a powerful address to the listeners' self-interests. They not only "saw" the details of the "Donora disaster" as it was called at the time, but they were made to sense the dangers extreme air pollution can bring to any community. Undoubtedly they were more ready to listen to Schalliol's plea that they, as individuals, assume responsibility for promoting cleaner air conditions throughout the United States.

*Descriptions should be short and their purpose should be clear.*

Description can serve you as a powerful clarifying and reinforcing tactic, but you will need to avoid two pitfalls which trap many describers. The first is describing at too great length and the second is failing to make clear what you want your listeners to *learn* from any description. Mr. Schalliol's description is concise. In slightly more than 100 words, which would take only a minute to deliver at a deliberate, emphatic pace, he summed up the main features of nearly a week's experience with extreme air pollution. Had he said more, he might have strained his listeners' interest and overburdened them with detail. And he quickly applied his description to his own subject with these words:

> The concern of public health officials is no longer for small towns like Donora. What happened there in 1948 is now happening in New York City, Los Angeles, and Washington.[5]

It was quickly apparent to listeners that Mr. Schalliol wanted them to project the description he had given on today's pollution problem in our great urban centers. When a description can serve your need to clarify and reinforce ideas, you will be well advised to emulate Mr. Schalliol's economy of words and his unmistakable indications of what listeners were to think about description now that they had heard it.

---

[4]Charles Schalliol, "The Strangler," *Winning Orations* (Detroit: The Interstate Oratorical Association, 1967), pp. 54–57. A full text of this speech also appears in Linkugel, Allen, and Johannesen, *Contemporary American Speeches*, 3rd. ed., pp. 260–264.
[5]*Ibid.*

## EXEMPLIFYING

Of all the clarifying and reinforcing tactics, exemplifying is probably the most available and useful. We have few ideas for which we cannot provide clarifying examples, and the great advantage of examples is that they render concrete ideas that might otherwise be abstract. How can you talk clearly about a concept like *freedom* without giving examples of what kind of freedom you are thinking of? "Like what?" your listener will be asking. Of course, examples need not always be real ones. Hypothetical, imagined instances can serve in the same way as actual instances. All of Aesop's fables are imaginary examples (usually in the form of anecdotes) which serve to illustrate and prove a moral. Consider Leon Zellner's joining of an actual example (snow) with an imaginary example (a flower) in this excerpt from the talk we cited in Chapter Five:

> . . . If we try to figure out the probabilities for the fact that it's now snowing here at this moment, it can be proved that it's infinitely improbable that it would snow here today. It is necessary for a whole complex chain of events to occur before it can possibly snow in State College. If the earth weren't rotating at its particular speed, we wouldn't be here with the snow. If the earth were not revolving around the sun as it is, perhaps the climate would be warmer and it would be impossible for it to snow here. If the masses of air had any other set of molecules than they have at this instant, it would be impossible for it to snow. This kind of argument can be applied to anything in nature. Take the existence of a flower in a particular spot. There are an infinite number of places where that flower could grow. So, for a flower you don't plant but which just happens to grow, it is infinitely improbable that that flower could grow where it does.

As Mr. Zellner was speaking, it began to snow. Wisely and with quick wit, he seized that real fact and used it as an example of his general argument that whether we talk of the earth's path around the sun or any other thing in nature, we can never prove scientifically that that is its necessary way of being. To this example he added the imaginary case of the wild flower, illustrating and further supporting the same idea. Whether examples are real or imaginary, then, they can both clarify and prove if you devise and apply them carefully.

*Examples should not distract the listener.*

Whether you are illustrating with an example or trying also to prove something with it, you need to be sure your example is not likely to draw attention in directions you do not want. Some examples can be so interesting they make listeners forget what is being exemplified. A journalism student in one of our classes once tried to explain what "spot reporting" is in radio journalism. He rightly thought that an example was needed to clarify this concept. Unfortunately he chose as his example a recording of a news reporter's almost hysterical, on-the-scene account of the murder of Lee Harvey Oswald, assassin of President John F. Kennedy. Naturally, when the recording had been played, none of the student's listeners had their minds on what spot reporting is as a form of journalism. None remembered what the example was supposed to clarify. All questions had to do with Kennedy's assassination and the details of Oswald's murder by a man named Jack Ruby. The example simply had too much drama and general human interest in itself to allow listeners to keep their minds on the kind of journalism the reporter's report illustrated. The speaker would have made his rhetorical point far better had he chosen a *quiet, un*dramatic illustration of spot reporting.

There is an important general point about exemplifying embedded in the journalism student's experience. It is that examples need to be very carefully chosen and presented so that they do exactly what you want them to do, no more and no less. Just *any* example will not do for purposes of clarifying and reinforcing ideas.

## QUOTING

*Quoting allows the speaker to "borrow" authority and language.*

It is sometimes helpful to quote other sources to justify and clarify ideas. Citing sources other than yourself can increase your credibility when you are not, yourself, an authority on a point you need to discuss. It also makes sense to quote others if they have expressed something better than you could. The two main reasons for adopting the tactic of quoting, then, are to "borrow" authority and to "borrow" language, in moments when your own authority or language would be inferior.

Mr. Schalliol, whom we just quoted, cited authorities on public health, a national conference on air pollution, United States Senate hearings, the Civil Aeronautics Board, environmental engineers, and several other sources whose access to facts and whose authority in interpreting data were superior to his own. He also quoted one source because that man had expressed an important point with special force:

> Athelstan Spilhaus of the University of Minnesota's Institute of Technology aptly sums up our air pollution problem in thirteen words: "We don't consume anything, we simply convert every product we touch into waste!"

Obviously at this point Schalliol gained both authority and advantageous language from quoting Mr. Spilhaus.

Inexperienced speakers tend to quote too much. If you examine your own listening habits, you will find that you soon tire of hearing "one quote after another." You expect to hear what the *speaker* thinks. You can read quotations for yourself. As a speaker, you ought to regard your listeners as having the same wishes. You will not offend them if you quote Albert Einstein's remark, "No amount of experimentation can ever prove me right; a single experiment may at any time prove me wrong." A great scientist expressed the limitations of his work and did it pithily. You could not match his authority or, probably, his language. But if someone named John Smith said, "Experiments don't prove everything," you hardly need the quotation. You could say it as authoritatively and as well. A good rule is: never speak someone else's words unless they will carry more weight than your own or their expression will help you make your own point in a unique way.

## REPEATING AND RESTATING

Repeating and restating are effective ways of emphasizing ideas, though they can become tiresome to listeners. By *repeating* we mean saying something more than once in the same way, and by *restating* we mean saying the same idea more than once but expressing it differently each time.

*Repeating must be done correctly if it is not to lose its effectiveness.*

Research indicates that with each of the first three repetitions of a thought you further increase the likelihood that your listeners will grasp and remember your idea. It also appears that *after* three repetitions, the amount of emphasis you gain from each successive statement becomes less and less. There is also evidence that it is especially effective to repeat an idea at several different points in your talk; this seems to be a more effective practice than repeating in series, as in, "The score is appallingly low. The score is appallingly low. The score is appallingly low." You're likely to irritate listeners if you repeat in this fashion, but you could refer back to the appallingly low score at several stages of your talk—if the point deserves that emphasis. You can, however, be effective if you *restate* an idea in series. Thus, you might say, "The score is appallingly low. It is a score that places our state forty-eighth in the nation. It is certainly not a score in which we can take any pride." "Lowness" gets emphasized by three successive remarks but varying ways of referring to it avoid monotony.

Randy Cohn effectively emphasized her purpose and promise to her audience when she said, "But I am going to give each of you, as individuals, *the chance to leave an imprint on the world, a chance to give of yourself, a chance to give the greatest gift of all*—the gift of life. . . ." By restating the opportunity three times she virtually ensured that no listener could miss her purpose. Here, she did not depend on restatement to prove anything; it was enough if it drew attention to her purpose. However, at the close of her talk (p. 240, paragraphs 11–13), she did depend on the tactic of repeating the terms "gift" and "give" to *urge* listeners to sign donors' cards. If the audience could be made to think of signing as giving, their interest in doing something generous would be aroused and more might take the trouble to sign.

Repeating and restating, then, can clarify or justify. If you make something easier to notice and remember by repeating or restating it, you make the idea more likely to affect your listeners' thoughts. If you can phrase restatements so they awaken strong beliefs and feelings in listeners, you evoke personal-interest justifications for what you say.

## QUANTIFYING

Numbers—statistics—clarify and often support or prove by expressing *amounts*. Therein lie the strengths and weaknesses of statistics when used in speaking.

You can tell someone of the nature of a famine in several ways. You can dramatize it by telling an anecdote about it or by describing it colorfully but concisely. You can clarify the famine's nature by comparing it to other kinds of catastrophes. You can also express the magnitude of a famine statistically. If you do that, you shift from dependence on word symbols to dependence on numbers as symbols. By this shift you gain precision in what you present to your listeners, but you lose much imagery and opportunity to evoke personal interest.

*Statistics can support ideas precisely.*

You can say there will be 10,000 deaths from starvation in a country with a population of 1,000,000. This is precise. If you convert these large and difficult-to-interpret numbers into simpler numbers, you can dramatize the magnitude of the famine somewhat by saying that 1 in 100 people will die. It may be very important to get this precise meaning across, but notice what you *cannot* convey through numbers: the conditions under which the 10,000 will die, the cause of the famine, and a good many other features. Through numbers you can communicate

*amounts,* and to do this you have to turn people into numbers in the example we are using. The point is that the tactic of resorting to numbers to clarify and reinforce ideas is an excellent choice when amounts are what you need to communicate; but numbers are abstractions, and you will often need to add nonstatistical information in order to bring the amounts to life.

The language of numbers has specialized rules—a kind of special grammar—which you also have to observe when you clarify and prove with statistics. What do the numbers really represent? How was the counting done? What conclusions is it safe to draw from numbers collected as these were? These are questions always raised when you clarify or prove by statistics.

*An audience needs to know how to interpret a given set of statistics.*

It is not enough just to give an audience statistics. You need to add—in *words*—how the statistics may and may not be interpreted. It does not help listeners to tell them that in 1960 Kennedy defeated Nixon for President by 118,550 popular votes. But it does help to tell them that Kennedy became President by a margin of 118,550 votes, which is fewer votes than there are people in Topeka, Kansas, or Paterson, New Jersey. Helping the audience *interpret* the amount of the margin shows them the real narrowness of Kennedy's victory—which would be the point of citing the figure itself.

Despite the limitations that statistics have as clarifying and supporting material, statistics are invaluable whenever quantitative sizes and relationships are what you must get audiences to see. Because they are so valuable for this purpose, it is all the more important that you remember: (1) you must often compensate for the dryness of statistics, and (2) it is usually not enough merely to supply numbers—you need to explain how they are to be interpreted.

One device that helps you to compensate for the dryness and technicality of statistics is to round off figures. For 775 miles say, "A little less than 800 miles." It is also helpful to present statistics visually as well as orally, for statistics are hard to remember if there are many of them. Usually it helps to *show* numbers as well as *say* them. Because concentrated clusters of numbers can be confusing, avoid clustering your statistics if you can; if you cannot, be sure to present them visually as well as orally and do all you can to simplify them. And, of course, because statistics only express amounts, be sure to use other, more vivid materials along with them.

## AUDIO-VISUAL AIDS

*Audio-visual aids can be introduced for four reasons.*

If you use them carefully, audio-visual aids can give your ideas clarity, vividness, and personal-interest and rational justifications. You ought to consider the tactic of introducing audio-visual aids (1) if they can save words or reinforce what you must say; (2) if they can help to bring ideas or facts into your listeners' fields of experience; (3) if they can help to make what you are talking about more concrete or specific than words can; (4) if introducing such aids will sustain your audience's attention by letting you vary the means by which you communicate and letting you move about in ways that specially emphasize your points.

Some people think only of charts and graphs when they think of visual aids, but your options are far more numerous. Audio-visual resources that can help you to communicate include photographs, maps, charts or graphs, models, mock-ups, blackboard drawings, assistants who help with demonstrations, sound movies, slides, videotapes, musical instruments, disc and tape recordings, and still more. But the most versatile and convenient audio-visual aid any speaker has is himself. This is a fact you should never forget. If you do, you will involve yourself with gadgets that are less effective than your own body could be.

*Using audio-visual aids has its own peculiar problems.*

One basic principle must be observed when deciding whether to clarify or vivify ideas with audio-visual aids: unless the aid is less complicated than the idea it is supposed to clarify, it will probably introduce more difficulties than it solves. Other, more specific things need to be thought about, too. Any aid you use must be relevant to your point and fit the specific situation in which you will use it. Think about your speaking situation to determine what physical or acoustical properties the aid must

have if it is to be easily seen, heard, and understood. Also, because you will be in a particular kind of *speaking* situation, you (or someone available to help you) must be able to manage and control your aids without disturbing the intimate relationship which you, as speaker, need to maintain with your listeners. Your aids must not dominate the occasion. If it is an occasion for speaking, the listeners will expect public speech and not some other kind of communication or display. For example, no speech can genuinely "contain" a ten- to twenty-minute film presentation, and a ten-minute speech will hardly remain a speech if half the time is taken up by music.

There seems no end to the ways in which audio-visual aids are misused in speaking situations; almost all mistakes happen because people disregard the fact that audio-visual aids can threaten a speaker's own mastery of purpose, audience, and situation. "Who is in charge?" is always a question when audio-visual aids are brought in. "A picture is worth a thousand words," it is said. But if pictures can convey your entire message, you ought to send the pictures and omit the speech.

Here are some *do's* which can help you choose aids that serve your purpose and manage them during speaking so that they clarify and support what you say.

1. Introduce audio-visual resources where you think that even your best verbal-personal presentation would otherwise fall short of complete clarity.
2. Always *verbalize* what your listeners are supposed to see, hear, and understand. Do this either *before* or *while* you use the aids.

3. Design or edit all aids to eliminate material that is irrelevant to your immediate purpose.
4. Use your aids where you need them, then get them out of the way so your listeners will not dwell on the aids when you want them to attend to what you are saying.
5. If possible, pretest sight lines, sound levels, and distances in your physical speaking situation, then design and use aids that suit these physical conditions.
6. Pretest your aids just before speaking to be sure they are convenient and in working order.
7. When using aids, give your main attention to your listeners, not to your devices. *You* are supposed to be the chief messenger. To understand your aids rightly, listeners need *your* attention even while they are receiving part of your message from the aids.
8. Always use the simplest audio-visual aid that can do what you need done. Keep machinery and details to the minimum that will serve your purpose.
9. Always position yourself so that (a) your entire audience can see whatever visual material you are using, and (b) you can give full, easy attention to your listeners as you discuss what your aid helps you to show. In short, keep out of your audience's way when using audio-visual material and talk to people, not your aids.

In public speaking *you* are presumed to be the principal messenger, so *keep yourself in charge and maintain close personal relationship with your listeners.*

## SUMMARY

An adequately researched and justified idea is not always in its clearest, most interesting, most potent form when you have assembled sufficient personal-interest, rational, and self-justifications to make it acceptable to an audience. You may be able to clarify and further support it by adopting one or more of the special tactics we have discussed in this chapter. A solid idea can perhaps be made more clear and interesting by adding an example; statistical information may need to be treated specially because of what numbers can and cannot do when orally presented; the sound idea can perhaps be made more persuasive by citing a familiar authority or by introducing visual material; and so on. These are the kinds of "finishing up" considerations to which we have tried to draw your attention in this chapter.

We have been saying that if you need additional clarifying, vivifying supporting material after you have assembled the basic material for a public speech, you can choose from among the nine ways of presenting ideas we have just discussed. Each is a special resource or tactic available to you as you give final shape and substance to the content of any speech.

As we discussed each special tactic we tried to show you what that way of presenting ideas can and cannot accomplish for and with your listeners. If you have understood us you now know:

1. What special force anecdotes can give to basic ideas and what cautions you ought to observe in using and telling anecdotes.
2. How comparisons and contrasts clarify and can be made to support major ideas.
3. What the most interesting, clarifying kinds of definitions are and what cautions to observe in presenting definitions that classify or explain by referring to historical meanings of names and other terms.
4. How to build descriptions that concisely clarify relationships among physical things while at the same time arousing listeners' self-interests.
5. Why examples make abstractions clear by introducing concreteness and how to use real or imaginary examples to illustrate and also prove.
6. When to "borrow" the words of others, or their information, in order to make what you say more credible and clearer or more striking.
7. How to insert repetitions and restatements into a speech in order to take advantage of the special emphasis these tactics can give to points you are making.
8. When to rely on numerical (statistical) information and how to handle statistics so they clarify and support but do not seem dry or confusing to listeners.
9. The main advantages and dangers that come from introducing audio-visual aids to clarify and reinforce ideas presented orally.

Knowing that these special tactics will do specific jobs of clarifying, vivifying, and proving lets you choose the resources that meet your special requirements, given the particular material you have, the situation you will enter, and your goal in speaking. No special tactic is helpful *always*. The question is whether what an anecdote or example or other tactic can *do* is what you need done with the speech material you have gathered. We have emphasized the positive and negative aspects of each tactic for precisely this reason. In composing your particular speech for any situation you have to weigh which tactic is best for the job you must do with each major part of your justifying material. Then there will remain one more major thing to consider in rhetorical invention. It is how your specific purpose in speaking can predetermine what tactics are best for the task you are undertaking. This is the subject of our next chapter.

## EXERCISES

*Written*

1. As you prepare your next talk, label in the margins of your outline what *kind* of supporting or amplifying material you are planning to use at each point. Then write a short paragraph contending that you have achieved the best degree of *variety* in supporting material that is open to you. Discuss your defense with your instructor or one or two of your classmates.
2. Identify and evaluate (a) the kinds of justification and (b) the forms of amplification used in the following excerpt from Leonard Bernstein's lecture, "The World of Jazz":

> But I find I have to defend jazz to those who say it is low-class. As a matter of fact, all music has low-class origins, since it comes from folk music, which is necessarily earthy. After all, Haydn minuets are only a refinement of simple, rustic German dances, and so are Beethoven scherzos. An aria from a Verdi opera can often be traced back to the simplest Neopolitan fisherman. Besides, there has always been a certain shadow of indignity around music, particularly around the players of music.
>
> I suppose it is due to the fact that historically *players* of music seem to lack the dignity of *composers* of music. But this is especially true of jazz, which is almost completely a player's art, depending as it does on improvisation rather than on composition. But this also means that the player of jazz is himself the real composer, which gives him a creative, and therefore more dignified status.[6]

3. Pair off with another member of your class and read a newspaper or study a series of television advertisements to see how many of the nine kinds of clarifying and reinforcing tactics you can find used there. Write a brief report of what you found and what you think these tactics did or did not accomplish for the user. Hand your report to your instructor for evaluation, or exchange reports with

[6]From Leonard Bernstein's televised lecture "The World of Jazz," *The Joy of Music* (New York: Simon and Schuster, 1959), p. 97. Copyright ©1954, 1955, 1956, 1957, 1958, 1959 by Leonard Bernstein. Reprinted by permission of Simon and Schuster.

another pair of students in the class and then discuss together what you have found out about effective and ineffective uses of these tactics in communication.

*Oral*

1. With a group of four or five classmates choose a subject to talk about. Almost any subject will do. Assign to each member of the group one of the nine ways of clarifying or reinforcing ideas discussed in this chapter. Have each member of the group make a one-minute talk on the agreed-upon subject, using primarily the single clarifying or reinforcing tactic assigned to him or her. After each talk, discuss the advantages and disadvantages of using that method in developing material for a talk.
2. Prepare and deliver a one-point informative speech in which you use at least four different tactics of clarifying and reinforcing.
3. Present an oral report on an advertisement or advertising campaign. Discuss especially the ways in which the advertiser has used tactics of clarifying and reinforcing. Indicate also what you think were the effects of these tactics and why.
4. With a group of four or five of your classmates, analyze the pitfalls that would face a speaker trying to use visual aids in the rooms shown in Figures 7, 8, 9, and 10 (pp. 219–222). Assume that in Figure 8 a chalkboard stretches across the rear of the raised platform and a chalkboard stretches across the full length of the wall behind the lectern in Figure 9. Assume there is no chalkboard available in Figure 7. Assume also that the furnishings are to remain as shown in the diagrams. What sightline problems, problems of size of visual aids, and problems of movement while using aids would a speaker face in these rooms? What would be the advantages and disadvantages of various kinds of visuals: chalkboard drawings, use of pictures from magazines, photographic enlargements, graphs, models—if they could be used at all in these settings?

   When your group has completed its analysis, have one of your number report the group's conclusions to the class.

# Invention in Relation to Purposes

# 7

In any public speaking situation, the sense of accomplishment that belongs to the successful speaker comes when he realizes that he has achieved his purposes. He is like a swimmer or runner who has won the race. He consciously sees that he has reached his goal.

In Chapters Four, Five, and Six we have been thinking about what the speaker does in preparing *any* speech no matter what its purpose. There, we did not consider whether your settled, reconsidered specific purpose for a speech will restrict your choices of what you can sensibly choose to say. This is what we shall consider in this chapter.

How will each of the goals you may have in speaking influence what you should choose to use from the proving, clarifying, and attention-getting material you have collected? Since we inform and persuade more often than we try to do anything else when we speak, we will give these two purposes the most attention. We shall, however, also give passing attention to what happens during invention when you adopt other goals.

## SPEAKING TO INFORM

There will be times when you will be satisfied if your hearers simply understand what you say. You have often given directions, explained processes, and described things, hoping for no more than to "get through to" your listeners. When a social worker explains a regulation to a client, he or she hopes simply to be understood. If a physician explains how a disease is treated, the goal is likely to be to achieve full and complete understanding. Teaching, too, aims at informing more than anything else.

What kinds of content are *peculiarly* appropriate when people talk in these informing ways? What are uniquely required are facts, ideas, statistics, examples, comparisons, and the like which help listeners to grasp attributes and relationships. Informing others is really helping others to understand attributes or features and the relationships things and beings have to one another. Of all the attributes and relations listed on pp. 71–72, the only one that is not likely to be discussed in talk that is primarily informative is *desirability*. The reason for that exception is that when talk gets into what is desirable, some persuasion is apt to be necessary too, for "goods," "bads," "betters," and "poorers" are usually matters about which there are many arguments.

*Listeners expect three kinds of information.*

What listeners look for when they are acquiring information are basically of three kinds: (1) information that is *accurate* in detail and proportion; (2) information that is *complete* enough to cover the subject as the specific purpose implies it should be covered; and (3) information that "fits together" or "adds up to" something that is intelligible as a *whole*. When the social worker explains a regulation, the client expects the information to be accurate, complete enough to cover the whole regulation, and add up to a "package" of information the client can think with and act upon. Bob Barth's listeners expected him to tell them the truth about jet engines and to give them at least enough information so they could understand the principles he promised to explain and could conceptualize a *whole* jet engine. In general, when we listen to information, we all ask ourselves whether what we are hearing is true, whether we are getting enough information for the purpose, and whether what we are hearing adds up to some unified understanding that is of use or interest to us. So it is with all listeners in all situations. Therefore, in finally choosing material for informing you will need to protect yourself against making mistakes which informants sometimes fall into.

## Mistakes in Explaining

If you set out to explain how tape recorders work, you would make a mistake if you left the impression that all recorders use cassettes. Many use reels. You would make a different kind of mistake if you left out any reference to the fact that recorders vary a great deal in the number of tracks on which they record and play and in the fidelity of their reproduction. Your explanation would be incomplete if you failed to touch on these matters. You would make still another mistake if you failed to recognize that virtually everything about a tape recorder is in one way or another connected with its basic functions: to preserve sound and reproduce it faithfully and conveniently.

If you made any or all of these mistakes, what would happen? First, some listeners would be well enough informed to notice your inadequacy as an informative speaker. They would lose confidence in you. They would judge you an incompetent explainer of tape recorders. With them you would lose credibility as an accurate, comprehensive, fully understanding speaker. A second unfortunate result would be that those among your listeners who did not understand recorders very well at the beginning would end with less understanding of tape recorders than they needed. So, using materials that are less than fully accurate, complete, and comprehensive costs speakers respect as informants and costs listeners understanding.

*Incorrect explanations cost the speaker his credibility and his achievement of purpose.*

It also is easy to be imprecise when giving information. Being especially clear to yourself about your purpose is your best protection against this kind of mistake. You ought to keep your subject sentence or specific purpose closely in mind as you choose materials for informative speaking. Be sure your material tells all but no more than you want your listeners to understand. A good practice is to write the words: "When I finish I want my listeners to understand *that*. . . ." Insert after "that" a single clause expressing just what you want to accomplish. You will then have expressed your rhetorical purpose and your communicative goal in a single statement that can guide you as you include and exclude available material. "When I finish I want them to understand *that* the Battle of Gettysburg was a battle of maneuver rather than of firepower" is a precise subject sentence that could keep you from becoming vague in speaking. "When I finish I want my listeners to understand the Battle of Gettysburg" is useless as a guide. It gives you no assurance that the material you choose for a speech on "maneuver rather than firepower" will keep listeners' attention focused on what they are supposed to learn.

Without an exactly stated purpose you may try to cover too much or too little, but you may also make another mistake. You may make it harder for even you to remember your plan. So, sheer efficiency and your own self-confidence are served by holding close to carefully formulated purpose statements as you compose informative speeches.

### Maintaining Interest

*Explanations must be interesting to be effective.*

Sometimes it is difficult to maintain interest when you are explaining. Many things that need explaining are in themselves abstract, static, technical, or impersonal. Much content lacks inherent power to command attention except from specialists, yet such matters have to be explained to laymen. When this is your problem part of the solution lies in what we have said in earlier chapters. You will need to select material that specially introduces such factors of attention as activity, familiarity, conflict, vitality, and humor. Interesting examples, comparisons and contrasts, brief narratives, real and figurative analogies can usually be found to arouse degrees of interest that your basic content cannot achieve in and of itself.

The anatomy of the housefly does not seem a subject on which to build an engrossing speech, but a student speaker made her explanation interesting by finding especially concrete and threatening amplifying materials. The housefly is hairy. This unexciting fact assumed significance when the speaker amplified it by saying that the fly's body hairs are easily befouled as he moves around filth, and the same hairs easily pollute human food when the fly later alights on it. The fly's digestive system is not fascinating to most of us, but this speaker centered her exposition on the fact that the insect's digestive system is not capable of handling dry matter. Thus it is necessary for the fly to salivate or regurgitate on dry food in order that he may wet it and make it edible. In explaining the mouth, legs, and wings of the fly, the speaker drew enlargements of these parts on the blackboard and in these ways she compelled close attention to detail. Her information on the fly's anatomy lacked neither accuracy nor the power to grip attention, and so she also astutely solved the problem of making basically dull material interesting.

Informative speakers often neglect another opportunity to make difficult ideas both clear and interesting. It is the opportunity to treat the subject *as if* it were something other than what it literally is. Usually this is a matter of finding a familiar analogy that will at least partly clarify and vivify the subject.

No one has ever seen a real sound wave. These waves do not behave precisely like the water waves we call ripples, but everybody has seen ripples. So, it is customary to explain part of the behavior of sound waves *as if* those waves acted like ripples spreading outward when a stone is dropped into the water. Some characteristics of sound waves can be explained in this way, though not all. The analogical treatment will serve as long as attention is confined to how sound waves spread from their source. If the "as if" treatment is used to this degree only, it can lend both clarity and interest to an explanation of sound waves.

The point of hunting for *as-if* treatments is that people build new knowledge upon the knowledge they already have—through comparison and contrast. Some aspects of a steel rolling mill can be made clear and interesting by thinking of the steel as if it were dough and the mill as if it were equipped with kitchen rolling pins. One must be careful that listeners understand that an as-if treatment is not a discussion of actuality; yet, informative speakers are well advised to search more often than they do for such ways of explaining. It is worth remembering that this method of thinking and explaining is standard in scientific communication because many concepts can only be expressed in as-if terms or through mathematical symbols.

### Informing and Persuading

We have been discussing informative speaking as if information giving really existed completely apart from persuasion. It seldom does, but we can talk clearly of only one thing at a time. Clear explanations persuade us to believe; they encourage us to seek more knowledge; and they are often entertaining in the sense that new learning is pleasing.

*Informing, in itself, is often persuasive.*

Informative speaking persuades us about speakers' intentions. For example, if a speaker explains methods of contraception, he or she will almost surely be interpreted as endorsing some or all of the methods explained. Listeners suppose the *reason for* the explanation is a favorable mental set on the part of the speaker. That may or may not be true, but "pure" explanation is almost impossible on controversial subjects because persuasive intentions will be projected upon explainers. It is further true that in some circumstances the strongest persuasion possible is just a completely clear exposition of how and why the facts are as you say they are.

For the reasons just given, you should be careful when informing to exclude materials which are not necessary to your explanation and which, if used, might imply persuasive purposes you wish to avoid. If your goal is purely to inform, choose material that will accurately, completely, and in a unified manner communicate just the ideas you want to communicate. Choose also whatever additional material is needed to keep your exposition interesting. Your object ought to be to give such a clear and interesting explanation that your listeners will think your version of "how things are" is the most "persuasive" they have heard.

## SPEAKING TO PERSUADE

The best explanations are persuasive, as we just said. But in many rhetorical situations you will have to *motivate* listeners to accept, adhere to, and act on what you tell them. Because this is true, it has become commonplace to consider "to persuade" a rhetorical purpose different from "to explain or inform." From the viewpoint of a listener, this distinction between "persuading" and "informing" is largely academic. He hears what is said; he decides "how far" he will commit himself to the content of the message; and whether the speaker thought he was persuading or informing is of little interest to the listener as he makes his decisions. However, the distinction between "persuading" and "informing" is *not* academic to *makers* of oral communications. They need to have very clear ideas of exactly "how far" they want to move listeners along the line from passive acceptance to changed views and, perhaps, even to action. When they seek change, communicators have to do things differently from when they ask only for acceptance.

*A speaker must know exactly how much he wants to persuade.*

Persuading—seeking changed belief or encouraging action—requires you to give special attention to the *justifications* for what you claim. Especially, your listeners' interests and needs must be used to justify change. It will not do merely to assert. The Scottish rhetorician, George Campbell, said quite rightly:

> . . . when persuasion is the end, passion also must be engaged. If it is fancy which bestows brilliancy on our ideas, if it is memory which gives them stability, passion doth more, it animates them. Hence they derive spirit and energy. To say that it is possible to persuade without speaking to the passions, is but at best a kind of specious nonsense. The coolest reasoner always in persuading addresseth

> himself to the passions some way or other. This he cannot avoid doing, if he speak to the purpose. To make me believe it is enough to show me that things are so; to make me act, it is necessary to show that the action will answer some end. That can never be an end to me which gratifies no passion or affection in my nature. You assure me, "It is for my honour." Now you solicit my pride, without which I had never been able to understand the word. You say, "It is for my interest." Now you bespeak my self-love. "It is for the public good." Now you rouse my patriotism. "It will relieve the miserable." Now you touch my pity. So far . . . [is it] from being an unfair method of persuasion to move the passions, that there is not persuasion without moving them.[1]

A twentieth-century psychologist might reject Campbell's technical distinctions among fancy, memory, and "passion," but he would agree that there is no changing the attitudes or feelings of mankind without engaging the desires that Campbell called "passions." The modern psychologist would agree with Campbell that "the coolest reasoner" must certainly fail to change views unless aided by feelings. This necessity of enlisting active desires is one of the special demands the persuader's aim imposes on you.

### Consulting All Sides

There is more than one side to anything we choose to persuade about. We would not try to persuade if there were no doubts

[1]George Campbell, *Philosophy of Rhetoric,* ed. Lloyd Bitzer (Carbondale, Ill.: Southern Illinois University Press, 1963), bk I, chap. 7, p. 77. Originally published in 1776.

*A speaker must be well informed about all opinions on his topic.*

"out there." Consequently there are sure to be many sources of information that are strongly committed to one side of an issue. You would not expect to secure the whole story of a labor dispute from either the labor union's headquarters or from officials of the disputing corporation. You certainly would not expect to get all the facts from hearing only one side of a court case. In general, then, in choosing persuasive material it is important that you weigh the biases of the sources from which you gather it.

When you prepare a persuasive speech you ought to have consulted all sides. You ought to have read *The Nation* and *The National Review,* and *The New York Times* and *U.S. News and World Report,* if your subject involves liberal-conservative controversy in politics. See that you have the perspectives of union, management, and public observers if your subject concerns a labor dispute. You are likely to come away from this kind of investigation with a good deal of extraneous information and much that is biased, but you will know where the interested parties agree and where they differ. Where they agree, you may probably accept; where they disagree, you must search for the *reasons for difference.* Therein may lie the most important thing to say about the controversy. Using all available sources and your own analytical and reasoning powers, you will be able to offer your listeners positions you can truly justify.

This advice may sound idealistic, but we give it because it is practical. Of all kinds of speakers, a persuader must be most jealous of his or her own reputation for good sense and integrity. Persuaders presume to lead and advise. They thereby place their own reliabilities at issue. As a listener, you do not readily accept the advice of people who know less about the matter than you do; neither will your listeners. You must thus choose material that will show you have thought much and carefully. To get belief from doubters, you have to show them that you understand your subject, can reason well about it, and that *their* interests are involved in it. The question you should ask about all your material when you persuade is: will this information, or this argument, or this way of handling ideas generate *as much* change as my purpose, sense of responsibility, and the situation allow?

### Limited Goals

You will not have failed if you achieve less change than you hoped for in speaking. Lincoln did not greatly cool sectional animosity between North and South by giving his "Second

Inaugural Address." Dr. Martin Luther King did not wipe out racial discrimination with his "I Have a Dream" speech. Yet we cannot say Lincoln and King failed as persuaders. They achieved about as much change *as circumstances allowed* at the moments of their speaking. The way to measure what you ought to try to achieve and what you finally do achieve through persuasion is the same. You should assemble material that will induce as much change as it is reasonable to expect *given the facts about your rhetorical situation.* To change attitudes and beliefs only a little is still to persuade. Speech that only reinforces beliefs and feelings or only unsettles them a trifle is all that can be expected in some circumstances. Here is an example of a classroom speech which almost certainly succeeded persuasively by "chipping away" at widespread, fixed beliefs.

*A persuasive speaker need not effect radical change to be successful.*

In 1967, a Purdue University freshman named Charles Jarrow spoke on "The Case for the Non-Voter." He wanted to diminish belief that having a high turnout in elections is highly desirable. To do this he first noted the widely held belief that raising the percentage of regular voters who cast ballots is a good thing. Then he showed that the highest turnouts of voters usually occur in totalitarian countries. But there, he said, elections "are actually meaningless." Relating "high turnout" to totalitarianism, Jarrow then set up a contrast between voting records in the United States and those of other democratic states. "Their voting percentages match ours quite closely," he said. Choosing still another set of data, Jarrow next showed that those who do not vote regularly in the United States are actually the least informed among the eligible voters; so, he said, "We have what might be termed a kind of 'natural selection' among voters," and we should be thankful for it.[2] By the end of his speech, Jarrow had affirmatively associated his listeners' admiration for democracy and informed voting with the *status quo* and associated their distrust of totalitarianism and ignorance with high turnouts at the polls. It seems likely that he unsettled some customary beliefs. To that extent he persuaded and probably achieved as much change as his rhetorical situation allowed.

Where achieving persuasion is difficult, as in Jarrow's case, the reliability of the persuader is always specially at issue. It becomes important that he show he is both an informed and a fair counselor. A good way to show fairness is to recognize that there are other views than your own. Experimentation has almost uniformly shown that recognizing opposing views has

*A successful persuader should recognize opposing views.*

[2]Charles Jarrow, "The Case for the Non-Voter," in *On Speech and Speakers,* H. Bruce Kendall and Charles J. Stewart, eds. (New York: Holt, Rinehart and Winston, Inc., 1968), pp. 229–231.

more durable, favorable influence than one-sided persuasion. Only when an audience already agrees or when it will never be exposed to "other sides" is it safe to discuss only one side of an issue. Even then, there seems no reason to think that persuasion which disregards other views is any better than persuasion in which the speaker points out that there are positions other than the one he advocates. With either an unsophisticated or a sophisticated audience, he can show fairness by considering ideas that are different from his.

Common sense and experimental findings also suggest that when you plan to mention and eliminate viewpoints other than your own, the best tactic is: *first present your own position* as attractively and persuasively as you can, *then* indicate the competing positions and show their inferiority. Another way of saying this is: *present constructive arguments before answering or refuting*. There seems to be no way you can lose by this tactic, and there is good evidence that this is the best method of arranging pro-con elements in persuasion.[3] At the same time you will show listeners that you *know* what has been said and thought about your subject.

*Constructive material should be presented before refutational.*

What we have just said implies that in research for persuasive speaking you should gather both constructive and refutational information, and in composition of persuasive speeches you should include both kinds of material. As a beginning speaker you can put your material together best if you follow these three principles:

1. No matter what motivational justifications you offer for your position, satisfy your listeners that you have not taken up your position irresponsibly. Give some kind of evidence that you have taken it for sensible and essentially rational reasons.
2. Your listeners will expect you to show them why the position you have adopted is *more* sensible and responsible than other positions they may have heard of (or may hear of in the future). Give your audience both rational and self-interest justifications for rejecting alternatives to the position you endorse.

---

[3]The classic studies of one-sided vs. two-sided persuasion were done during World War II and were reported by Carl I. Hovland, Arthur A. Lumsdaine, and Fred D. Sheffield in *Studies in Social Psychology in World War II*, vol. 3: *Experiments on Mass Communication* (Princeton: Princeton University Press, 1949), especially pp. 201–227. There has been little investigation of whether persuasiveness is affected when opposing views mentioned are or are not *directly* refuted. Concise discussions of modern experimental research on these tactics appear in Ralph L. Rosnow and Edward J. Robinson, *Experiments in Persuasion* (New York and London: Academic Press, 1967), pp. 69–70 and 99–104.

3. The ultimate justification for any position you endorse will be your constructive proof that your position is *better for* your audience. Hence, the bulk of persuasion is *constructive*.[4]

A persuasive speaker needs to recognize that he seeks a special degree of change in his listeners. Therefore, a good question to ask about the persuasive material you include in a speech is, "Has this item enough promise or threat for my listeners so it will tend to shift their thinking?" Another good question is, "Can I *increase* the promise or threat of this item by presenting it in a special way (e.g., by setting up a contrast, including examples, or using especially vivid words)?" A persuader needs also to be especially sensitive to the observation we quoted earlier from George Campbell: "That can never be an end for me [as listener] which gratifies no passion or affection in my nature." When you are building a persuasive speech, you dare not stop developing your material until you have included substance which will contribute *psychologically* to change in listeners' beliefs and attitudes.

## OTHER PURPOSES

Giving information and persuading are the goals speakers most commonly set for themselves. But these goals sometimes become intertwined. At times we deliberately set out to get others to inquire for themselves or to entertain listeners. In a first course in speech you are unlikely to try to *induce inquiry* or *entertain* as frequently as to inform or persuade. Nonetheless, we shall give passing attention to these purposes because you may find yourself in speech situations that require you to adopt these goals, at least in part.

### Inducing Inquiry

You will not always "have the answers" and yet you may need to speak. In some rhetorical situations the need is to define a problem clearly and canvass possible "answers" in anticipation of choosing one later. If you become chairman of a committee assigned to perform a task, you may find it necessary to sit down with the committee and explain what you understand the "problem" to be. Or your job may be to motivate the committee

[4]An excellent, more extensive treatment of these principles appears in Douglas Ehninger and Wayne Brockrieder, *Decision by Debate* (New York: Dodd, Mead, 1963), especially pp. 81-95 and 252-266.

to try to solve the assigned problem. In more formal situations a city manager or an engineer may need to tell a group of citizens about a water-supply problem which *they* must act upon if there is to be a solution. Or an industrial supervisor may need to draw his or her staff together to create plans for a new production assignment.

If talk in these kinds of situations is to be a fitting response to the rhetorical situation, it must give information about the "problem" and persuade listeners to want to do something about it. In Chapter Eight we shall outline the pattern of organization that is characteristic of this kind of speaking. Here, it will be enough to point out that speaking to induce inquiry requires you to treat your subject sentence in a special way and is apt to require you to pay special attention to introducing features of interest into your speech.

*To induce inquiry, the speaker must have a precise subject sentence.*

The subject sentence of any speech to induce inquiry is best stated when it contains an expression of the precise question that has to be answered by those who will listen. The sentence might be phrased: "When I finish, I want my listeners to be prepared and motivated to answer the question, '——————'?" The words "be prepared and motivated to answer" are needed to remind you that you have *both* informative and persuasive tasks. Whether you incorporate these reminders in your subject sentence or not, it is still the case that a precisely stated *question* needs to be included in your subject sentence. If you are to try to induce inquiry, you will be asking your listeners to *answer* something. We do not answer propositions; we answer *questions*. Both you and your listeners will need to be very clear about *what* is to be answered.

If you say to yourself or to listeners that you are "raising the problem of amnesty for conscientious objectors," you are being vague about what is being asked and what is to be answered. You and your listeners would know what you are "up to," however, if you said: "When I finish I want them to be prepared and motivated to answer the question, 'Under what conditions, if any, should the federal government grant amnesty to conscientious objectors who refuse to serve in military forces during time of war?'" You would be similarly clear if you said, ". . . to answer the question, 'What steps need to be taken to improve the check-out services of our college library?' " Or, ". . . 'What can we five people do to reduce thefts in Doolittle Hall?' "

*To induce inquiry, the speaker must explain, motivate, and identify.*

In short, when you plan to speak to induce others to engage in inquiry, you must prepare yourself to (1) explain, (2) motivate, and (3) identify the *specific* question to be answered. Phrasing an exact subject sentence containing the question to be answered is a way of clarifying your purpose and a way of checking up on whether you have the materials with which to do what you must.

Another special problem arises in speaking to induce inquiry because this kind of speaking asks listeners to suspend judgments—to delay answers—until a *problem* is fully analyzed and all the optional answers have been systematically examined for advantages and disadvantages. For many people this withholding of judgments produces anxiety or boredom. They would rather "jump to conclusions," which is exactly what speaking to induce inquiry seeks to prevent them from doing. Because these things are so, anyone attempting this kind of talk needs to give special attention to keeping the *problem* interesting. Hence, as you prepare to induce inquiry you will need to look for material that will make the problem vivid. And in building your speech you will need constantly to ask yourself whether you have introduced enough interest-evoking features such as we have discussed in Chapter Three (pp. 56–58). If you can get your listeners truly interested in the problem you are presenting, they will, almost automatically, become *motivated* to answer the question you pose.

*In speaking to induce inquiry, an interesting problem is all-important.*

**Speaking to Entertain**

In many situations it is expected that whoever speaks will divert the listeners' attention from matters of high seriousness to lesser, but more interesting, subjects. This kind of situation does not occur regularly in classrooms, but it develops frequently elsewhere: at banquets, in convivial social groups, and other places where "Just interest us!" becomes the order of the moment.

What entertains? Narratives and colorful descriptions. These may or may not be humorous. A first-rate travelogue can entertain. So can a striking description of a mountain, if it is not too long. Any subject—any theme—that will hold attention agreeably in a diverting rather than a highly serious manner is at least potentially entertaining.

*Speech that entertains differs from other speech primarily in the way subject matter is treated.* The more diverting the amplification and delivery of ideas, the more entertaining the speech is. Once again, then, if you undertake to entertain listeners, you will need material that provides a heavy mix of the resources discussed on pp. 56–58.

Purpose statements are less important for entertaining speech than for more serious speaking. They are usually assertions and express your attitude toward the subject to be discussed. The reason they need not be framed as formally as other

*Purpose statements are not so important in entertaining speeches.*

subject sentences is that *the pleasure of your audience is more important to you than the logic of your subject.* This simply means that the diverting parts of your topic may be as important as the whole and that complete accuracy is not crucial. Neither you nor your listeners will care very much whether you cover all stages of mountain climbing in an entertaining speech on mountain climbing. What counts is whether the aspects of climbing which you do mention are engagingly and colorfully presented. When you entertain, you can choose what happens to be fascinating; when you explain, you must show you are covering the subject *fully.* This is a significant difference in what the two different purposes require of you.

It is well to remember that we may not always be entertained by interesting speeches, but entertaining speeches must always be interesting.

*While good humor is always entertaining, entertainment does not necessarily have to be humorous.* Storytelling is one of our most basic forms of entertaining communication. On the other hand, humor is usually expected in social situations where entertaining speech is anticipated. So the processes of distorting reality which are basic to humor are major elements of humorous speakers' resources. "The Conspiracy against Lefty" was the title of a delightful talk a left-handed student gave. The speaker's basic method was to exaggerate what it is like to be left-handed in a right-handed world. An imaginary cause (conspiracy) was offered to account for these difficulties. The speaker deftly twisted relationships to "establish" that the entire horse breeding, training, and equipping industry is managed by "right-wing plotters" who "brainwash" every newborn foal to resent all left-handed persons who try to approach in a "natural and convenient manner." This, of course, "explained" the speaker's many difficulties in trying to become a horsewoman. When you want to entertain by amusing, this speaker's devices are basic: treat inconceivable or barely conceivable attributes and relationships as "real" and treat the exceptional as "natural."

*Entertaining speech should have a thematic structure.*

*Entertaining speech pleases most when it has some kind of thematic logic.* Listeners are more gratified when pleased by *something* than by some *things.* Even nightclub gag men recognize that their audiences want a semblance of structure in entertainment. The most artful among them separate their mother-in-law jokes from their insurance-company jokes, giving each group of gags the status of a thought unit within the patter. And modern audiences seem especially partial to monologists who treat single themes in each monologue. Rambling is not a virtue in entertaining speech; conciseness and specificity are.

## CLASSIFICATIONS OTHER THAN BY PURPOSES

In this chapter, we have treated speeches according to their purposes. In doing so we have used but one method of classifying. It is a system, however, that is fairly inclusive. That is, all speeches have one of the purposes we have described as their dominant purposes.

We have not dealt with speeches as they have been classified according to types, places of delivery, or occasion. We have not talked about the characteristics of eulogies, inaugurals, nominating speeches, or keynote addresses. Nor have we described the special features of speeches of presentation, farewell, acceptance, or welcome. And we have not mentioned the common features of sermons, television reports, or classroom lectures. Your teacher may wish to explore these special types with you, but in all cases the purposes of the speeches you will examine in these other classifications will be those we have discussed.

## SUMMARY

The central idea of this chapter has been that some of your choices in deciding what to say in any speech are dictated by whether your goal is to inform, persuade, or influence your listeners in some other way. It would be a mistake to infer from what we have said on this theme that public speech never contains mixed purposes. In fact, informing, persuading, inviting listeners to inquire, and entertaining appear as mingled objectives in almost all first-rate speaking. But if listeners are to have a clear and satisfying sense of why you speak, your material must also communicate your *main* goal: whether to get listeners to understand what is said, change their views, cause them to inquire into a problem, or please and divert them. Listeners seek for "*the* point" in all public speech (though they are also interested in your making other, lesser points if you do so incidentally).

We have tried to show you that audience expectations shift as their sense of what is chiefly expected of them changes. We have pointed out that audiences wonder especially about accuracy, completeness, and the point of it all when they think they are being informed. They wonder especially about the fairness of their persuaders. They wonder, too, about their persuaders' knowledge, reasonableness, and about how genuinely they are interested in their listeners' concerns.

If you understand the points we have made, you will recognize that your speeches will be uniquely tested by your audience, depending on what your chief purpose is. We have just mentioned tests for informing and persuading. In listening to speeches to induce inquiry, audiences look for information justifying a true state of perplexity. When they are being entertained, their questions will have more to do with *how* you treat ideas than with the ideas themselves.

Each communicative goal we have discussed makes certain kinds of speech material more important than others. Each goal makes some invitations, assurances, and emphases more important than others. In Chapters Four and Five we talked about what speakers have to do in inventing speeches of *any* sort. Here, we have focused on the speaker's purpose as it defines the relevance and importance of the available speech material. Not everything relevant to your subject should be included in any speech. What you say must be chosen because it suits the subject and also fulfills the unique expectations that surface in the minds of hearers when they realize what your main goal is. What you seem to want them to do alters the kinds of ideas they will be most interested in. We have been stressing how a difference in purpose affects the choices you must make in order to move your public in the direction you want it to go.

## EXERCISES

*Written*

**1.** Write a brief essay on differences between speech materials that "prove" propositions and those that "amplify" ideas.

**2.** Choose a general topic such as "The Cost of Living" or "Clothing" and outline three different kinds of speeches that could be given on some aspect of the topic. For example, outline a persuasive, an informative, and an entertaining speech on "The Cost of Food Is Rising."

**3.** Read a speech of your own choosing and write a critique in which you:

a. Identify what seems to have been the speaker's dominant purpose in speaking.

b. Identify any subsections of the speech in which the purpose of communication seems to have shifted temporarily (e.g., from a dominant purpose of informing to a subordinate purpose of entertaining or persuading).

c. Evaluate the speaker's success in making shifts from primary to secondary aims and back to his primary aim. (Did he indicate to his listeners that he was shifting purpose? Did he indicate why he was doing this? How successful was he in keeping his dominant purpose clear despite temporary shifts? Was the impact of his speech strengthened or weakened by temporary changes in purpose? If weakened, how might this effect have been avoided?)

*Oral*

1. With two other members of your class, choose a simple topic such as earth, tools, books, or some other. Let each member of the group prepare and give to the class a two-minute talk that makes three points about the chosen topic, one talk giving information, another persuading, and the third entertaining. Afterward compare and contrast the different kinds of material each speaker used and the different ways he or she used them.
2. Among the more difficult topics on which to inform are those in which abstract or aesthetic concepts have to be made clear. For practice with this kind of speaking prepare and give a two-minute talk on how people should go about "understanding" or "appreciating" some specific artistic object (a statue, piece of jewelry, architectural form, bit of poetry, or other).
3. Prepare and present an oral report on the kinds of content used in a speech to entertain which you have read or heard. Indicate also what special treatment was given this content. (Speeches by Mark Twain or Will Rogers, or recordings by such entertainers as Bob Newhart, Mort Sahl, or Stan Freberg might be chosen for discussion in this exercise.)

# 8 Disposition: Organizing Materials

Nobody enjoys listening to a speaker when it is difficult to follow his train of thought. Just as we are bothered by the chaos of a cluttered, messy room or the disheveled dress of a classmate, we are disturbed by a speaker who seems to have dumped his ideas on us with no regard for our abilities to comprehend. Many lecturers, sadly enough, think we ought to sort out what they say. They do not help us by showing which of their ideas are primary and which are secondary or by revealing the relationships among their thoughts. They hinder our perceptions by spewing forth thought that flows like a river filled with debris, or they set before us a Mulligan stew of ideas.

Happily, most things we talk about in public *can* be spoken of in structured forms that are easily understood. We all share conceptions of relationships we call time, cause, effect, contiguity, succession, repetition, and so on. This makes it possible to communicate the basic connections among our experiences and thoughts. Even listeners who are not good organizers can understand us if we emphasize interconnections among ideas. This is fortunate because listening is not a very efficient way of taking in information or of getting relationships straight.

Listeners, like everyone else, like progression and variety in what they hear. They want clarity plus cumulative, psychologically satisfying effect. Communicative speaking, therefore, needs to build—point by point. Somewhere a climax must be reached, usually near the end of what is said.

*The content of a speech will often dictate how it is to be organized.*

Content will often suggest how your speech deserves to be organized. When you have selected the material for a speech, you are apt to find that your examples, statistics, authoritative statements, anecdotes, and the like tend to group under particular topics, headings, or arguments. Randy Cohn's outline for a speech on "The Artificial Kidney Machine" (pp. 172–175) seems to have been organized according to a series of natural questions about the process of dialysis. The main divisions concern *what the machine is,* how it *works,* and how a *person* uses it. Any listener-centered speaker would be likely to organize Ms. Cohn's data in a similar manner: moving from the impersonal machine to its service to people to people's use of the machine. In other circumstances, you would probably find that information about the Swiss Alps invited spatial organization which would also make description a major method of clarifying and vivifying. On the other hand, historical information virtually demands to be handled chronologically. In short, you will frequently find that your information suggests very strongly that one kind of organization is more reasonable than any other.

*The speech situation will also affect organization.*

The circumstances under which you expect to speak can also affect your choice among organizational structures. You may have to discard the least important and least interesting ideas because you will not have time to present them. You may have to organize to *exclude* unessential information—for other good reasons. Exclusion may be painful but it is not always unfortunate. Franklin D. Roosevelt found it necessary to cut his 1932 speech accepting the presidential nomination. His plane from Albany to Chicago was late and his audience was sure to be weary. Samuel Rosenman, who assisted him with the speech, wrote:

> With each radio report, we were falling further and further behind schedule: and more and more paragraphs came out of the acceptance speech. This lopping off of material on which we had worked so long and so hopefully was a painful process. I know that there were some jewels dropped on the airplaine floor that day. It is likely, though, that the cutting process hurt us more than it did the speech.[1]

---

[1]Samuel I. Rosenman, *Working with Roosevelt* (New York: Harper and Brothers, 1952), p. 75.

As Rosenman says, cutting and rearranging speech material is sometimes painful. But the tightening that often comes from cutting can enhance the structural unity of what is said. Focus is especially important in speaking, and eliminating dispensable details sharpens focus.

When you are preparing to speak, it is easy to misconceive the relations and relative importance of ideas, at first. On reflection, however, you are apt to discover that what formerly looked like six or seven points of equal importance can actually be fitted under just two or three main heads. Excellent! From an audience's point of view the fewer the main points that must be remembered, the better.

*The fewer main points in a speech, the better.*

You should remember, too, that the positions in a sequence of ideas are not equally impressive. Knowing that audiences are apt to pay close attention and to be least tired at the beginning of talks, you may want to put a very important idea first in the body of a speech. But knowing that the ideas listeners hear last are also apt to be remembered may cause you to put an important point last in another speech. These are the two strongest positions, first and last. Your final decision on what to put into those positions will really be a kind of bet that one position is likely to be stronger than the other for your particular audience.

*The first and last ideas presented will have the most impact.*

Arrangement of ideas in speeches ought not be random, but arrangement cannot be settled by rule, either. Look at Randy Cohn's image of the structure of her speech as she reported it in her subject registration paper (Appendix, pp. 229–230), then examine the three main headings of the body of her speech as she actually gave it (Appendix, pp. 234–235). There is a resemblance between the two plans but only that. Randy appears to have reconsidered the nature of her material and decided that emphasizing the donor program was *most* important in the body of the speech. Thus she put her appeal in the final position. She seems also to have thought it would be psychologically wise to move from (1) history to (2) present advances in transplantation of organs to (3) "what you can do." Thus she achieved a structure both logically and psychologically sound for the purpose she describes in her "Diary."

## MAIN COMPONENTS OF A SPEECH

Today's convention is that a speech should have an *Introduction*, a *Body*, and a *Conclusion*, *unless* there are good reasons for building it otherwise. Clear connections are needed to link these main parts. These linking parts are called *transitions*. We shall now consider each of these parts of a speech.

## Introductions

*An introduction should fulfill four functions.*

An introduction should: (1) attract initial, favorable attention to you and your subject; (2) provide any background the audience needs in order to comprehend what will follow; (3) take the occasion into account; and (4) contribute to your ease during the crucial first moments of adjusting to your speaking situation. In addition, an introduction ought to be clearly related to the body of the speech. It certainly should not seem to be a detached preamble or prelude.

At the outset of speaking you need to gain attention for yourself and your subject in such a way that your listeners will want to hear more. It may be useful to connect your subject with the speaking situation or with something else the audience already knows. On the other hand, special circumstances may dictate what you should say at the very beginning. You may need to begin with greetings, for example. Or, as Randy Cohn seems to have tried to do, you may need to begin by rousing your hearers, refocusing their attention (pp. 236–237). Generally, relevant anecdotes, striking assertions, unfamiliar ideas or statistics, and direct references to listeners' special interests will help you create curiosity or suspense if that is what needs to be done at the beginning. Where you can create common ground with your audience by referring to your own and their interests, this is a practical way of making the audience want to listen to you. Sometimes a modest statement of your qualifications for speaking on the subject you have chosen can make your listeners want to hear more.

The things that can be done in introductions are many, but the basic fact is that most audiences have to be given reasons for listening. They are always ready to ask, "Why should *I* listen? What's in this for *me?*" And usually they want some directions about what to listen for. This is why you will need to give them background knowledge when they do not have the information that will let them see their own relations to you and your subject.

Once you have aroused interest in yourself and what you are talking about, there are other things you *may* need to do in an introduction. It may be important to define unfamiliar terms associated with your subject or to clarify special meanings you will give to familiar terms. It may be helpful to you and your listeners if you say something about what you will *not* deal with in the body of your speech. And if you plan to pass over items the audience will expect you to treat, you ought to explain why these are irrelevant items or otherwise deserve to be "waived." For this purpose it is usually enough to state that you will not consider the ideas and give reasons.

If there are no reasons for not doing so, you ought to include your subject sentence in your introduction or as an initial item in the body of the speech. If you look at Randy Cohn's "The Gift of Life" (p. 237), you will find a statement of her specific purpose very early in the introduction.

*In certain circumstances an introduction is not needed.*

In some circumstances no introduction will be needed, such as when the audience is already attentive and interested in your subject, when they expect you to speak and know what you are going to speak about, when they already possess all the background information they will need, when they are highly motivated, or when the occasion requires no special accommodations from you. For example, a college lecturer can often safely dispense with introductions after the first few class meetings. The point is that when audiences are already oriented and motivated, all but the most perfunctory introductory remarks become superfluous. You should be cautious, however, about omitting introductory material. Introductions can rarely be omitted when you speak to an audience for the first time, and never when your audience is not entirely ready to pay attention to your central idea.

**The Body of the Speech**

*The body of a speech contains three elements.*

The body of any speech comprises (1) the main points, (2) the material that supports or amplifies these points, and (3) transitional phrases or sentences. This is true whether your speech is formal or informal.

*Main points should be phrased in certain ways.*

When you have sorted and selected materials, arrived at main points, and determined their psychological weights and placements, your next task is to phrase your main points. If you word them in parallel phrasings, they will be easier for you to remember. Main points for informative speeches should be phrased as simple, clear assertions. For speeches of inquiry, the main points should contain the questions to be explored or answered. Main points for persuasive speeches should be phrased as assertions which express your points of view and which support the main proposition contained in your subject sentence. Persuasive main points should be thought of as "contentions" or "reasons" which function as foundation stones upon which your core idea rests. Where your goal is entirely to entertain, the entertaining idea is usually best stated as an assertion, though the assertion may not be meant seriously.

Once you have phrased your main points, you need to develop them by organizing your supportive and amplifying material. When this is done, you will have, in skeleton form, the body of a speech consisting of main points which support or amplify a single subject sentence and the developmental material which, when attached to the main points, makes those points credible, interesting, and appealing. With this much sketched out in rough outline form, your next concern should be with how you can connect these organized units of material to one another.

*Listeners need transitions for optimum understanding.*

*Transitions.* Listeners cannot easily review what you say after you have said it. They might turn back and reread, had you written your message. They cannot do this with a speech. So, you will need to help their understanding by planning careful transitions. *Transitions are words, phrases, sentences, or groups of sentences which join ideas together and direct thoughts along paths you intend them to follow.* Transitions are like signposts. They tell an audience where you have been, where you are, or where you intend to go. They are particularly needed between the main divisions of a speech and at the ends of main points in the bodies of speeches. You may also need to insert them to emphasize connections among subsidiary points or even as phrases pointing out the significance of single sentences.

Internal summaries can function as transitional materials. They point ahead to next ideas. They commonly contain such wordings as:

Since we have already considered that . . . , we should adopt. . . .
In addition to . . . there is another reason (element, factor, consideration, fact) . . . .
We have seen . . . , yet it remains for us to observe. . . .
But . . . is only one viewpoint. Equally important is. . . .
Since . . . is so, what can be said of . . . ? (Questions can often serve as useful transitions.)

If you want to point out connections between subpoints, phrases, or even single words, "so" or "yet" may be adequate to tie ideas together. Some other common transitional phrasings are:

More important is the fact that. . . .
In contrast to. . . .
Looked at from a different angle, the problem is. . . .
This last point raises the question of. . . .
What was the result? Just this. . . .

On the other hand....
When this has been done....
And so you can see that....

In phrasing transitions, try to avoid using only stock phrases or repeating the same ones over and over. It is a mark of an unpolished speaker to use only "and," "also," or "like" as transitions. A speaker who does this gives the impression of having tacked his ideas together, of having joined them carelessly. But even *he* is in a better communicative position than the speaker who melts from point to point, leaving the impression that he is groping for a path or train of thought.

*There are four criteria for good transitions.*

Good transitions (1) show that you are moving from one idea to another, (2) put "periods" to completed ideas, (3) identify how ideas relate to one another, and (4) remind you of your own sequence of thought. The last of these points is very important to you. If you have planned clear transitions or "bridges" from point to point you will be unlikely to lose your way when you talk with your audience.

## Conclusions

The final segment of your speech ought to perform whatever functions your audience and you still require. At the end of sustained talk an audience normally expects (1) some restatement of the central idea of the talk or (2) a summing up of the main points used to clarify or support the main idea.

*Conclusions should drive home the central idea.*

Almost any set of ideas needs to be finally rounded off in a way that fuses subject matter with the communicator's intent. The final moments of speaking ought to drive home your central idea. Read the conclusion to Randy Cohn's "The Gift of Life" (p. 240). Did she achieve the greatest impact possible, given her purpose? What is said at the end of a talk ought to echo the beginning, completing the thought forecast by the subject sentence with the fullest appropriate force. We cannot say how this is to be done in specific situations but indicating that you have fulfilled your promises is a wise move in any conclusion.

It is conceivable that you will speak in a few situations where you need not utter "concluding words." These circumstances will be rare. The most common ones will be when someone else will conclude what you have said, as when one person explains that the treasury is empty, knowing that a colleague will make an appeal for money.

On the whole, "thank you's" and other remarks of appreciation detract from otherwise strong final impressions. They seem tacked on when they occur at the end of a speech. Such amenities are better handled at the beginning. Your ending ought to stress your *message*.

## USEFUL PATTERNS OF ORGANIZATION

*Four factors determine a speech's pattern.*

Four factors usually combine to determine what the most appropriate pattern for a talk will be: (1) the type of response you seek from the audience; (2) whether the audience is favorably, unfavorably, or apathetically disposed toward your subject, your central idea, and you as a speaker; (3) how much your listeners already know about your subject; and (4) how you can best relate your specific purpose to the interests and desires of your audience.

Patterning the ideas which make up the body of a speech is not an either-or affair. You are likely to have more than one choice among ways of organizing. If so, you ought to pick the pattern of organization that will give your particular audience the clearest and most emphatic understanding of the logical and psychological relationships among your ideas. The commonest structures for accomplishing this are briefly discussed below.

### Chronological Pattern

*The chronological pattern treats topics in the order in which they happen.*

If you talk about occurrences in the order in which they happened or will happen, you place them in a chronological or time pattern. This arrangement can be used in all kinds of speech units. Segments of speeches developed chronologically can be found in the narrations of circumstances leading to crime, as in Clarence Darrow's famous summation at the trial of Leopold and Loeb or in Daniel Webster's classic speech for the prosecution in the Knapp-White murder case. Mary Collins's speech "The Big Fraud," which is outlined on pp. 175–177, is structured in this way. She treated social security's past, its present worth, and its future.

One weakness of putting ideas in chronological order is that such important considerations as cause, effect, desirability, and form cannot easily be emphasized without interrupting the movement through time that gives chronology its chief interest value.

### Spatial Pattern

If you describe how something looks or is "laid out," you adopt a spatial pattern. You describe left to right, top to bottom, bot-

*The spatial pattern treats how things are "laid out."*

tom to top, or front to back. Randy Cohn's subpoint I.B. on p. 173 is developed in this way. She describes the artificial kidney machine from top to bottom. You might describe the control panel in an airplane by first discussing the centered instruments that are most important and most often referred to, then moving out toward the surrounding instruments which are less frequently referred to.

In any spatial arrangement, whether in a part or in the whole of a speech, you will need to cover parts or aspects of the thing discussed *systematically*. Haphazard coverage makes spatial relationships especially hard to understand.

Spatial structures are particularly useful in giving information. A fire extinguisher might be described from top to bottom; a painting from left to right; the floor plan of a house from front to back or from story to story. Which portion of space you should discuss first depends on your estimation of how you can make the whole system of relationships clearest. If these standards leave you more than one good way of describing spatially, choose the one that is easiest for *you* to *remember*. This will improve your command of your material when you speak.

### Topical Pattern

*The topical pattern treats topics logically.*

The label "topical" is given to organizational schemes that we cannot otherwise account for. Some call these "classification patterns." Others say "topical patterns" are those that arise from subject matters—from the internal "logic" of the thing discussed. Whatever language is used, the ways these structures are discovered are clear. A speaker asks himself what "standard headings" people are used to when they analyze his kind of subject. The answer may be like that Randy Cohn produced for her speech on transplantation of organs (Appendix, pp. 233–236): (1) the nature of transplantation, (2) recent advances, and (3) what donors of organs accomplish. When devising a topical pattern you try to locate a *special* way of "cutting up" material that suits both your subject and your listeners' probable ways of thinking about it. You could discuss social, political, and economic aspects of a subject or you could treat roles that public and private interests play respecting the same subject. Now, you have a choice. The question is: which of these two *arbitrary* ways of organizing ideas best fits your purpose, your listeners' habits of thought, and the situation? An engineer discussing construction will find it almost mandatory to treat the topics, *mass* and *tensile strength* of construction materials, at some point. But if he is going to speak to someone who is going to *buy* a construction plan, he will also treat the further topics of *cost* and *desirability* if he is wise.

Certain "topics" are regularly discussed in connection with some speech subjects; other sets of "topics" emerge as necessary in particular kinds of rhetorical situations as our example of the engineer illustrates. Your job is to decide whether a particular structure is "standard" for either your subject or in circumstances like those you will face in speaking. For example, kinds of *type faces* are a necessary "topic" if you discuss printing as a practical art, but not if you discuss the publishing business generally. You would probably make *economics* one of your "topics" of discussion if you spoke of the *consequences* of liberalized abortion, but you would not emphasize this "topic" if the *morality* of abortion were your subject.

## Ascending and Descending Orders

*Ascending-descending structures arrange ideas from least to most or most to least—important, familiar, etc.*

Sometimes you will feel it wise to move from most to least important or from most to least familiar ideas. You will then be treating ideas in a "descending" order. The same will be true if you decide to start with common ideas and move into unfamiliar territory. To take an example, you might explain how pulp is processed for the manufacture of paper by taking up the most commonly used process: the ground-wood process. Then you might successively move to the soda, sulfite, and alkaline processes, which are less frequently used and are less familiar to most listeners.

An opposite, "ascending," structural system is also open to you. In some circumstances it is helpful to move from the least familiar or the least important idea to the most familiar or most important. For example, you can sometimes make costs seem most impressive by starting with the smallest and gradually moving toward the most costly aspect. Similarly, you might move from the least attractive to the most attractive feature of a building or a policy.

Ascending-descending structures are suitable for all kinds of speaking except speaking to induce inquiry. The reasons speeches of inquiry do not accommodate this kind of organization will be clear from the discussion on pp. 162–163.

## Causal Sequences

*Causal patterns treat cause-effect relationships.*

Causal patterns occur when one set of conditions is given as the cause for another set. Everyone is familiar with cause-effect relationships, hence arrangements that emphasize causality are relatively easy to follow. To create such a pattern you might begin with a set of conditions and say that these will produce certain results or effects; or you could present a set of conditions and hold that they resulted from certain causes which you then identify.

The most common use of causal patterns is to urge elimination of causes in order to get rid of undesirable effects. You can show listeners undesirable effects first, then show their cause(s), then argue for removal of the cause(s), or you can show the cause(s) first, then the undesirable effects, and finally argue for removal of the cause(s). In either case you will need to persuade your audience of one or more of these: (1) that the effects you describe are really undesirable to them; (2) that the causes you present are truly responsible for the effects you speak of; and (3) that elimination of the causes will not produce other, undesirable effects. The first two concerns must either be evident to the audience, or you must prove them. The third may sometimes be safely disregarded, particularly if you have no reason to think your listeners will anticipate bad effects from removing the causes you talk about.

Although causal patterns are widely used to advocate removal of some condition, they can be used as structures for arguing that certain conditions should be encouraged. You can show how something desirable to your audience (effect) will or could result from something else (cause); therefore, you can contend that listeners should set the causes in operation in order to secure the desired effect. For example, you could contend that we all want peace in the world, that peace is likely to come about as a result of strengthening the United Nations in some way, and therefore the listeners ought to act as you advise to strengthen the United Nations. In explaining processes, too, causal patterns are useful; for example, X-rays have such and such qualities (cause) which produce certain effects in human tissue.

In all causal structures the most important single thing to accomplish is to show that there is a genuine cause-effect relationship between the two sets of conditions you talk about. The entire success of this plan of organization hinges on the listeners' seeing and believing this relationship.

### Problem-Solution Sequence

*The problem-solution sequence treats topics psychologically.*

Especially in speaking to reinforce belief and feeling or to persuade, it is often useful to structure what you say so that you first present a problem and next propose a way to solve it. Success here hinges on your ability to show that the solution can be put into effect without negative results. Normally in treating the solution you will want to show that it is (1) practical, (2) desirable, and (3) an action which will not introduce new disadvantages of its own. Problem-solution structures work well in the following situations.

1. If your audience is aware of the problem and is interested in finding a solution to it, you can advocate one solution as the best of several possible answers. Although you will probably need to outline the problem briefly, most of your time will be spent in showing how your particular solution will solve the problem.
2. If your audience is only dimly aware of a problem, you can first heighten their awareness, outline your solution, and then argue its practicability. Randy Cohn's "The Gift of Life" (Appendix, pp. 233–236) could have been given this structure. It might be a useful experiment to construct the outline she might have made had she chosen to address her listeners in this way. To take another example, you might explain the extent of child abuse as a social problem, offer a plan for easing the problem (perhaps family clinics), show that where the solution has been tried it has proved workable, and contend that the solution should be applied generally.
3. If your object is simply to make your listeners see how something happened in the past, you can make yourself clear by showing how people were faced with a problem and by what steps they solved it, or tried to solve it. Had Mary Collins chosen to explain how the Social Security Act came about, she could have expanded item III under "Body" on p. 175 into a complete speech using this kind of structure. In speaking on child abuse you might seek understanding of what has happened by explaining the extent of child abuse in city X and then explaining how family clinics were set up as a solution and how they worked. If audiences are not expected to take action, this "historical" problem-solution structure may be useful.

### Withheld-Proposal or Indirect Sequence

*The indirect sequence treats supporting materials first, and later gives the subject sentence.*

Sometimes the withheld-proposal or indirect sequence is the only pattern that will enable you to persuade. Following this pattern, you would first give your audience examples, facts, and arguments based on the common ground of agreement you have with your listeners. Only late in your speech would you put forward the conclusion toward which you were indirectly working. This strategy is a standard one for dealing with hostile and firmly indifferent listeners. One way of using this pattern is to pile up examples (of what is good or of what is bad) until a listener's own logic forces him to agree with your initially withheld assessment of a situation—which the listener did not at first care to recognize. Another method is to establish a set of premises or assumptions which you know your listener will agree to, then show him that his own logic forces him to a conclusion which you have withheld up to this time.

The first of these choices is one Mary Collins might have used in developing her speech, "The Great Fraud." She might have discussed all of the inequities said to exist in Social Security insurance and then revealed her charge of "fraud" (see pp. 175–177). In a speech using the second option you might show that emergency aid to the poor and malnourished is generally approved and has been helpful, and then you could apply that principle to the case of migrant workers' camps and argue for direct action aimed at improving the economic and nutritional status of these workers.

Indirect approaches are chiefly useful when listeners would not accept your proposal if it were revealed at the outset. If listeners are generally favorable toward you, nothing is gained and some clarity may be lost by withholding your specific purpose in speaking.

### Open-Proposal or Direct Sequence

*The direct sequence gives the subject sentence first, and then the supporting materials.*

A simple and familiar way of presenting ideas is to tell your listeners what your purpose is and then proceed to support it. You urge the audience to accept a proposition on the grounds which you then supply. Using this pattern, you might say that you favor a certain piece of legislation, explain it, and then argue that it is practically beneficial, legal under the Constitution, and morally right. In explaining, you might announce that you seek understanding of road building and then cover route planning, grading, surfacing, and so on.

In general, an open-proposal pattern of presentation is most suitable where listeners are fairly familiar with your subject and where they have favorable or open-minded attitudes toward your position. A special advantage of the pattern is that it is easy for your listeners to see what you are doing and how you are going about it. However, there are usually few surprises and little suspense in this kind of organization. Above all others the open-proposal plan is forthright and clear, but special efforts may need to be made to keep this kind of presentation interesting and motivating.

### Reflective Sequence or the Pattern of Inquiry

*The reflective sequence presents a problem but leaves the solution open.*

The reflective sequence or pattern of inquiry is an organizational structure that requires you and your listeners to suspend judgment about a problem and its solution. Your own state of mind is usually your justification for adopting this way of presenting ideas.

If you are in doubt about what "the answer" really is, you can do little else but invite listeners to join you in a quest for solutions or best answers. Under such circumstances you will probably need first to make your listeners feel the problem is their problem, not yours alone. This done, you do all you can to give the audience and yourself a better basis for coming to a sound decision. Coming to a decision is the essential goal in a speech of inquiry.

To orient your listeners to your subject, you will need to help them understand the dimensions of the problem as you see it. You explain its symptoms, its underlying causes, perhaps its historical development. You do not stop there, however. You next consider the criteria which an acceptable solution must meet. This is an important stage of discussion that is often missed, but unless you satisfy your listeners that you have offered the right standards for separating a "good" from a "poor" solution, you will have lost your control over their channels of thought.

When you have clarified a problem and said what is needed concerning standards for judging solutions, you ought to present whatever reasonable, alternative solutions exist. This usually ought to be the most important section of your talk. Unfortunately speakers often allow themselves too little time to discuss the advantages and disadvantages of the different solutions to their problems. As you examine the pros and cons of different solutions, you must, of course, remind listeners again of the criteria by which solutions are judged.

If you seriously want to encourage your listeners to inquire, you will conclude your talk by encouraging them to weigh the different solutions that you have identified. Their reflection should not stop when you have finished your presentation. One way to encourage them to think further is to close your speech by presenting some challenging questions for your listeners to consider as they work out their own answers. Another way is to point out the *direction* in which you think, or other people think, the best answer(s) probably lie. Still another is to end your talk by inviting discussion of what seems to be the best solution.

The reflective sequence is a pattern of thought people follow naturally when they want to inquire. *The* answer is not provided by the speaker; questions that encourage further thought, and leadership in subsequent discussion of the problem, are the behaviors with which talk to induce inquiry ends.

When does one use this pattern of presentation? When he knows there is a problem but does not see a clear answer and, therefore, would like assistance in searching for an answer. Perhaps the most familiar place where such a presentation is called for is the committee room. Again and again, chairmen must say to their committees: "Our difficulties are these. What shall we do?" Wherever your speaking situation is of this general sort, in or out of a committee room, you will have little choice but to structure your remarks in the reflective sequence—if you wish to be clearly understood.

### The "Motivated Sequence"

*Five organizational steps help motivate listeners' responses.*

Professor Alan H. Monroe of Purdue University proposed some years ago that the way to motivate listeners' responses to speakers' purposes was to organize talk in a sequence of five steps. The steps are these: secure attention, create a sense of need, assure satisfaction, evoke visualization of results, and appeal for action by the listener. Monroe urged speakers seeking to persuade to develop talks that carried out all five of these steps. The persuader would (1) draw attention to the subject, (2) establish a need for some sort of change, (3) show how the change could be brought about or the need could otherwise be satisfied, (4) visualize what would happen when the need *was* or *was not* met—picturing probable results, and (5) appeal directly for action, either mental or physical.

If a speaker's goal is simply to inform, Monroe advised him to use only the first three steps: getting attention, establishing the listeners' need to know, and creating satisfaction in knowing. In a speech to entertain, Monroe suggested that effort might be devoted almost entirely to securing and holding attention. Entertainment in some cases might be provided by parodying the developmental stages of speaking to inform or persuade.

This way of organizing speaking, more than any other, is psychologically planned to lead listeners' thinking naturally and easily from a vague interest in a subject to a definite acceptance of the attitude or action advocated. Each step is built on the preceding ones. Here is how the pattern might be used if your were selling a vacation tour:

I. You deserve better vacations than you have had. [Attention.]
II. Isn't it privacy and comfort you want? [Need.]
III. Maurice Island has long, quiet beaches, luxury living at moderate prices, and come-as-you-are attitudes. [Satisfaction.]
IV. There are four beach hotels on twelve miles of tropical, sandy beach, each hotel offering a different nation's night-life once the sun has set. [Visualization.]
V. Miss Krider is here to take your reservations for a one-week visit; better still, she will accept your check and assure you of the vacation you have been waiting for. [Action.]

You have been exposed to this pattern of presenting ideas before! Do not miss the fact that it is psychologically sound for promoting international cooperation as well as vacations, for rousing lethargic voters, for showing people how to study better, and even for giving a speech to entertain.

### Elimination Order

*The elimination order presents several "solutions," and then eliminates all but one.*

Sometimes it is effective to present several possible interpretations of a subject or problem and then to show that all but one must be eliminated as undesirable, impractical, or incorrect. This strategy is called the "elimination order" or the "method of residues."

By this process what would otherwise be a reflective sequence can be turned into a persuasive pattern. If you apply agreed-upon criteria to available solutions, you may be able to show that only one solution is actually worth considering. The strategy can also be incorporated into a problem-solution structure as a way of eliminating all solutions except the one you advocate.

For this kind of organization to work effectively, both you and your listeners must be willing to investigate more than one kind of solution or answer to a difficulty. Also, time must be available for full explanations and for testing the various possibilities in order to discover the grounds for rejection. A talk built on principles of elimination could be made concerning "Maurice Island," the subject we imagined in the section on "motivated sequences" just above:

Maurice Island offers more privacy and comfort than any other spot in Laguna Sea. [Subject sentence.]

I. Seaward Island has beaches and luxury but at luxury prices and with white-tie-and-tails conditions.
II. Seaward Island has four hotels per beach mile to Maurice Island's one hotel per three miles of beach.
III. Only on Maurice Island can you find the combination of privacy, comfort, moderate prices, and come-as-you-are attitudes.

You have seen and heard that pattern before, too. It is effective provided you are confident that the advantages of one solution will seem greater than the advantages of the other choices.

## OUTLINING

*An outline is a visual representation of a pattern of thought.*

No matter what pattern you use in structuring a speech it will be very valuable to you and whoever advises you if you make a *visual* representation of the structure of the talk you plan. That is what an outline is: *a visual representation of a pattern of thought.* Outlines are skeletal maps of intended communications. They allow you and anyone helping you to review your organizational plan and its logic to see whether it makes sense."

### Functions of Outlines

In classrooms and in some other situations you may be asked to construct outlines in order to show a teacher or some other adviser your basic plan for speaking. This practice is not peculiar to speech classes. We know of religious groups, corporations, and governmental agencies which routinely require speakers to submit outlines of their plans. These are then reviewed for content and organization by experts in communication and in the special subject treated.

*Full-sentence outlines are best for the beginning speaker.*

If you have no need to communicate your plans to anyone but yourself, you will be free to construct *full-sentence, phrase,* or *key-word* outlines, depending on the degree of preciseness and refinement you demand of yourself as a planner. But if you are a beginner at speaking publicly, or if you must communicate your speech plans to someone else, you will find full-sentence outlines the most useful way to represent your plans. Full sentences express the complete thoughts to be presented. If you get each thought fully in mind, then whoever reads your plan will understand it and be able to advise you

clearly. Most beginners are handicapped if they develop only shorthand outlines. Too often the brief notes resemble grocery lists of unrelated points. Not even your best friend is likely to be able to translate your shorthand notes or test whether your plan makes sense.

The point in submitting an outline to a teacher or other adviser is to secure advice about the plan. An outline prepared for others to read is not a private paper. Therefore, the full nature of ideas and the characteristics of their relationships need to be clear both visually and verbally. This means you and your adviser must understand a common system of representing ideas and relationships. If there is to be communication, full sentences and an agreed-upon way of outlining are necessary in most cases. You may know what you intend to say when you write the word "Economic" and list "Cost" and "Profit" as supporting ideas, but another person seeking to advise you will not see clear-cut connections among such sketchy symbols. In fact you, yourself, may really have slipped in thinking. So, for your own sake and a reader's sake, you ought to prepare outlines carefully so that ideas are fully represented and their relationships are unmistakable.

Outlines are skeletons of speeches showing the relations among the parts and places where the flesh of discourse will be added. These things need to be symbolized in some conventional way that allows clarity despite brevity.

### Common Practices in Outlining

No hard and fast rules govern outlining, but certain customs are commonplace. If followed they help anyone to read an outline quickly and intelligently. Here are some specific features that can make your outlines useful to you and to any other reader.

*There are seven "rules" to keep in mind when outlining.*

*Show clearly the basic divisions of your speech: Introduction, Body, and Conclusion.* These labels are not part of the idea structure; they are technical names of parts of typical speeches. Therefore, they are not normally given numerical or alphabetical symbols. Numerical and alphabetical symbols are usually reserved as indicators of relationships among ideas intrinsic to the speech. It is a good idea to place these names of the basic divisions of your speech in a center position without accompanying symbols. In the infrequent instances where no introduction will be needed, the absence of the heading "Introduction" will be quickly apparent; so, too, with "Conclusion."

*Use a consistent system of symbolization and indentation.* The system of symbols you use is up to you; what is essential is that you use them consistently and that each time a certain type of symbol occurs it signifies that the idea associated with it is of approximately the same importance as every other idea associated with the same type of symbol. If you follow this principle, it will matter little whether Roman numerals, capital letters, or Arabic numerals are used to indicate main heads and subheads.

*Follow the rule of one symbol, one idea.* This will remind you to break up compound ideas and guarantee that you distinguish your thoughts from one another. Especially if you make phrase outlines, you will need to check carefully to see that each symbol stands beside a single idea rather than beside a fragmentary idea or beside a phrase which actually represents—for you—several ideas.

Indentation, the physical arrangement of ideas on paper, is another way of representing visually how ideas relate to one another. Ideas subsidiary to other ideas should be placed under the thoughts they support to show they are subordinate. This lets you see at a glance which ideas are major and which are supportive or developmental. Logical indentation will also let you see at a glance *how many* ideas develop a subsuming concept or argument. You will need this visual guidance when rehearsing for a public presentation and when speaking in public.

*More than one piece of information is usually needed to develop a point adequately.* It is possible that one definition, one example, or one opinion will suffice to clarify or prove an important idea. Whether this is so depends on how much your listeners require as "sufficient proof" or "adequate amplification." However, most ideas of importance are best reinforced if listeners are given more than one supporting thought or datum.

Therefore, an outline that contains single subpoints should be viewed suspiciously. Only when you are sure that one and only one bit of proof or amplification is necessary should a subpoint be allowed to stand alone.

*Ideas must be discrete.* A major reason for making an outline is to show yourself and others how *individual* ideas relate to one another. The following muddle of notions does not do this:

**A.** The Federal Employment Service has more than 2,400 local offices and it placed more than four and one-half million people last year.
- **1.** It gave help to old, young, inexperienced, minority, and handicapped applicants for work.
- **2.** It assisted in developing manpower resources in this nation, in meeting emergencies, countering disasters, and assisting other countries.

The compound sentence and the strings of terms and phrases not clearly interrelated show that the maker of this fragment of an outline has not sorted out the thoughts jumbled together in the sentences. There will not be clear, direct thinking in speech based on this structure. Had the maker of the outline followed the rule, "one idea per symbol," he would have been forced to straighten out his thinking. This is sounder:

**A.** The Federal Employment Service has more than 2,400 local offices.
**B.** Its services go to a wide variety of incapacitated people.
- **1.** It assists those whose age affects prospects for employment.
  - **a.** It helps the aged to find work suited to their abilities.
  - **b.** It helps young people who lack work experience.
- **2.** It assists those who are physically or otherwise handicapped.
  - **a.** It helps people held back by belonging to minority groups.
  - **b.** It helps to find work that physically handicapped people can do.

**C.** The Service tries to develop manpower resources here and abroad.
- **1.** It trains people in skills needed to meet emergencies such as national or local disasters.
- **2.** It develops training programs in types of skills now needed or likely to be needed in the nation's future.
- **3.** It even offers training in skills needed by other nations.

A speaker or other reader can scan the second outline and see quickly and exactly what specific points are to be covered. He can see where more supporting material may be needed, and he can see how much time is likely to be needed to cover points A, B, and C sufficiently to satisfy an audience. He can tell *none* of these things by scanning the first outline! Why? Because in that outline specific, discrete ideas are not visually separated; in the second case they are. This is the reason you should be wary of inserting compound sentences and numerous "and's" and "or's" in any outline. Follow the general principle, "one symbol, one idea," and you will force yourself to think clearly, to represent fairly the whole of your thinking, and to be able to evaluate your thinking and the relations of ideas.

*Clearly symbolize and place your subject sentence.* Your subject sentence or central idea is the most important statement in your talk. It therefore deserves highest rank in your system of symbolization. It should stand out as the governing idea for all else. The name you give this statement is not important nor is the symbol or other designation you assign to it. The important thing is that this statement appear as the precise, one-sentence summary of your whole, planned communication. In outlines of deductively organized talks, this central idea usually appears near the end of the Introduction or near the beginning of the Body of the speech. (Notice its placement as point II of Randy Cohn's outline on p. 173.) In outlines of inductively organized talks, the subject sentence or central idea may not appear until the end of the Body or even in the Conclusion. In either case, the important thing is to place the statement *obviously* to help you keep your mind on the main business of the whole speech.

*Include transitions in outlines.* Setting off transitional statements or phrases by using parentheses will remind you of how to "bridge" from one thought to another. Notice how this is done in Mary Collins's outline on pp. 175–177. If you do this, you will have another way of visually reminding yourself of what to say and when. You will be visually drawing your own attention to how you plan to move from one point or subpoint to another.

If you follow the practices we have just suggested, a diagram of your outline will look about like this:

Title

Introduction

**I.** ..........................................................
    **A.** ..........................................................
    **B.** ..........................................................
**II. (Central Idea)** ..........................................................
        **(Transition:** ..........................................................**)**

Body

**I.** ..........................................................
    **A.** ..........................................................
    **B.** ..........................................................

1. ..........

a. ..........

b. ..........

2. ..........

a. ..........

b. ..........

**(Transition: ..........)**

**II.** ..........

**A.** ..........

1. ..........

a. ..........

b. ..........

c. ..........

2. ..........

**(Transition: ..........)**

**B.** ..........

1. ..........

a. ..........

b. ..........

(1) ..........

(2) ..........

(3) ..........

(a) ..........

(b) ..........

c. ..........

2. ..........

a. ..........

b. ..........

**(Internal Summary: ..........)**

**III.** ..........

**A.** ..........

1. ..........

a. ..........

b. ..........

2. ..........

**B.** ..........

**(Transition and/or Internal Summary: ..........**

**..........)**

Conclusion

**I.** ..........

**A.** ..........

**B.** ..........

**C.** ..........

**II.** ..........

Bibliography
(or Statement of Sources)

Two items appearing in this diagram remain to be considered: title, and bibliography or statement of sources.

### Titles

In informal speaking situations, titles for talks are less necessary than in situations where you will be formally introduced or where your speech will be announced in advertisements or in news accounts. A title provides those who report your speech, record it, or otherwise refer to it with a label that identifies what you will or did talk about.

*A title should be brief, relevant, and provocative.*

Titles are normally composed after speech composition is completed. Then you can cast your mind back over all you have planned and decide on a phrase that will characterize it. A title is a good one if it is (1) brief, (2) relevant, and (3) provocative. William Jennings Bryan's famous speech might have been titled "Silver *vs.* Gold" instead of "The Cross of Gold." The first title would have announced Bryan's subject more precisely and relevantly. The "skeleton" in a speech that was titled "Skeletons All?" represented a nonvoter; the speech might better have been given the title "Present but Not Voting." Brevity and provocativeness would have been retained, but relevance to the real subject would have been improved. On pp. 175–177 you will find the outline of a speech titled "The Big Fraud." What fraud? We suggest a better, clearer title might have been "Social Security or Insecurity?"

### Bibliographies

There are good reasons for appending bibliographies to the outlines of speeches. One is that, however informal your public speech, you ought to be able to account for its sources should anyone ask. Another reason is that you may want to give all or a part of a good speech again. If that should happen, you need to have a clear way of recalling what was most useful to you when you originated the speech. A bibliography, then, is a natural acknowledgment of other people's contributions to your work and a ready reference which you can use at some future time when the odds and ends that were your original notes have disappeared.

There are many forms for making bibliographical entries. The important standards to meet are that your entries be complete and consistent in form. Appended to the outlines that follow you will find examples of ways in which personal obser-

*Bibliographic entries should be complete and consistent.*

vations, interviews, books, magazine articles, newspaper items, and pamphlets can be identified clearly for you or any other reader. These forms meet the criteria we just cited; they will serve you as guides if you have no other way of citing your resources.

## SAMPLE OUTLINES AND SPEAKERS' NOTES

The two outlines that follow illustrate outlining procedures and preparatory methods that are functional, even though not every detail will meet a perfectionist's demands. The first outline was a plan for a speech to inform, six minutes in length. It presents a clear, overall structure, and the mechanics of outlining are generally good. It may be more detailed than some speakers and advisers find necessary, but it can serve as a model from which abridgements can be adapted.

### THE ARTIFICIAL KIDNEY MACHINE[2]

Introduction

**I.** Although we haven't made any giant steps in controlling air or water pollution, we have found a way to eliminate body pollution.
- **A.** What is body pollution?
  - **1.** Body pollution is the loss of function in both kidneys.
  - **2.** This results in the inability of the person to filter out the wastes from the blood.
    - **a.** Uric acid begins to pollute the body.
    - **b.** Excess water is also built up within, due to the lack of efficient urinary output.
- **B.** How has body pollution been eliminated?
  - **1.** Through the use of the artificial kidney machine, the blood is purified.
  - **2.** Hemodialysis or simply dialysis is the term given to this process of cleaning the blood.

(Central Idea)

**II.** Living without kidney function is not only possible, it is safe, painless, and relatively simple, if one has access to an artificial kidney machine.

---

[2]Adapted from an outline prepared for an informative speech in a beginning course in public speaking at Herbert H. Lehman College. City University of New York. The author of the outline was Miss Randy Cohn. Used by permission.

Body

**I.** What is the basic structure of the artificial kidney?

- **A.** I will limit my discussion to the Drake-Willock Kiil combination dialyzer, since it is the one used most frequently in the United States.
- **B.** The artificial kidney consists of two main parts.
  - **1.** The upper part is made up of three boards and a frame.
  - **2.** The electrical portion composed of the heater, delivery system, and trouble detecting devices make up the bottom half of the unit.
  - **3.** (Visual Aid Number 1—Picture showing the main parts of the artificial kidney machine.)

  (Transition: After seeing the artificial kidney, one cannot help but wonder how it operates.)

**II.** How does the dialyzer work?

- **A.** The dialyzer works on the principle of osmosis.
  - **1.** Osmosis is the tendency of a fluid to pass through a semipermeable membrane in order to equalize concentrations on both sides of the membrane.
- **B.** The upper portion of the kidney is set up in such a way that it can be compared to a double-decker sandwich.
  - **1.** The boards would be the bread.
  - **2.** The dialysate or cleaning liquid would be the butter.
  - **3.** The membranes would be the lettuce.
  - **4.** The blood ports, through which the blood flows, are in the position of the meat.
- **C.** By realizing this positioning, it is easy to see that the membranes serve as the semipermeable membrane through which the blood passes its unwanted wastes and excess water into the dialysate.

  (Transition: In order for the machine to be effective, the person must come in contact with it.)

**III.** The blood of the person being dialyzed can be sent to the machine in one of two ways.

- **A.** The shunt is a piece of flexible silastic tubing which is embedded into an artery and a vein of the arm or leg.
  - **1.** It has a portion which is visible.
  - **2.** The visible piece of tubing is separated at a connecting piece; much like two drinking straws attached by a smaller piece of straw.
- **B.** The other method is by the use of a fistula.
  - **1.** A fistula is an internal operation.
  - **2.** It requires the use of needles to be inserted into enlarged veins of the arm.

  (Transition: In conclusion, I would like to remind you that people who have lost complete kidney function may lead a normal life.)

Conclusion

**I.** Dialysis can be carried on at night.
  **A.** Depending on the machine used, dialysis takes either 6 or 10 hours.
  **B.** The person may sleep without fear, due to a complex alarm system sensitized to the slightest problem.
  **C.** There is no pain involved.

**II.** We should value our health and protect it.
  **A.** There are signs we can all look for in order to determine possible kidney trouble.
    **1.** Puffy eyes and swelling ankles are significant.
    **2.** Intense thirst and low back pain are also present.
  **B.** To protect your kidneys you can do a couple of very easy things.
    **1.** Make sure you drink a few glasses of water a day.
    **2.** Strep throat is the number one cause of kidney infection; therefore, take care of all sore throats.

## Bibliography


**Observation:**

Since March 1969, I have been involved with the hemodialysis program at Grasslands County Hospital, Valhalla, New York. The majority of my knowledge comes from this experience.

**Interview:**

I have had the opportunity to speak with Dr. S. Weseley and Mr. Roger Smith, both prominent members of the staff at Grasslands, along with other people and patients involved in the program.

**Books:**

Longmore, Donald, *Spare-Part Surgery* (Garden City, N.Y.: Doubleday and Company, Inc., 1968), pp. 53–59.

**Pamphlets:**

*A Chance to Live,* U.S. Department of Health, Education, and Welfare (Washington, D.C., 1968).
*Instruction Booklet #2,* Drake-Willock Mobile Dialysis Machine operation and maintenance.
*The Modified Kiil Dialyzer,* Cobe Laboratories, Inc.

**Newspaper:**

"Mobile Unit Aids Kidney Patients," *The New York Times* (February 17, 1974), p. 50.

This outline illustrates suitable procedures for outlining a persuasive speech. It was prepared for an eight-minute presentation.

## THE BIG FRAUD[3]

### Introduction

(Central Idea)

**I.** Beware of Social Security: a poor investment.
- **A.** Students preparing to enter the work force will be most affected and have the least to gain from Social Security Insurance.
  - **1.** They will contribute for 46 years at the highest rates in history.
  - **2.** Their contributions will far exceed what they could ever hope to achieve in benefits.
- **B.** They must be alerted to the inequities of this system.
  (Transition: Before telling you more about this fraud, I'd like to mention a few of the facts.)

**II.** Social Security Insurance was born at the height of the depression when 22 million were unemployed.
- **A.** It was a crash program to free citizens from economic fear, care, and want.
  - **1.** It provided money with dignity to those in need.
  - **2.** The requests for welfare were reduced.
- **B.** The present system is not fulfilling the promise made back in 1935 with regard to financial security.

### Body

**III.** In the beginning Social Security Insurance was a good deal.
- **A.** Until 1939, whatever money the worker contributed was returned to either the retired worker or his estate.
  - **1.** This "money-back guarantee" was cancelled in 1939.
- **B.** Ida Fuller was the first person to receive benefits and is still receiving them—$12,000 later.
  - **1.** She paid in less than $70 to the plan.
  - **2.** She participated in the plan for only two years.
  (Transition: For *Ida* it was a good deal; for *you*, it's *not!*)

**IV.** Under present law Social Security Insurance is not a good deal.
- **A.** A person now 18 will contribute approximately $19,270 by the time he reaches 65 and will not receive interest on his money.

---

[3]This outline was submitted by Mary M. Collins. Used by permission.

1. If deposited in a bank, the contributions could earn presently 5½% interest.
2. Money doubles every 14 years in a bank.

**B.** The maximum benefits one could receive assuming one lived till 79 years of age would be $80,888.

1. Internal Revenue actuarial tables show life expectancy at 71.9 years.

**C.** There are many inequities in this system.

1. Participation is compulsory.
2. This "insurance" does not have the restrictions and regulations imposed on private insurance plans.
3. The plan used is "pay as you go"—no reserves.
4. Funds can be used for any purpose the government decides upon.
5. This "gift" can be revoked, increased, or decreased by Congress.
6. There are gimmicks attached which prohibit receiving checks under certain circumstances.

**V.** The solution is to get the government out of the insurance business.

**A.** Encourage growth of private investment plans rather than hamper them.

**B.** Manage your own money in your own way rather than entrusting it to Uncle Sam.

Conclusion

**VI.** After three decades the promise of financial security is still unfulfilled.

**A.** Constant clamoring for more indicates that Social Security is not enough.

**B.** Let's do all we can to abolish Social Security Insurance.

**C.** The fraud is being perpetrated on *you*. Beware!

Statement of Sources

1. Anonymous, *Social Security—Medicare Simplified* (Washington, D.C.: *U.S. New and World Report*, 1969).
   [This book was easy to understand and provided basic material. Pages 219–223 were especially useful.]
2. Douglas, Paul Howard, *Social Security in the United States* (New York: Arno Press, 1971).
   [This volume contained historical material which I found useful, in part.]
3. Ellis, Abraham, *The Social Security Fraud* (New Rochelle, New York: Arlington House, 1971).
   [Ellis suggested leading arguments and some of the wording of main points. My title was also suggested by this source.]
4. McKinley, Charles, and Robert W. Frase, *Launching Social Security: A Capture-and-Record Account, 1935–1937* (Madison, Wiscon-

sin: University of Wisconsin Press, 1970).
[I found most of this book much too technical, but it was an aid on the historical aspects of my topic.]

5. Miller, Roger LeRoy, "Social Security: The Cruelest Tax," *Harper's Magazine*, CCXLVIII, No. 1489 (June, 1974), pp. 22–27.
[The section of this article headed "A Time for Change" provided material for my conclusion.]
6. Scheibla, Shirley, "Memo to Young Workers," *Barron's National Business and Financial Weekly*, LI, No. 27 (July 5, 1971), 5ff.
[Figures under IVA and B came from this source.]
7. *Social Security Benefits for Students, 18–22,* United States Department of Health, Education and Welfare, Social Security Administration Pamphlet No. SS 1-48 (Washington, D.C.: U.S. Government Printing Office, October, 1969).
[Some of this material aided me in adapting to my specific audience.]
8. *Social Security Benefits—How You Earn—How to Estimate,* United States Department of Health, Education and Welfare, Social Security Administration Pamphlet No. SS 1-47 (Washington, D.C.: U.S. Government Printing Office, January, 1970).
[This pamphlet was an easy to understand, valuable, authoritative source.]

The speaker's notes for the speech outlined above might have looked like those below.

### SPEAKER'S NOTES: THE BIG FRAUD

**Intro:** Beware of Social Security = poor investment
Students entering work force—you—most affected
  Contribute 46 yrs. at highest rates
  Contributions exceed benefits
Program born at height of Depression, crash program

**Body:** In beginning, good deal!
  Money-back guarantee—cancelled
  Ida Fuller, example—how worked well
At present, *not* good
  18 yr. old, by 65 = $19,270 *vs.* money in bank
    (doubles every 14 years)—no interest on yours
  S.S. maximum at 79 = $80,888
Six inequities of system:
  1) Compulsory
  2) No regs. (as there are for private ins. co's)
  3) Pay as you go—no reserves
  4) Funds can be used for any purpose
  5) Congress can revoke—increase or decrease
  6) Gimmicks
Solution: *Get Gov't out of business!*

**Concl:** Promise—still unfulfilled. Don't let it happen *to you*. Beware!

Notice that these notes could be placed easily on two or three 3″ x 5″ cards which could be used conveniently and therefore unobtrusively while talking to an audience.

## SUMMARY

In this chapter we have discussed the normal parts of speeches presented in public, described and evaluated standard patterns of organization, and considered conventional ways of outlining as a phase of planning for speaking. You can adapt all human beings' needs to order their perceptions only if you shape what you say to suit people's habits of perceiving and thinking. In considering eleven patterns of organization and habitual practices in outlining we have been considering the everyday habits of human beings as consumers of public communication. They expect to find familiar forms and structures in what they hear. They expect to discover relationships among ideas easily. By adopting familiar structural patterns and by testing the interrelationships of your thoughts through careful outlining you meet those expectations and improve the prospects that you will be understood as you intend.

Indirectly we have also been considering how you can become more confident when you speak. A clear and familiar structure that is easily followed from a carefully made outline is easy to fix firmly in your mind. You then have less reason to worry about forgetting your talk. Anything you do to help listeners see the relations among your ideas will help you to see and remember them too. We all remember best the orderly and logical; we forget most easily that which lacks system, order, and unity.

## EXERCISES

*Written*

**1.** a. Choose a subject area, such as air pollution, current methods in secondary education, or the Democratic party in America today.
b. Carefully write out the subject sentences for the subject chosen. One sentence should be devised for a speech of *information*, the other for a speech of *persuasion*.
c. Write out the main heads for each of the subject sentences you have composed.

**2.** Write an essay in which you evaluate the following introduction according to the requirements for a good introduction found on pages 152–153.

**Drunken Drivers**

From the wreckage of the crash, two persons extricate themselves. The first seems to be an elderly, well-dressed businessman, who, after surveying the wreckage, pulls out a young man and helps him to his feet. The young man obviously needs help; his gait is unsteady, his eyes are bloodshot and bleary, and his speech is almost unintelligible. The onlookers are convinced by these signs that he is drunk, which is confirmed by the strong smell of alcohol which is obvious a few feet away.

As the police cars pull up, the crowd is assured that the young man will get what is coming to him. He can get out that his name is William Schultz, and he is a taxi driver, but he is unable to give the police his address, does not know where he is by a few miles, yet insists that he had nothing to drink. The officers dutifully administer a test commonly known as the "Balloon Test" to him. After the balloon is blown up, the contents are passed through a tube containing a purple liquid on what looks to be a wad of cotton. The purple color disappears if the air passing through it is filled with alcohol, the policeman explains, and the faster the color disappears, the drunker you are. At the end of the test, however, the purple color is still there, causing some bewilderment among the spectators and the policemen. Some more tests will be taken down at the station.

It is now the older man's turn for examination. As expected, he gives a good account of himself. He is Milton P. Jones, an executive, on his way home from a business conference. He admits to having had a few drinks two hours earlier with his lunch, but the policemen are unable to smell alcohol on his breath. He is also asked to take the balloon test, and, within a fraction of a minute, all color disappears in the glass tube. Befuddled, the policemen take them both down to the station for further examination.

From the evidence placed before you, every person in this room must have some thoughts as to who the guilty party is. Young Mr. Schultz appears to have all the physical attributes of a drunk, while Mr. Jones is surely the victim of this terrible crime. We'll come back to these men and their particular case in a few minutes.[4]

**3.** Assume that the following sets of main heads have been taken from the "bodies" of outlines for speeches. Evaluate each set for (a) the wording of the main points, and (b) the overall pattern of organization. Give detailed reasons for your judgments.

a. I. Every speech should have an introduction, body, and conclusion.
   II. Should the introduction get attention and make the speaker's purpose clear?
   III. A conclusion should summarize and put the entire speech into focus.

---

[4]This introduction was composed by Renee Ehrlich for an introductory course in public speaking. Used by permission.

b. I. The social, political, and economic instability of underdeveloped countries is a potential breeding ground for Communism.
   II. We must increase our financial aid and technical assistance to these countries to head off the threat.

c. I. Economical and efficient means of smoke prevention have been devised.
   II. Heavy smoke darkens the sunlight.
   III. Smoke is harmful to public health.
   IV. Smoking is a bad habit.
   V. The annoyance, filth, and unhealthful effects of smoke have caused an agitation for smoke prevention in large cities.
   VI. Gas and electricity may replace coal for many domestic uses.
   VII. Imports of residual oil cause much unemployment in coal fields.
   VIII. Since smoke is injurious and preventable, immediate steps should be taken toward its elimination.
   IX. Efficient smokeless furnaces have proved a success.
   X. Smoke hinders good ventilation.
   XI. Smoke prevention in large cities should be compulsory.
   XII. Electric locomotives may be used in place of steam.
   XIII. Many fires are caused by faulty furnaces.
   XIV. Coal smoke damages the lungs.
   XV. One important step is to sign the Anti-Smoke League petition.

**4.** Arrange the eleven statements below as an outline for a main point in a speech. There is no title, introduction, or conclusion. Select the sentence containing the main point and give it proper place and status in your outline.

Political bribery may be increased considerably due to heart transplants.
Some feel the poor man deserves it.
The families of the poor cannot afford prolonged private care without surgery.
*Saturday Review* of February 3rd reports an incident in which a prominent New York politician used his influence to have a half-hour conference with Dr. Christiaan Barnard when he was in Washington, D.C., in order to discuss the possibilities of his securing a heart transplant.
Heart transplants are ethically questionable.
Some feel the rich man who can afford surgery should receive it.
The poor are the only means of support for their families.
The January 6th *Science News* states, "A million dollars could buy a patient almost anything . . . including a new heart."
There are inequalities shown in deciding whose lives are to be saved through the miracle of heart transplants.

How many other unreported incidents of this sort will be revealed in the near future?
Some feel it should be the man or woman with special talent.

5. Make a list of suggestions for improving the outline entitled "The Big Fraud" (see pages 175–177).
6. In a sentence or two evaluate each of the following speech titles:
   a. "What You Must Do"
   b. "Acres of Diamonds"
   c. "Billy the Kid–Juvenile Delinquent?"
   d. "A Case for Euthanasia in the United States Today with Special Emphasis upon the Role of the General Practitioner in the Rural Areas"
   e. "From Trees to Paper"
   f. "Drug Addicts: The Living Dead"

*Oral*

1. a. In class discussion choose several subject sentences for impromptu speeches. Such sentences as: "The automobile is primarily a vehicle for human transportation"; "Donation of blood to the Red Cross is worthwhile"; "Grades in college should be abolished" will serve.
   b. Assign each of the subject sentences chosen to three different members of the class, and also assign to each of them *one* of the usable patterns of organization discussed in this chapter, e.g., chronological, spatial, problem-solution, causal.
   c. Allow time for each of the three students to prepare two-to three-minute impromptu speeches using the pattern assigned.
   d. After hearing the speeches, discuss the suitability of each pattern to the subject sentence assigned. Also evaluate the speaker's ability to produce a recognizable pattern of organization on short notice.
2. Outline a speech by one of your classmates as you listen to him deliver it. Arrange for a conference during which you compare the outline you composed with the outline he used. Look for similarities and differences between the outlines and discuss why these occurred as they did.
3. Here, in proper order, are the items of a "blank outline." Choose a suitable subject, organize the items of the outline with proper symbols and indentations, and fill the blanks with ideas appropriate to the subject you have chosen. Be prepared to give this short speech extemporaneously at your next class meeting.
   I wonder whether you have thought enough about __(subject)__.
   I would define __(subject)__ like this: ______.
   You can see what I mean by thinking of these examples:
   My first example is: ______.
   Another example is: ______.
   What causes [or results from] ______ is this: ______.

An example of how this happens is ______.

Another example is _____.

We usually think of ______ as something remote from our everyday lives, but there are cases where it makes a lot of difference to people like you and me.

One everyday influence it has [had] is [was] ______.

Another influence is [was] ______.

My conclusion is that the next time we hear people talk about ______ or think of it ourselves, we ought to remember it is no vague thing but something that can touch our lives as closely as in (refer to examples used) .

# Choosing Language

# 9

*Style of speaking influences listeners' understanding.*

The expression of a speaker's inner self probably emerges more clearly in style than in any other aspect of his communicative acts. Indeed, *style,* as we define it, *is the personal manner of utterance or expression giving ideas impact and movement.* Speech consists of the particular ways we convert ideas into word symbols. In part, at least, each idea is represented by the words we use to express it. When all is said and done, the way we choose words, their capacities to stir meaning in our listeners' minds, and the influences of their combination are our ideas as our listeners understand them.

*How* we say something matters a good deal, then. There is a great difference between saying: "A poor, old man stood at the entrance to the church, a container in his hand, waiting for a rich person to come by" and saying, "An ancient beggar leaned against the doors of the cathedral, clutching a broken dish, biding his time until some wealthy nobleman appeared." Some people would see most of the words in these two sentences as synonyms—as words having substantially the same meanings. For example, some people would think such words as "old" and "ancient," "church" and "cathedral," "rich" and "wealthy" are

*Words are chosen to create nuances, which influence meaning.*

equivalent in meanings. But it is very easy to see that while the sentences themselves are similar in idea, they do not communicate exactly the same meanings. The words and their combinations create nuances (shades of meaning) that change the message you receive. And such changes are very important to speakers because in public speech the primary goal is to arouse exact or nearly exact meanings in listeners. So it is that if we are to be practical we must give attention to style, to our choice of words, and to the ways we combine them.

How useful your spoken language is depends, in the first place, on how clearly you have thought. It is only when your idea is clear and precise *to you* that you can know what words you need. Then you can choose from all the words you know just those which will say accurately and appealingly what you were thinking. George Henry Lewes was right when he wrote:

> . . . a genuine style is the living body of thought, not a costume that can be put on and off; it is the expression of the writer's mind; it is not less the incarnation of his thoughts in verbal symbols than a picture is the painter's incarnation of his thoughts in symbols of form and colour. A man may, if it please him, dress his thoughts in the tawdry splendour of a masquerade. But this is no more Literature than the masquerade is Life.[1]

Lewes was thinking of writing, but what he said applies even more forcefully to public speech.

In speech, as in writing, you already have a personal style—a way of expressing your mind. Your style may be excellent, but we have yet to meet a speaker who could not handle language better. So, in this chapter we shall consider three things: *how* you can develop and improve your personal, oral style, the *goals* you ought to have in choosing language for specific speeches, and some *differences* between oral and written style, as people in our culture use the two ways of communicating verbally.

## IMPROVING YOUR PERSONAL STYLE

You will notice that members of your speech class and your other friends have individual verbal habits. One person you know may use more imagery than most others. Another may talk tersely; he may not amplify ideas and repeat them enough to allow you to understand without special effort. Other people

---

[1]George Henry Lewes, "The Principle of Beauty," in *Representative Essays on the Theory of Style*, ed. William T. Brewster (New York: Macmillan, 1921), p. 217.

you know may seem to talk abstractly. Some pepper their talk with meaningless "like's" and "y'know's" or use so much slang that you are not always clear about what they are trying to say. Certainly, too, you know some people you think "too glib" and others who speak just as you would like to speak. Our point is that every speaker has habits that favor particular kinds of language and specific sets of stylistic devices. The goal of a speech class is not to make all these people sound alike. It is to encourage all to enrich and improve their own styles by taking fuller advantage of the resources language offers to everyone.

*Every speaker has a unique style that can be improved.*

Clear and interesting speakers tend either to have fallen into the habit of using the full resources of language or to have learned to think ahead as they talk. They choose words carefully before uttering them. Thinking ahead and choosing words carefully are possibilities for you, even if you are not colorful or precise by habit.

Extemporaneous speaking offers excellent opportunities for perfecting your personal, oral style. In rehearsal for this kind of speech you can experiment with alternative wordings as you practice from your outline or speaker's notes. You need not commit yourself to any particular set of words. Your object ought to be to build a variety of alternative, effective phrasings, any of which "will do." In this way you show yourself what your options are and at the same time build a reservoir of stylistic structures that will permanently enlarge your verbal resources. Over the long run, this is what you should gain linguistically from a speech course: an enlarged repertoire of ways of saying well the things you normally want to talk about.

Acquiring a wide vocabulary is important, of course. You have a vocabulary at some stage of development. Your background, prior education, and experience in writing and speaking have influenced this aspect of your personal style. The question is: Is your vocabulary sufficient for the needs you will face in the future? No doubt some of your habits of expression are good ones for any purpose. They need to be emphasized as you develop your verbal style. Build on your strengths! Almost certainly you have other habits that interfere with thoroughly effective communication. With what shall you replace these weaknesses? With language that has the qualities we shall discuss in the next section of this chapter. You cannot expect to improve your language permanently by preparing one or two speeches, but you can expect small, permanent improvements from speech to speech if you adopt a systematic program for refining your habitual ways of talking.

To improve the style you now use in speaking:

*Seven methods will help improve speaking style.*

1. *Become language conscious.* Think about the precise meanings of words and pay conscious attention to what *are* and *are not* conventional grammatical constructions. Get reminders from classmates and others of your grammatical uncertainties, of moments when you were not as vivid as you could have been, of malapropisms (ridiculous misuse of words) and clichés (trite expressions) you have fallen into the habit of using. Listen carefully to the best speakers you can hear, not to imitate them but to learn what they achieve through best choice of words.
2. *Increase your speaking vocabulary.* It is a fact that you know more words than you are in the habit of using. Try to extend the numbers of these words and phrasings that you use naturally in talk. Do not try to master unusual words and unique phrases; try to put to oral use the language you normally encounter. Keep a dictionary handy, too. Refer to it when you see and hear unfamiliar words. This will increase both your reading and speaking vocabulary. But in developing an improved speaking style your goal should be to get full, practical control over all the language of your ordinary experience, not to dazzle with unusual expressions.
3. *Write.* It is true, as we have said, that the language of good writing differs from the language of good speaking, but practice in writing is an excellent way of improving vocabulary and grammar. By expressing yourself on paper you can choose words more carefully and consciously than in most speaking. And you can revise as much as you want. Writing begets consciousness of language, and what you learn through writing will stay with you as a resource for speaking.

4. *Rehearse.* Rehearsal is a preventative against stage fright. It is also an experience in which you can experiment with language in ways that will give you both confidence and a larger linguistic repertoire. You ought to expect to rehearse any important speech (certainly orally and perhaps in writing). The best speakers who have spoken from manuscripts put their speeches through several drafts. As we pointed out earlier, Franklin D. Roosevelt, a masterful public speaker, put some of his speeches through many drafts before he was satisfied. Much of this revisionary effort went into perfecting the language of the speeches. Benjamin Disraeli composed, rehearsed alone and before friendly critics, and rewrote his speeches—in order to speak extemporaneously! In rehearsal you ought to give specific attention to smoothing out phrasings, correcting unclear constructions, rearranging statements. Writing helps here, for you can *see* as well as hear your language, but your goal should never be to *fix phrasings permanently* if you are to speak extemporaneously. Then, it is always to build your fund of language and refine your *habits*.
5. *Study published and live speeches.* Note what seems to make for success and failure in style. Take cues from successful models. Avoid the faults of bad ones. Do not study other speakers to copy them; study them to borrow their best attributes, incorporating those qualities in the distinctive, personal style you are developing for yourself.
6. *Speak in public.* You can refine your oral habits in conversation. You should try to do this because in conversation you have many opportunities to correct yourself and to try new and better phrasings. It is in public speech, however, that you test your mettle. Then you can see whether your refinements of verbal habits are firm enough to stay with you under pressure, in "one-shot" communications. Speak as often as possible. The more you speak, especially extemporaneously and impromptu, the more experience you will gain in finding ways to finish phrases and statements effectively—no matter how you started them.
7. *Think.* Thinking and phrasing are inseparable processes when one is working with words. You can never say a thing well until you understand it well, though it may be the case that you understand things you cannot say well. In any case, it takes concentration to develop an idea clearly enough in one's own head so the "right" words for its expression can be found. It takes concentration, too, to locate the *best* words for an idea you have formulated. An efficient, versatile, personal style does not just happen to very many of us; it grows slowly

from discriminating thought about ideas and verbal symbols—and especially about "right" ideas and symbols for *particular* listeners in particular times and places. What, then, should be your goals or targets as you concentrate on the words you choose for public speech?

## GOALS IN CHOOSING LANGUAGE

A useful way of thinking about what language to use in a particular speaking situation is to think of the *qualities listeners want* in the talk they hear. Some of those qualities are so universally sought that we can say they are needed in virtually every situation.

*A speaker's word choice should be aimed at accuracy, clarity, and liveliness.*

Theorists writing on style point to attributes such as *propriety, force, economy,* and *striking quality.* We will mention these attributes in the pages that follow, but the three most important attributes, we think, are *accuracy, clarity,* and *liveliness.* Your listeners will always be asking themselves whether what you say *accurately* expresses what you mean. They will also ask whether what you are saying is *clear*—fits their experience and knowledge. And they will want what you say to be *lively,* capable of sustaining their interest. These are such basic demands they ought to guide you whenever you choose one word, phrase, or expression over another.

### Being Accurate

*Accuracy depends on situational exactness of words and grammar.*

Whatever you say is bound to seem accurate, fuzzy, or mistaken as your listener hears you. Accuracy depends on whether the words you choose will represent as exactly as possible what you want your listeners to understand. How well you make such choices depends on how well you know the conventional meanings of words and on the range of your vocabulary. If you say "infer" when you mean "imply," listeners will not get your meaning precisely. If you say "I contacted the safety division" when you could have said "I telephoned the safety division," you will have been less specific and therefore less accurate than you could have been. You will be most accurate if you concern yourself with specificity and concreteness. The more abstract words and phrases are, the more ambiguous and subject to misinterpretation they are. So, stick to words for which both you and your listeners have precise, concrete, conventional meanings. Then listeners will give you credit for speaking accurately.

Grammatical accuracy—observing the grammatical conventions your listeners respect—ought also to be one of your goals as you fashion words into meaningful clusters. Modern experiments have repeatedly confirmed that what listeners take as "slips" in grammar cause them to think less well of the speakers who "slip." If you talk to educated listeners, you ought to remember Cicero's observation:

> . . . nobody ever admired an orator for correct grammar, they only laugh at him if his grammar is bad, and not only think him no orator but not even a human being; no one ever sang the praises of a speaker whose style succeeded in making his meaning intelligible to his audience, but only despised one deficient in capacity to do so.[2]

There are many private and some public speaking situations in which unconventional grammar does *not* interfere with listeners' favorable judgments of speakers, but you ought to be very, very sure you have strong reasons for doing so before you abandon grammatical conventions in public situations. You ought to remember, too, that in the vast majority of rhetorical situations conventional grammar is *always* acceptable—even to people who are ungrammatical themselves. The heart of the matter is that "ain't," "I be," "with she and I," and expressions of this kind are taken as "accurate" in *some* places; but "is not," "are not," "I am," and "with her and me" are almost never rejected as "inaccurate."

Another kind of accuracy that is expected by listeners is accuracy to the requirements of the situation. There are rhetorical situations in which only one form of expression is "accurate," even though there are several, equally grammatical ways of expressing a single idea. For example, in a parliamentary situation "I agree with George's idea" is an inaccurate way of expressing a *parliamentary* meaning, even though the statement may be an accurate, grammatical statement of your attitude. The *parliamentary* meaning must refer to a parliamentary motion, so the accurate expression would be: "I support the motion offered by George Green." It is equally possible for an abstract or technical expression to be accurate in one situation but not in others. The most convivial gathering of space scientists would allow—even demand—levels of technicality that would be bafflingly imprecise if used in a high school science class. And the same is sometimes true of the "in language" of motorcycle buffs, philosophers, ethnic groups, and so on.

[2]*De Oratore*, trans. by H. A. Rackham (Cambridge, Mass.: Harvard University Press, 1948), pp. 41–42, bk. III, ch. 14.

In speech, then, what is accurate enough to be efficient is always partly determined by who speaks, to whom, on what idea, and under what circumstances. Your language will be accurate only if you choose it to meet all the tests imposed by these elements of your rhetorical situation. But it is easy to exaggerate the differences among the demands of speaking situations. Though they *allow* different standards of verbal accuracy, very few situations exert demands that make "inaccurate" the kind of verbal expression that would satisfy moderately educated, alert listeners *anywhere*.

**Being Clear**

*Clarity goes beyond accuracy and takes into account the listeners' needs.*

What listeners demand as clarity is more than denotative accuracy of terms and grammatical conventionality. They want language from which they can get pertinent meaning in the easiest, most concrete ways. This is what Aristotle had in mind, it appears, when he wrote: "Clearness is secured through the use of name-words [nouns and adjectives] and verbs, that are current terms. . . ."[3] His judgment is still sound. Listeners get the most meaning from the names you give to things and beings, from the adjectives with which you modify names, and from the actions your verbs say occurred. But your nouns, adjectives, and verbs need to be in current use by your listeners. In short, the more directly you say what you mean, the more likely you are to be clear, provided your listeners are used to the terms you employ.

What your listeners are *ready to understand* is another factor to consider when you decide how to express ideas. How far you can go in giving detailed explanations depends on how much your listeners already know. For listeners who know very little about jazz, you would not be clear if you tried to analyze the different "schools" of jazz. These listeners must first understand the basic musical forms that make jazz jazz. In such a case you would be clear only if you explained what jazz *is* and left exposition of the "schools" for another talk.

To put the above points another way, you can be accurate about an idea and still be unclear to a particular group of listeners. This is especially important to remember when you deal with technical materials. Unless you have sophisticated listeners, clarity will require you to give numerous, simply explained definitions, analogies, contrasts, and examples.

---

[3]From *The Rhetoric of Aristotle*, translated and edited by Lane Cooper, p. 185, bk. III, chap. 2. Copyright 1932, renewed 1960 by Lane Cooper. Reprinted by permission of Prentice-Hall, Inc., Englewood Cliffs, New Jersey.

Still another fact to weigh in choosing language is that you may communicate clearly but convey *mis*information. We pointed out earlier that in explaining the transmission of sound it is accurate and clarifying, up to a point, to ask listeners to think of sound waves as ripples spreading out when a stone is dropped into water. This comparison and the language you have to use when talking about water can help an uninformed listener. But if that listener is allowed to think of sound waves as behaving entirely like ripples, he will be misinformed. The "water language" must be abandoned once the notion of circular spreading has been established in the listener's mind. After that, "water language" conveys *mis*information, and new language must be found in order to establish that sound waves travel through walls as water waves cannot.

As our examples suggest, you can find clear language only if you work with a full understanding of your particular speaking situation. *Your* preferences for language should influence you least in choosing language. There is the rub! Your own sense of clarity, for yourself, will tempt you to forget your listeners' clarity. This is why being clear becomes a matter of *self*-discipline. Good speech is always adaptive, not self-serving; and so it must be with oral language.

## Maintaining Lively Interest

*Liveliness depends on economy, vividness, and simplicity.*

Liveliness in speech comes from creating vivid images in economical ways. The text of Randy Cohn's "The Gift of Life" (Appendix, pp. 236–240) contains many excellent examples of language having both of these qualities. Notice the exactness of language, yet the economy, of Randy's story of the amputation and transplantation described in paragraph 7. The narrative could scarcely be told in fewer words, yet the words used let listeners know the church was a "shelter" for the victim of cancer, that both drugs and surgery were used in the amputation, that one brother "rushed to a nearby cemetery" to secure a Moor's leg for transplantation, and that the victim awoke to find he had one white and one black leg, both healthy. Such, said Ms. Cohn, is the "black-leg legend."

You can discover Randy's achievement in language in this narrative if you examine it in detail and then experiment with it. Can you remove any words from the narrative without injuring its clarity? Do you need any more, or any different, words to "see" the series of events that took place, according to the legend?

What would happen to the effect of the story if you inserted additional modifiers or additional details to such a

statement as: "As he slept, Cosmas and Damian came to him in a dream bearing drugs and surgical equipment"? If you try to answer the above questions for yourself, we think you will conclude that there are few changes that can *safely* be made in this telling of an incidental story.

Ms. Cohn did not always achieve such economical pictorialization in her speech, but this passage illustrates what your goal should be in choosing language for liveliness. You need the fewest words that will evoke the image you want in the mind of a listener. Ms. Cohn achieved this goal in narrative, where it is often moderately easy to attain. But she achieved it in another way in paragraph 11. Here she was trying to impel action by showing how easy it is to register as a donor.

Notice that although the subject is not a "story," Randy Cohn has injected *actions* into what she needed to say. You do not have to *"go"* to a bank or organization. You can *"change* your mind" and *"rip up* your card." But you would *"destroy"* your "gift." She will *"present"* you with a card and pamphlet. You are to *"think* about the program" and *"sign"* the card, *"remembering"* the *"living."* Everything said here could have been passive—involving no actions except, perhaps, the handing out of cards. But in every sentence save the first, Ms. Cohn has created movement—of people. Here is another secret of lively speaking: create images of activity wherever a choice of language allows.

We suggest that Ms. Cohn's quotation in paragraph 12 does *not* have the qualities of either economy or imagery.

Would she have been wiser to have said the thoughts of this paragraph in her own words rather than in the words of Francis Moore?

Liveliness in language also arises from grammatical simplicity. Modern research in linguistics and stylistics has shown that the easiest and most forthright construction in English is the simple order: subject-verb-object. This is the form you experienced when you first read, "I see the ball." Insert ideas between "I" and "see," and you will complicate understanding and lose force. "I, to the best of my judgment, see the ball" is harder to take in than "To the best of my judgment, I see the ball." True, more complicated constructions than "I see Jane" may be necessary if you are to be accurate (e.g., "The measurement, taken at seventy degrees Fahrenheit, is sixty millimeters"), but to be interesting and lively you ought to put words together in the simplest way accuracy allows. When you must use complicated constructions—as you will have to do—seek other ways of compensating interestingly. Do, perhaps, as Randy Cohn did in paragraph 11: use active, simple words that create images in listeners' imaginations.

Some words are more forceful than others. The number of "interior" meanings a word contains can diminish force and interestingness. Rudolf Flesch explains:

> Language gadgets . . . are of two kinds: Words by themselves, like *against*, and parts of words (affixes), like *dis-*. The more harmful of the two for plain talk are the affixes, since the reader or hearer cannot understand what the gadget does to the sentence before he has disentangled it from the word it is attached to. Each affix burdens his mind with two jobs: first, he has to split up the word into its parts and, second, he has to rebuild the sentence from these parts. To do this does not even take a split second, of course, but it adds up.[4]

You need not avoid all affixed words, but when you have a choice you ought to prefer the simplest words that will be accurate. The student who said, "Your response is a variant of the teleological argument for the existence of God," would have been clearer and more interesting had he said, "Your answer is like the argument that since the world seems orderly, a God must have organized it."

Simplicity of language is associated in the best speaking with accuracy and liveliness growing out of economy and

---

[4]Rudolf Flesch, *The Art of Plain Talk* (New York: Harper and Brothers, 1946), p. 42.

imagery. As our examples from Randy Cohn's speech show, college students *can* achieve precision, clarity, economy, and liveliness, but examine the language chosen by an unusually brilliant speaker of considerable fame:

> Remember, I said that jazz was a player's art rather than a composer's. Well, this is the key to the whole problem. It is the player who, by improvising, makes jazz. He uses the popular song as a kind of dummy to hang his notes on. He dresses it up in his own way, and it comes out an original. So the pop tune, in acquiring a new dress, changes its personality completely, like many people who behave one way in blue jeans and a wholly different way in dinner clothes. Some of you may object to this dressing-up. You say, "Let me hear the melody, not all this embroidery." But until you accept this principle of improvisation, you will never accept or understand jazz itself.[5]

Notice that the player "*makes*" jazz, he "*uses* the popular song" to "*hang* his notes on." He "*dresses* it up," and it "*comes out*" an original. The tune "*changes*" like people who "*behave* one way in blue jeans and a wholly different way in dinner clothes." People say, "Let me hear the melody," but if they insist, they "will never *accept* or *understand*." No verb is in the passive voice in this passage. *All of the verbs are in the active voice!* Most images are of *people doing* something. Again, we have the kind of language listeners respond to eagerly—active language about people, and even things, *acting*, and there is not a word, concept, or verbal construction in this entire passage that *you* could not use naturally in any talk!

You can take your audience with you as you relive the suspenseful moment when your boat capsized or your car crashed. Let the audience feel the tape breaking across your chest at the finish line of a race, or the pull of your muscles as you lift a rock or kick a football. If you describe a process, let your listeners *see* your swimmer learning to swim or the cars moving along the assembly line. Let your appeals be especially to *sight, touch, taste, hearing,* and *smell,* to *thermal* and *kinesthetic sensitivity*. Like Bernstein, express experience in the present tense when you can, producing passages like, "I smell the pines. The morning air is clear, and I hear the crunch of snow beneath me as I walk up the path. My ears tingle with the cold." In this sequence four kinds of sensory experiences *(imagery)*

---

[5]From "The World of Jazz," a televised lecture first published as part of Leonard Bernstein's *The Joy of Music* (New York: Simon and Schuster, 1959), pp. 94–119. A full text of the lecture also appears in Carroll C. Arnold, *Criticism of Oral Rhetoric* (Columbus: Charles E. Merrill Publishing Co., 1974), pp. 320–334. This excerpt appears on pp. 330–331 of the latter source. Copyright © 1954, 1955, 1956, 1957, 1958, 1959, by Leonard Bernstein. Reprinted by permission of Simon and Schuster.

combine to form a pattern of human activities that brings a moment of life into *present* being again. Experiment with animating what you say. Try out sensory images and concrete, realistic terms. What you say can run to its goal rather than limp to a conclusion.

The qualities that contribute liveliness are important in all verbal communication, but they are especially necessary in your speech. We have said in several connections that listening is not a very efficient process for acquiring information and that listeners attend waveringly at best. This makes it uniquely important that as you refine your mastery of language for speech, you seek to accumulate the resources that will allow you to achieve accurate, clear, and lively talk. That it is *talk* and not writing that you are developing is in itself important. Consider the basic differences between oral and written style.

## ORAL AND WRITTEN STYLE

Speaking is not writing. Effective oral style is not entirely like written style. Choosing language for the ear is not entirely the same as choosing language for the eye.

*There are at least sixteen differences between oral and written style.*

The experimental research that has been done on differences between oral and written style argues that there are significant differences of degree, though not of kind.[6] There seem to be at least the following differences between common practices in oral and written language. In contrast to written prose style, effective *oral* style uses:

1. More personal pronouns.
2. More variety in kinds of sentences.
3. More variety in lengths of sentences.
4. More simple sentences.
5. More sentence fragments.
6. More rhetorical questions.

---

[6]See Gladys L. Borchers, "An Approach to the Problem of Oral Style," *The Quarterly Journal of Speech,*XXII (1936), pp. 114–117; Gordon Thomas, "Effect of Oral Style on Intelligibility of Speech," *Speech Monographs,* XXIII (1956), pp. 46–54; Joseph A. De Vito, "Comprehension Factors in Oral and Written Discourse of Skilled Communicators," *Speech Monographs,* XXXII (1965), pp. 124–128; James W. Gibson, Charles R. Gruner, Robert J. Kibler, and Francis J. Kelly, "A Quantitative Examination of Differences and Similarities in Written and Spoken Messages," *Speech Monographs,* XXXIII (1966), pp. 444–451. Gibson, Gruner, Kibler, and Kelly provide a valuable survey of contemporary studies of oral and written style. See also Joseph A. De Vito, "A Linguistic Analysis of Spoken and Written Language," *Central States Speech Journal,* XVIII (May, 1967), pp. 81–85.

7. More repetitions of words, phrases, and sentences.
8. A higher ratio of monosyllabic to polysyllabic words.
9. More contractions.
10. More interjections, retractions, and self-corrections.
11. More indigenous or colloquial language.
12. More connotatively used words.
13. More euphony, alliteration, and other acoustical devices.
14. More figurative language.
15. More direct quotations.
16. More words that are widely familiar.

No doubt there are other differences between good speaking and good writing, but this list is sufficient to show that if you apply only the standards of writing in preparing communication for the ear, you will use a number of irrelevant standards and fail to apply other important criteria of realistic *talk*.

Not only are ideas phrased somewhat differently in everyday speech and everyday writing, but thought units are uniquely structured in oral communication and the principles of creating "form" or "shape" are unique. For example, the principles of paragraphing have limited relevance to oral communication. Speakers break up their thought units by movements, by vocal inflections, and by formal transitions. They have no means of indenting or setting ideas apart from one another in *space*. They work entirely in *time, sound,* and *action*.

To apply writing's standards to sentence construction in speech is to expect oral communication to "hold together" by the same principles that give black marks on a page meaningful interrelationships. Speech does not work that way. Consider the fragment below from Franklin D. Roosevelt's address, "The Philosophy of Social Justice through Social Action." Notice how little the language resembles polished writing *for the eye*. Notice the broken "sentences." Notice how repetition of the words "crippled children" is used to reinforce where expert writing might achieve emphasis in more subtle ways. This is a carefully established sample of the *oral* style of one of the most successful political speakers in the history of the United States, and this is the way he *talked:*

> Take another form of poverty in the old days. Not so long ago, you and I know, there were families in attics—in every part of the Nation—in country districts and in city districts—hundreds and thousands of crippled children who could get no adequate care, crippled children who were lost to the community and who were a burden on the community. And so we have, in these past twenty or

thirty years, gradually provided means for restoring crippled children to useful citizenship; and it has all been a factor in going after and solving one of the causes of poverty and disease.[7]

Speech reduced to print sometimes looks strange until one remembers that meaningful pauses and appropriate vocal inflections can divide or connect seemingly strung-out thoughts. Relationships that cannot be shown by black marks on white pages can be "announced" by pauses, inflections, or even gestures. Read paragraphs 6 and 8 of Randy Cohn's "The Gift of Life." Try to listen to a fairly tall, slender brunette *saying* these thoughts and making these "broken" (to the eye) thoughts become whole, reasonable, fully understandable comments in a college classroom. Can you *hear* and *see* that these paragraphs are *not* at all "sloppy" *talk?* You must think this way about your own language as you refine a personal style in speech. Oral language is made up of *verbal* cues, *visual* cues, and *acoustic* cues to structure, stress, and meanings.

Speech usually contains fewer subtle qualifications and more quick, verbal pointers to the connections among ideas than one finds in expert writing. In speech there are apt to be fewer "howevers," "thuses," and "therefores" than in writing but many more words and phrases like "but," "and so," "the result is," and "the reason is." These last are the simpler, more blunt connectives of normal conversation. Because speech is *heard* it ought to contain few indefinite pronouns. "This" and "that" are ambiguous words. They require listeners to remember some noun used earlier, but it is often hard to recall that the "this" now heard actually means the "cathedral" mentioned five or ten seconds previously. And speech is personal if it is "real." Good oral style lets the speaker's attitudes toward his subject show through. Effective speakers do not talk of "human organisms," they talk about *people;* they do not "consume food," they *eat* it, and they either *relish* it or *dislike* it. It is normal for speech to express more of the creator's attitudes than writing usually does, and listeners come to expect that personalized quality.

*Speech is unique for its personal character.*

The fundamental uniqueness of the language of speech can be traced to the fact that, if effective, speech creates a living relationship between persons who are directly sharing one another's experiences. Speech is brought *by* someone *to* someone. It *must* be personal in intention—it needs to be verbally and

[7]The passage is excerpted from a text reconstructed by L. LeRoy Cowperthwaite and is based on an official stenographic report, Roosevelt's own manuscript, and a recording of the speech as given.

structurally personal. This is the kind of language experience you should experiment with as you plan, rehearse, and present formal and informal talk in your speech class. But remember, effective speech is not sheer *self*-expression. The human relationships of effective speech have to be created and sustained within the conventions of language and behavior which your listeners can and will share with you.

## SUMMARY

In the foregoing pages we have discussed how thought is symbolized in language that is spoken, and we have called attention to the fact that thought and linguistic expression of it cannot be separated in the experience of a speaker. We have suggested that you can improve the personal, oral style you now have if you become conscious of language, increase your vocabulary, rehearse orally, study speeches, practice writing for oral communication, and think. We have proposed as your goals in refining speech: accuracy, clarity, and liveliness. Finally, we have pointed to some of the ways oral and written language differ. In all of this we have tried to show that to speak effectively you must search always for those words and verbal structures that say what you mean in ways that acknowledge the human relationships on which your oral communication finally depends.

## EXERCISES

*Written*

1. Below are the first, second, and final versions of a statement from Lincoln's "Gettysburg Address." In a paragraph or two discuss what language problems Lincoln tried to eliminate as he worked on the speech and which of the successive changes seem to you to have yielded gains (or losses) in effective communication of the ideas of the statement. Be sure to say *why* each change was an improvement or a regression in stylistic effectiveness.

   *First draft:* We have come to dedicate a portion of it as a final resting place for those who died here, that the nation might live.

   *Second draft:* We have come to dedicate a portion of it as a final resting place for those who here gave their lives that that nation might live.

   *Third draft:* We have come to dedicate a portion of that field, as a final resting place for those who here gave their lives that that nation might live.

**2.** Rewrite the following sentences for oral delivery:

a. Therefore, it is evident that before you can provide an elucidation of the operational functions of the system for the propagation and dissemination of information, you would be required to make a thorough investigation of the public relations branch of the corporation.

b. If one had one's preference, one would be likely to hold a preference for one's own photographic equipment with which to photograph one's own favorite subjects.

c. Easily seen is the fact that the playing field is surrounded by a large metal fence over which the ball often passes when a home run is made.

d. Even although I had been selected to represent my college, had planned my itinerary to the meeting, which incidentally was held sixty miles from the college itself, had packed my clothing for the journey, which I did the night before, had reserved my seat in the airplane, which was a jet and was flight 107, and had persuaded my close friend, whose name was Mark Smith, to convey me to the airport, I was still in fear that the weather would prevent my going to the convention at all.

e. "Like I said," she said, "Jane's cheeks looked as red as roses, however, I discovered that the effect was all due to the application by her of cosmetics in large quantity."

**3.** Rewrite the following paragraph in such a way as to give it the qualities discussed in the section of this chapter devoted to liveliness.

My most embarrassing experience was when I was a boy. It was the result of my getting into a place I had no business being. I had crawled under our old back porch and had found some paint cans. I pried off the tops with a stick. Then I had put my hands into one can after another. First I put them into a can of green paint. Then I put them into a can of red paint, and then into a can of yellow. The color which resulted was an ugly brown. When I finally finished, my clean clothes had paint dribbled all over them. I was a mess. What was embarrassing though was that I couldn't get the paint off. After a licking by my mother, a bottle of turpentine was given to me, and I tried to get the paint off with that. I rubbed and rubbed with a cloth, but there was so much paint it just wouldn't come off. I was embarrassed for a whole week because it was summertime, and I looked as if I were wearing a pair of brown gloves. I guess I felt most foolish when my piano teacher came to give me my lesson, and I had to explain why my hands were as they were. I also felt very foolish on Sunday. I was sure that everybody was looking at my hands when I was up there singing in the choir.

*Oral*

**1.** Using a speech you delivered during a prior session of your class and drawing upon what you now know about style, rework the speech or a portion of it and deliver it again. Discuss the effects of your deliberate stylistic changes with your listeners.

**2.** Some subjects are harder to talk about in words than others. For example, it is more difficult to find words to describe an abstract painting than it is to find words to describe an automobile. As an exercise in expanding your awareness of linguistic resources, prepare a short talk on one of the following subjects or a comparable subject:

a. How abstract art tries to communicate.
b. *Form* as communication.
c. Red and yellow are "warm" colors.
d. "Quick hands" are essential in a basketball player.
e. Charisma is a quality public leaders need.
f. Here's what to look for in (a statue, a piece of jewelry, tailoring in clothing, a top quality first baseman, or other quality-oriented items of a similar sort).
g. The reason this (car, book, movie, music group) was the best I've seen or heard is. . . .

# Delivery

# 10

When we were discussing stage fright (pp. 34–36), we pointed out that nervousness about public speech is familiar to everyone who takes speaking seriously. A good reason for that may be that we all know subconsciously that whenever we speak we reveal things about our minds, our social adaptiveness, our integrity, and even our muscular coordination. Knowing this, it becomes important to all of us to behave while speaking in ways that create "good impressions." So, we are all more or less interested in what the "best ways" of delivering speech are. As a matter of fact, no subject concerning speaking has been more written and talked about than delivery. Across the centuries there has been attempt after attempt to find the *rules* of "good" delivery.

*There is no one prescription for good delivery.*

It would not be at all unusual if you enrolled in your present speech course hoping to "get rid of my nervousness" and "learn now to deliver a speech *right.*" If you hoped you would learn some prescriptions for becoming poised in public situations, your hopes were like those of millions of people as far back as the fifth century B.C. But no one has ever found prescriptions for delivery in speech which work for everyone and which are appropriate for all speaking situations—even public ones. Where does that leave you, then?

Think about delivering speech. What determines what is the "best" way to tell someone else an idea? Isn't "how to say it" determined by (1) how you feel toward your listener, (2) how you feel toward your idea, and (3) what your listener is used to and willing to accept? What do *you* want to hear and see when you listen to a speaker? Isn't it (1) signs that the speaker is interested in *you* and in whether you can understand what he is saying, (2) signs that the speaker is interested in his idea and *means* what he says, and (3) signs that the speaker will talk and behave in ways more or less like those you are used to and that you find clear and easy to understand? We think you will have to say "Yes" to most of these questions. If so, then we have located the most important single fact there is about delivery in speaking: *Physical delivery of speech is the management of body and voice in speaking. It is adaptation to meanings, people, and situations if it is effective.* Delivery, if it is "good," is *adaptation*, just as finding and selecting ideas, organizing, and choosing the right language are ways you *adapt* to your own ideas, to your particular listeners, and to your particular speaking situation. Let's consider what that notion implies practically.

*"Good" delivery is adaptation.*

## DELIVERY AS ADAPTATION

Voice and action must *support* your meanings in ways that are right for your situation. When they do not, they interfere with your meanings. How then do you regulate voice and action so they *will* support other aspects of your message? The bulk of your vocal and bodily behaviors in any setting where you relate to other people is predetermined by your attitudes toward those people. How you sound, look, and act reflects what you are feeling and thinking about *your* relation to *them*. Unless you are a very good actor, you cannot hide these reflections of attitudes. They will show through.

When we get to the very bottom of things, we have to realize that what we sound like and look like in speaking are manifestations of our mental and emotional conditions *relative to others*. When we are mentally and emotionally adjusting to other people, our vocal and bodily behaviors will tend to show this—unless we have acquired unusual habits. *Whether* our vocal and bodily behaviors fit a speaking situation is fundamentally determined by whether we are adapting mentally to those situations—are fitting our thoughts to the situations. For fitting thought, hence delivery, to many different situations for public speech there can be no rules. However, some principles or guidelines for thinking about communication do tend to make physical behaviors support ideas if the guidelines are followed.

## General Principles

*Seven guidelines will help the speaker fit his behavior to the speaking situation.*

The governing premise for all realistic thinking about delivery is this: *Delivery that is "good" helps listeners to concentrate on what is being said; it does not attract attention to itself.* If your behavior is to conform to this overall principle, you will need to do the following things.

1. *Remember that you are trying to communicate, not to perform or exhibit yourself.* Voice and action are means to ends, not ends in themselves. *What you have to say* is your reason for speaking. During public speaking the message is the most important thing to be exhibited. It is more important than you are. Your mission should never be to show off your body, your grace, or your clothing. Any notion of performing takes your mind away from your basic meanings, and this is precisely what undermines your ability to communicate. Delivery then becomes a problem in your mind and in your behavior.
2. *Realize and feel your meanings fully as you utter them.* Keep your mind on your subject, your supporting ideas, and what you want them to *do* to and for listeners. Here is the motivation for your plan to speak to this audience. Your awareness of the meanings of what you say must last from the first moments of preparation through the last syllable of speaking. Professor Winans, who formulated this precept, put your needs well when he said:

   > . . . there should be full and sharp realization of content. And this includes more than bare meaning; the implications and emotional content must also be realized. The reference here is not merely to those striking emotions commonly recognized as such, but also to those attitudes and significances constantly present in lively discourse: the greater or less importance of this or that statement, the fact that this is an assertion and this a concession (with an implied "granted" or "to be sure"), this is a matter of course while this has an element of surprise, and so on through all possible changes.[1]

[1]From *Speechmaking* by James A. Winans. Copyright, 1938, D. Appleton-Century Company, Inc., p. 25.

If the ideas of your speech plan are firmly in your grasp and you are alert to what you want your listeners to *do* about those ideas, your bodily action and vocal inflections are likely to support your meanings conventionally, largely without your being conscious of the fact. You had a reason for bringing this subject to your audience when you planned your speech. Now, your rhetorical situation and the people in it are immediate, responding reasons for recreating your preparatory work. The process of speaking is a creative process if the speaking is done well. You recreate former thoughts and feelings about ideas for the people who listen. Catch this spirit and attitude, and you will be so busy creating *for people* that most of your physical expressiveness will care for itself.

3. *Intensify your sense of communication in all possible ways.* This is a matter of attitude, as we have said. Professor Winans phrased the injunction: *cultivate a keen sense of communication.* How do you do that? Thinking about speaking as dialogue rather than as soliloquy helps. Talk *with* your audience, not *at* them. Try to feel what you experience during informal verbal exchanges with your friends over the dinner table, on the athletic field, or in bull sessions. You experience this genuine sharing of thoughts and feelings daily. Trying to recapture the same sense in public speaking releases normal communicative behavior. As Professor Winans said:

> We should make sure in our efforts to bring this communicative tone into our delivery that it springs from mental attitudes; for it . . . should [not] be assumed as a trick of delivery. The attempt to assume it is likely to result in an over familiar, confidential, or wheedling tone which is most objectionable.[2]

4. *Be direct.* If you *mean* what you say and are genuinely interested in communicating it, you probably will be direct. Look at your audience. If you look at them, they will look back at you. Then the natural signs of personal communication will have been established. Looking at a spot on the back wall signals that you are avoiding communication, and it shuts away your listeners' signals to you. Similarly, if you talk to just one side of the audience, you deny communicative relationship with a section of your listeners.

   Perhaps in early speeches you will think it awkward to look at an entire audience in a direct manner. If so, try looking at a few people in a particular area of the room as you develop one idea. When you have finished with that idea, and as you start on the next one, direct your gaze to another

[2]Ibid., p. 28.

part of the audience. As you move to subsequent ideas, refocus each time. Then you will talk *with* your audience, not at them or past them. In time a natural impulse to cover the whole of every audience will evolve.

5. *Keep yourself free to punctuate and support your ideas with your body and your voice.* Facial expressions, gestures, pitch changes, variations in vocal rate and volume, pauses, shifts in posture, and walking take the place of the commas, italics, exclamation points, indentation, and question marks of written communication. You cannot be fully clear in speaking without these special signals of meaning, and yet if you try to "coach them in" you will destroy natural communicative patterns. Notice, in rehearsal, exactly where you need to "punctuate" meanings in special ways. Experiment with these physical "punctuations," but *fix* none of them as planned behaviors. Build a reservoir of different but useful ways of reinforcing your meanings, but when you actually address your listeners, simply keep your body free to move as meaning impels. It is entirely likely that if you keep yourself physically free to act and if you concentrate on your meanings and on how your listeners are responding, a good many useful, emphasizing, physical behaviors will occur naturally. To repeat, you can build up a reserve of punctuating behaviors in private—just as you build vocabulary—but you must not try to "edit them in" during speaking. If you try to "act" your meanings, your mind will slip from the main business at hand—communicating as one earnest human to others.

6. *Strive for conversational quality.* If the ways you say things have the features we discussed under the five headings above, your speech will tend to be much like your best conversation: meaningful, reflective of content, clearly intended for a specific group of listeners, and supported by natural physical and vocal behavior. The goal in speaking publicly is not to reproduce one's conversational behaviors exactly. The larger your audience and the more formal your situation, the more your presentation will need to differ in detail *but not in quality* from everyday conversation.

   Effective formal speaking retains important characteristics of good conversation: directness, spontaneity, animation, and emphasis. But it is conversational in *quality* not in its *manner*. The manner of delivery must recognize that the communicative setting is larger than that of intimate conversation. Perhaps it must recognize that the setting is marked by formal features and expectations. Public speech needs to sound like conversation enlarged—more systematic, including more people in its reach, and, therefore, probably more forceful than ordinary conversation.

Again, *attitude* is the condition that controls speaking appropriately or inappropriately. If you are thinking of your listeners as individual people whose understandings and interests are of genuine importance to you, what you say to them will have the *quality* of conversation. You will sound direct, spontaneous, and personal because you will feel that way. And if you feel that way, it will be almost as easy for you to relate to a number of people as to relate to one or two. You will naturally enlarge your manner of address to include all. Conversational *quality* will remain, but you will "reach out" to address all. These must be your goals.

7. *Monitor your listeners and respond to their emotional and physical experiences.* Your delivery needs to show that you are receiving and adapting to your listeners' signals. Just concentrating on maintaining lively contact with listeners can make your behaviors more natural; you will then reveal that you are communicating, not soliloquizing. A recent experiment showed that inexperienced speakers, who had merely *discussed* using feedback from listeners, afterward spoke with dramatically fewer "ahs" and other vocal signs of uneasiness than did other speakers who had given no special thought to observing and making use of "feedback cues."[3] In short, just remembering that there *are* messages for you "out there" and determining to respond to them are likely to help your behavior become natural and communicative.

## THE RESOURCES OF DELIVERY

*Private drill will improve delivery.*

We have just surveyed the principles that govern the adaptiveness of delivery in public speech. We implied several times that delivery can be improved by practice, but we cautioned you against carrying on your practice in delivery while you are making actual speeches. The strategy of learning we urged is not unlike that which a basketball or gymnastics coach would urge on his players or gymnasts. He would call for drill "on the fundamentals"—the basic moves on which expert execution of complex plays and moves depend. He would not pretend, nor would his charges, that the drills "on basics" were like the game or the final gymnastic performance. The drills would be *special* exercises to fix *as habits* certain capacities on which executing

[3]Steven C. Rhodes, "Some Effects of Instruction in Feedback Utilization on the Fluency of College Students' Speech," Unpublished M.A. thesis. The Pennsylvania State University, 1972.

more complicated maneuvers depends. We want to think with you in this section about the "fundamentals of oral delivery," treating them as a coach would the fundamentals of a sport. The things we are about to discuss are *not* things you should think about while you speak to audiences. We are going to discuss how to develop yourself *for* speaking through privately testing and exercising yourself on these fundamentals.

The fundamental resources we use in oral delivery are bodily and vocal action. If you understand how these activities serve speech, you will have basic knowledge with which to improve by private drill. Private drill develops habits that become resources for actual speaking. We shall consider the two kinds of activities separately.

### Bodily Action

*Listeners respond to both overt and covert actions.*

Any speaker's bodily actions are of two kinds: *overt* and *covert.* Overt action is that which listeners can easily see. Covert action is that which is largely concealed. An audience responds to both kinds. Listeners can sense and respond even to covert action. For example, an audience can detect that there have been hidden contractions of the muscles in a speaker's throat, arm, or leg. Listeners need not be able to locate the specific muscular activity itself to respond to a speakers' tensions in cases like these.

All action associated with speaking expresses something. It is all at least potential communication. The practical question is whether the actions express meanings that are relevant to what a speaker is saying. It has been reasonably established that whenever actions seem to contradict the meanings of words, the actions will be believed more than the words. So, it is important whether your overt *and your covert* actions support or deny your verbal meanings. If you clench your fist when you mean something intensely, the action can reinforce your meaning whether the fist can or cannot be seen by your listeners. But if you are standing limply on one foot while telling listeners something is important, they will probably doubt what you say because, as experiments have shown, they trust physical communication more than words when the two are in conflict.

### The Qualities of Communicative Action

The resources of communicative action are most prominently these: eye contact, posture, movement of the entire body, facial expression, and gestures by movement of hands and arms.

Beginning speakers' questions indicate that they are fully aware of these resources but tend to view them as problems. Speech teachers hear: "How shall I stand?" "How and when shall I walk?" "What shall I do with my hands?" "Where should I look?" "How do you look interested?" There can be no prescriptive answers to such questions. The basic answers must be those we have already given: *mean* what you say and mean to *communicate* to and for the people who are with you. Then bodily action will become much less a "problem." In addition, some statements can be made about the qualities actions have when they are truly communicative. These are standards you can use in judging and perfecting your communicative actions in private practice or in day-to-day conversation.

Bodily actions support and reinforce verbal and emotional meanings if they:

*Five criteria will help the speaker judge whether his actions are communicative.*

1. Fit the mood of listeners well enough to intensify relevant thoughts and feelings.
2. Suit the conventions of the occasion.
3. Help to describe or illustrate.
4. Direct the listeners' attention to meanings.
5. Express verbal meanings and at the same time contribute to the speaker's comfort.

The functions of bodily movement in communication, then, are: (1) to illustrate or describe what is talked about, (2) to express attitudes and feelings toward what is talked about, and (3) to release your own energies and feelings toward your subject and your audience.

It is entirely possible for you to improve and increase (if you need to) your communicative activity. Set yourself some private exercises that make you aware of the kinds of activities that are natural but which you have not thus far used very much in public communication. Try the oral exercises on pp. 224–226 in private, perhaps before a full-length mirror.

One other point needs to be made about the qualities of communicative bodily action. Mental and bodily activities are coordinated if they are natural. It is this coordination that you are apt to lose if you *plan* bodily activity for public speech, but you *gain* it if you develop good habits of physical expression. Coordinated action expresses a speaker's concern for his meanings as the action helps to express those meanings.

Feelings and attitudes are especially well expressed by action. There are both communicative and psychological boons in this fact. Coordinated mental and physical activity are means of tension release. At the same time action conveys *meaning*, it drains off tension and makes the speaker feel more comfortable.

An entirely sound reason for trying to develop more communicative activity in speaking is that you can thereby reduce your nervousness.

## Demands for Action

*Action fulfills the audience's desire for change.*

Aside from the fact that action can clarify and reinforce messages, the psychology of listening makes bodily activity desirable. Change is the key to human attention. Actions are changes. They therefore draw attention inconspicuously if they are judicious. Actions can *show* meanings that listeners are also hearing; sound *plus* sight is apt to have better impact than sound alone. In short, listeners like animation, and they like to *see* meaning as well as hear it. You can, then, speak and at the same time "show" your message.

For some audiences, of course, action is more necessary than for others. Very young listeners demand more action than older listeners. Children's attention spans are short, and they are usually highly imaginative. A teacher of young children will need to explain how a flower buds and opens with vastly more physical activity and vocal variety than a teacher of botany teaching a group of college students. In general, the younger your audience, the more plentiful and obvious your bodily action ought to be. The older the audience, the more likely it is that reserved and subtle action will serve.

Each message, too, imposes special demands for bodily action. Some material requires special bodily action for proper description or emphasis. You can hardly explain how to paddle a canoe without some descriptive action. Nor will talk about being tired make much sense without some bodily expression of fatigue. Often, too, important turns of thought in a speech are emphasized best by taking a step or two in a new direction as a transitional statement is uttered. Similarly, where it is important to enumerate points, the enumeration is sometimes helpfully reinforced by "counting off" on one's fingers. There are many such moments when the character of an idea genuinely calls for bodily as well as verbal communication, and you should be on the watch for such moments.

Finally, occasions sometimes dictate certain bodily actions, as in religious ritual. And sometimes occasions exert regulative influence. Quick, jerky movement in a softly lit, sedate, ceremonial setting would normally be as inappropriate as lazy, languid movements would be at a rally. Even the time of day may be an influence. When it is late and an audience is tired, speakers do well to increase the flow and variety of their movements.

Action is a communicative resource available to all speakers in all rhetorical situations. Its possible functions and meanings are too numerous to identify in full, but the immediately important point is that a very broad range of bodily activities can serve you. It will be unwise for you to "plant" actions in your speeches, but it will be even more unwise not to drill yourself privately on the "basics" of communicative action. What you need is a reservoir of naturally communicative actions that will "happen" in coordinated fashion when you *convey meaning* in communicative speech.

### Vocal Behavior

*There are three requirements of vocal behavior in speech.*

The minimal vocal requirements in public speech are: (1) you must be able to make yourself heard easily, (2) the words you utter must be easy to understand, and (3) your speech ought to be free from annoying vocal habits and distortions. Most of us can fulfill these minimal requirements by using fully the natural abilities we acquired in growing up.

Ideally, a good voice does not attract attention because of peculiarities—"peculiarities" as listeners choose to define them. We cannot deal here with such matters as regional dialects, problems of articulation and of vocal quality, or speech pathologies and physical abnormalities. Problems of these sorts deserve diagnosis and treatment on an individual basis. If such problems hamper you, you should seek expert assistance through your instructor.

Our supposition must be that you have typical vocal mechanisms for your sex and age and that you can meet the minimal requirements to which we just referred. Given that much, you have a range of vocal resources which you may or may not be using to the full. To know what these resources are, you need to consider how the sounds of the human voice are produced, the ways those sounds are articulated to yield oral language, and the modifying forces of rate and vocal quality.

### Voice Production

*The speaker should have knowledge of the basics of voice production.*

Each of your speech organs has some primary purpose beyond producing speech. Breathing and swallowing, for example, are more fundamental bodily functions than speaking. In order for you to speak, the following things have to happen. You breathe. During inhalation air rushes into the lungs through the nose and/or mouth. (See Figure 5.) The air passes through the pharynx (throat), the larynx (voice box, vocal folds, or Adam's

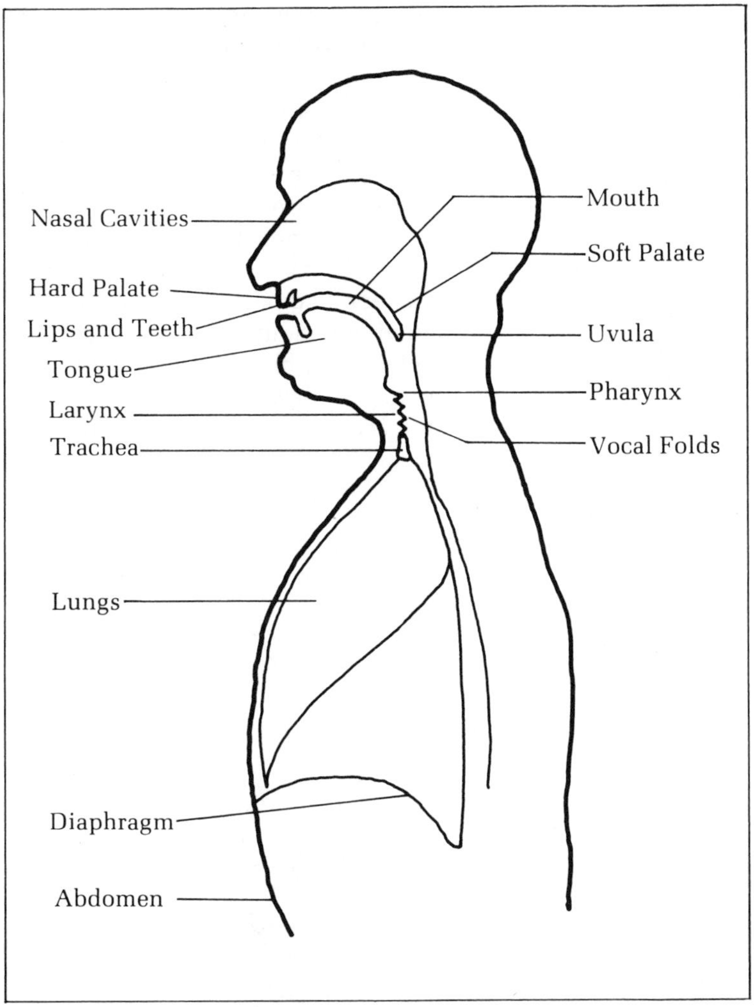


**FIGURE 5. Diagram of the Vocal Tract.**

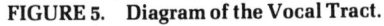

apple), the trachea (windpipe), the bronchi, and bronchial tubes. As the air fills the lungs, the lungs expand; the chest walls within which they are contained move outward and upward to create a partial vacuum that causes this lung expansion and allows the air to flow in at the start. The muscles that control the actions of ribs come into play in this raising of the ribs. During the same action the front wall of the abdomen expands as the diaphragm—the muscular floor of the chest and roof of the abdomen—moves downward compressing the visceral organs. When the rib muscles and the diaphragm relax, the diaphragm moves upward and the ribs move downward in a recoiling action. The size of the chest cavity is reduced, and air is forced out of the lungs and through the trachea, as exhalation takes place. Air passes between the vocal folds in the larynx, causing them to vibrate and produce sound as the air is forced through whatever opening is allowed between the folds. The length and thickness of the vocal folds and their state of tension determine the pitch of the sound produced, and the extent to which they are parted controls the quality of the sound to some degree.

Voiced and unvoiced sounds produced by air passing between the vocal folds during exhalation are given further character and quality as they are resonated from the surfaces of the pharynx, mouth, and nasal cavities. (See Figure 6.) Sound is reflected from these surfaces and reinforced by them. Finally, certain of these sounds are turned into consonants and vowels by the articulators: the tongue, the teeth, the lips, and the soft palate which controls the passage of air between the mouth and nose. These sounds are combined to form words, and the cycle is complete.

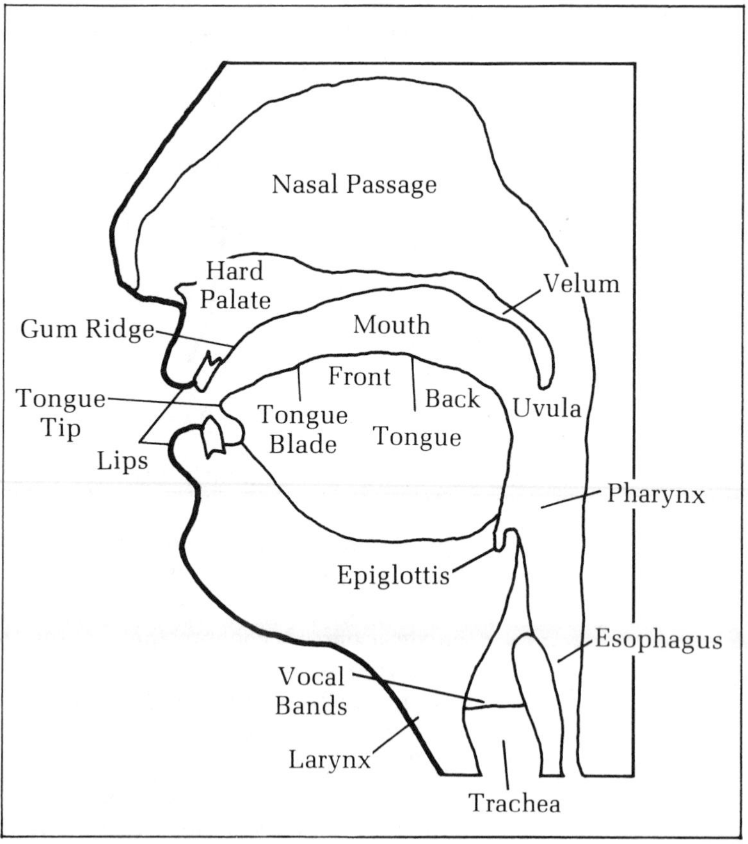


**FIGURE 6. Diagram of Speech Mechanism.**

The cycle we have just described is repeated over and over during speech, and what happens at the various stages of the cycle is responsible for the distinctive attributes of each human voice. It has been argued that our voices are as distinctive as our fingerprints. Whether or not this finally proves true, we all know that by the sound of the voice we know who is at the bottom of the stairs or around the corner.

Among the reasons we recognize one another's speech are the facts that we articulate differently, alter volume differently, speak with somewhat different variations of rate, use different pitch patterns, and generate different acoustical qualities because our speech mechanisms are formed and used differently. These differences that set us apart from one another are not wholly subject to our conscious control, but some of them are open to deliberate management. That is why you should understand your options in these respects.

*Articulation.* The special characteristics of your articulation are determined by how you modify vocal sounds as you manipulate your tongue, your teeth, your lips, and your soft palate. Since your oral language must be understood clearly if you are to have efficient communication in public speech, your goal ought to be a reasonably high degree of clear, distinct, but unpretentious articulation of sounds. The most effective speakers aim for distinctness that is not artificial. The *standards* of distinctness are not precisely the same in the various dialects of British and American English. This presents problems to speakers of some dialects because listeners may not be fully attuned to the distinctions peculiar to dialects other than their own.

*Good articulation is clear but unpretentious.*

*The inference must be that if you need to work at all on your articulation you should work in the direction of increased precision in the ways you enunciate the standard vowels and consonants of English.* You need not adopt the articulation of a mid-Westerner who uses the dialect "General American Speech," but you ought to aspire to clear, businesslike utterance that generally follows the usages reported in dictionaries, the uses of community leaders, and the kinds of enunciation recommended by experts in the field where a given word is commonly used. Unaffected precision is invariably a beneficial resource in public speech, no matter what dialect of English is natural to you.

*Volume.* If you cannot make yourself heard where public address systems are not required for everyone, you are probably tapping less than your full vocal resources. When they err,

*Volume should be controlled for maximum effectiveness.*

beginning speakers tend to make three kinds of misjudgments respecting volume: (1) they do not project their voices all the way to the back row of the audience; (2) they suppose they must reach *beyond* the farthest listener and so they speak too loudly; and (3) they suppose that tensing their throat muscles is essential to producing a reasonably loud vocal sound. If you have the first problem and do not quite reach your farthest listener, recall what we have already said about watching for "feedback" from listeners. Are your farthest listeners frowning, leaning forward as if to catch what you are saying, or sitting back indifferently? If so, relax your throat a little more and make a slightly louder sound. If you get a reaction, and you should, you have found a proper level of volume. If you speak in a large space and have not been able to make preliminary tests of the sound levels required, it may be a simple act of courtesy to ask, "Can you hear me?" before you begin to speak seriously. To do this unnecessarily is foolish, but there are times and places where such a query is important and proof that you want to relate to everyone.

On the whole, fewer beginning speakers use too much volume than too little. But there are those who unnerve listeners, erroneously thinking that all speeches ought to be delivered loudly. This is to forget the real resources of intense oral communication. Emotional intensity is more often achieved in a very quiet way, influencing people by the fact that the voice is only moderately loud but tense and specially soft.

Experienced speakers "test the hall" whenever possible. By doing so in advance of speaking, they can "tune themselves" to the amount of volume that comes across as "loud," "medium," and "soft" where they will speak. This is the best way of discovering which levels of volume you must call upon in a given case. Do not forget that, as a room fills with people, somewhat greater volume will be needed than when the room was empty.

*Variety is of prime importance to speaking rate.*

*Rate.* The typical rates of American speakers seem to fall in the range of 125–200 words a minute, but those are *averages*. Anyone speaking constantly at substantially the same rate will quickly bore his or her listeners. Variety is what is required in all effective speaking. Utterance needs to be paced to meaning. *We ought to slow down or speed up as ideas and feelings require.*

Beginning speakers tend to speak either too fast or too slowly. Sometimes they fail to vary pace because they are in a hurry to "get through." The best remedy for this failing is to concentrate on the fact that you are speaking to create and sustain a communicative relationship with other people who are trying to catch your meanings. Slowness of speech is often the result of insufficient preparation. If you are trying to remember words or laboring to recover next thoughts, you will, of course, talk more slowly. The remedy for this is simple: prepare thoroughly and rehearse!

You cannot choose a rate of speech arbitrarily. The rate at which you speak in any moment must be a conventional rate for *this* meaning, expressed in *this* mood, in response to whatever cues you receive from your audience. If this is your attitude toward rate, your pacing will be varied and will probably reinforce your thoughts and intensify your relationships with your hearers.

*Pitch.* More can be said about pitch as a vocal resource than about rate. Several facts stand out clearly. (1) Everyone has a basic pitch level that is natural and normal for him or her. (2) Monotony of pitch destroys the meanings of even the best ideas for even the most willing listeners. (3) A variety of pitch patterns is necessary in any speaking because it seems characteristic of humans that they significantly reflect their emotions and attitudes in alterations of pitch-rate patterns.

*A variety of pitch patterns is also necessary in public speaking.*

Each of us has a natural, normal pitch level, Hanley and Thurman say. "Research findings for superior young adult male and female speakers are that their average (habitual) pitch levels are $C_3$ and $G\#_3$ respectively . . . or one octave and two musical notes, respectively, below middle C."[4] These authors further add:

> Your average level changed from infancy to childhood to young adulthood, where you now stand. In the absence of better information, we believe, it should be assumed that your physiological maturation has been as normal in the larynx as it has been in your upper arm, or ankle, or any other anatomical locus. If this is true, if you have normal cords that vibrate under normal tension, then the frequency at which they vibrate most often is the best, most effective, most efficient frequency, the optimum pitch level, the one at which you can produce sounds longest, with least effort.[5]

These facts about "natural pitch levels" should have special importance for you if you have experienced vocal strain from only moderately long periods of ordinary talk, or if you have been told you "speak in a monotone." Some speakers unintentionally adopt pitches too high or too low for their laryngeal

---

[4]Theodore D. Hanley and Wayne L. Thurman, *Developing Vocal Skills*, 2nd ed. (New York: Holt, Rinehart and Winston, 1970), p. 184. By permission of Holt, Rinehart and Winston, Inc.

[5]Ibid., p. 185.

physiology. Error in either direction can produce soreness in the throat and inevitably makes it difficult to inflect upward or downward from too high or too low a basic pitch. If you experience these kinds of difficulties, you should consult a specialist on voice improvement to discover whether or not you have misplaced your basic pitch. This is not a casual matter. Chronic soreness or chronic monotony can also be a manifestation of conditions deserving medical attention.

Whatever causes it, monotony seems to inhibit oral communication very seriously. As pitch variations diminish toward monotone, listeners assign less and less credibility to both male and female speakers.[6] It is difficult to say precisely what "vocal variety" is in the judgment of a listener, but it is clear that whoever approaches monotone in speech is not using the vocal pitches listeners expect him or her to use.

*Vocal quality is the product of changes in the shapes and sizes of the resonators.*

*Quality.* Vocal quality is the product of changes in the shapes and sizes of the resonators: pharynx, mouth, and nasal passages. It is common to say that a speaker's voice is breathy, nasal, denasal, pectoral, guttural, metallic, strident, or orotund. These terms are attempts to say something about what is happening along the path of the breath stream. None of the terms describes the events that made the voice as it seemed. None describes or explains the psychological responses listeners make to these qualities. Nonetheless, some of these terms allow us to communicate *about* the vocal experiences of speakers and listeners.

When speakers exert inadequate control over the breath stream producing voice, others tend to say their voices are *breathy.* What is often happening is that the speaker is not *firmly* approximating the vocal folds during speech; the air passing between the folds causes *some* vibration but also some sheer escape noise that sounds somewhat like whispering. Assuming a healthy larynx, there is no need for this to happen. Exercises under the guidance of an experienced speech teacher can change matters. And change is desirable, for in both men and women what people describe as "breathiness" they also associate with undesirable personality traits. They may be wrong, but they do so anyway.

The ways in which speakers tense their muscles can also produce a *metallic* quality (too much vocal tension) or *nasality* (too little muscular tension). Again, if the mechanisms are

---

[6]See for example, David W. Addington, "The Relationship of Selected Vocal Characteristics to Personality Perception," *Speech Monographs,* XXXV (November, 1968), pp. 492–503, and Addington, "The Effect of Vocal Variations on Ratings of Source Credibility," *Speech Monographs,* XXXVIII (August, 1971), pp. 242–247.

healthy, then supervised exercises can solve such problems. And again, this is desirable because both qualities are associated by listeners with negative attributes of personality.

*It is possible to eliminate negative vocal qualities.*

Vocal qualities that are effective in public speaking cannot be assumed at will, but it is usually possible to eliminate what Hanley and Thurman call "negative tonal characteristics" and what Thompson calls "deficiencies" which listeners "consider unpleasant." To eliminate these qualities, if you have them, takes self-analysis, advice from experts, discipline, and retraining. The objective facts are that breathy, nasal, and metallic or otherwise harsh vocal qualities cause unfair perceptions of the personal qualities of speakers. Fortunately most of us have found comfortable vocal patterns which only need full use, not correction. For most of us the only question about quality of voice is: am I relaxed yet "strong" enough to use my muscles and cavity walls fully to control the sound that emerges from my vocal folds? An affirmative answer to that question is usually possible only when we can also say we are intent both on our meanings and on getting other people to understand them. Once more, for most speakers, effectiveness is a matter of attitudes—toward ideas and toward communicating with fellow human beings.

## DELIVERY AND RHETORICAL SETTINGS

*If a speaker does not adapt to his setting, he may be dominated by it.*

In every speaking situation speakers must either adapt their speaking to physical circumstances or be dominated by them. Though you have seldom thought of it, every utterance you make to another human being is in some degree modified or qualified by the physical space and the physical things you and your listener happen to share at that moment. Speakers always *share* space and objects with listeners. To ask whether the speakers use their surroundings or are used by them is always a fair question. If you use all your resources in delivery, you will adjust the amount and character of your action and the manner of your utterance to the physical spaces and objects around you. If that is awkward, you can sometimes alter the space and the furnishings.

If you and your listeners share ample space that is open, you will ordinarily move considerably more, speak with greater authority and command, and use broader gestures than if you communicated in crowded circumstances. If you spoke or read from a platform in a stadium or field house, you would need to make large, wide gestures, move in what would otherwise be exaggerated ways, and speak in a loud voice at a fairly slow rate. In the intimate circumstances of a small lounge, with a small audience, you might not even rise to speak, and your vocal behaviors might be very conversational in *style*. In either case your controlling concern ought to be that your manner show that you recognize the space and things you and your listeners share.

Communicators' and listeners' responses to space and physical things constitute significant parts of all orally communicated messages. We suspect you have often passed up opportunities to look, before speaking, at the spaces and furnishings that were available for your use. Not to take note of such resources and constraints is almost as mistaken as failing to organize one's thoughts before speaking.

*Physical surroundings can offer opportunities or limitations to the speaker.*

Expert salesmen, lecturers, and office managers often study systematically, and in advance of oral encounters, what positions, postures, and furnishings will give them advantages and disadvantages in relation to clients and audiences. But we also know lecturers, teachers, and student speakers who take little account of these matters. They fail to test the kinds of vocal modulations rooms demand; they fail to estimate what the physical arrangements of rooms will allow and require them to *do* in speaking; they fail to consider what listeners in different parts of rooms will be able to see. Not to check up on such things is to disregard opportunities and constraints of rhetorical situations. Almost always, ordinary alertness to physical surroundings and using common sense in making adaptations can improve communication.

One cannot give rules for adjusting to the physical features of settings for public speech. The settings are simply too variable. All we can do is urge you to consider *in advance* what space and furnishings will *do to you* as a speaker and how *you* can manage them to your advantage. If there is no lectern or desk to provide a physical focus for your audience's attention, what shall you do? You can still succeed. One way is to remember that you, yourself, are the best and most important "physical furnishing" an audience can focus on. Desks and lecterns are artificial "aids" to communication. You are the "real thing." So an easy answer is to get on with your communicating, taking advantage of the Spartan conditions by making yourself the entire focus of listeners' thoughts.

Reflection about what is communicatively possible will solve most problems of physical settings. Consider the problem situations in Figures 7, 8, 9, and 10. They are diagrams of rooms in which we have made speeches and taught. We have watched students like yourself and faculty members try to make speeches and conduct meetings in these spaces. Some succeeded and some did not. Those that failed did not perceive obvious communicative opportunities. Any kind of speech purpose can be accomplished somehow in these spaces.

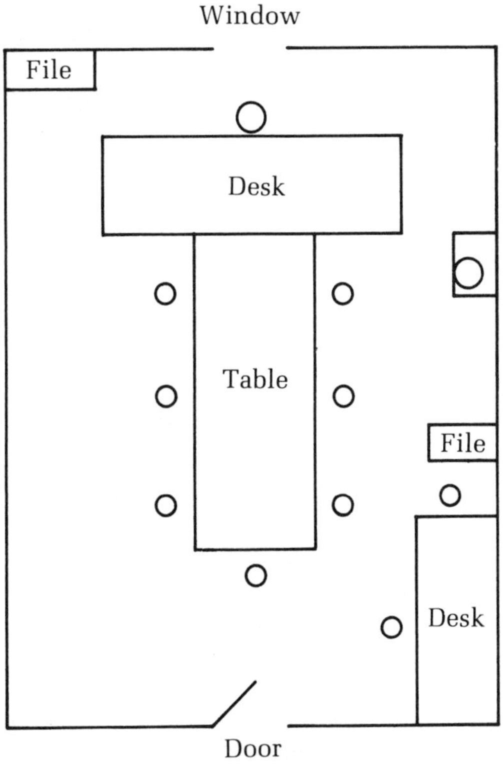


**FIGURE 7.**

We invite you to consider the following questions. (1) What does the arrangement of the office space pictured in Figure 7 "announce" about the two faculty members occupying this space? (2) How would you want to rearrange this office if you and the occupant of the other desk wished to communicate to others that you were of *equal* importance? (3) How would you rearrange the furnishings if you wanted to make the room suitable for seminar discussion?

Consider further how a sensible speaker ought to direct his movements behind and around the lectern as it is placed in Figure 8. How ought a public speaker move about to maintain effective personal communication with the audience in the setting shown by Figure 9? Where would you position yourself in

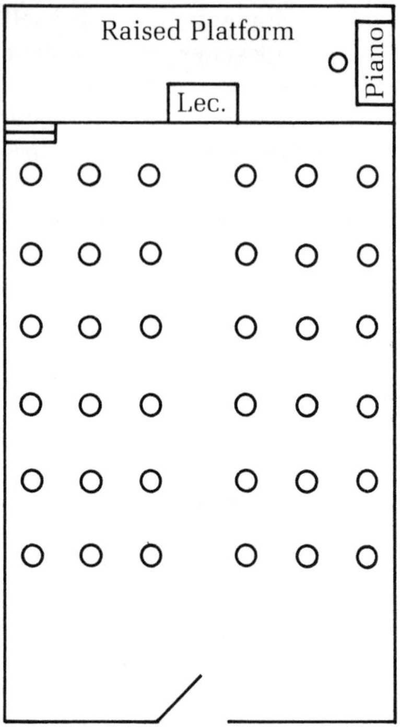


FIGURE 8.

Figure 10 if you were to preside over a meeting or make a report to ten people gathered in the room with the furniture arranged as indicated? Would you prefer to move any furniture? Why or why not? Now suppose there are twice as many seating spaces as are shown in Figure 10 and that you are to rearrange the room so eighteen or twenty people could become an audience for a visiting lecturer. What would you do then, and why?

If you will make your judgments on these matters, discuss them with friends, and study other settings with which you are already familiar, you will have begun to sensitize yourself to the uses (and abuses) speakers can make of the physical settings in which they talk. In the process you will become aware that physical settings often have persuasive effects of many different kinds.

You undoubtedly know of meeting rooms and halls in which portraits are displayed at the front. Why are they there? What do those specific portraits say, beyond what any speaker says? Why the flags, bunting, emblems of brotherhoods or unions, of parties and patriotism, that adorn the walls and platforms of other meeting halls? Is it not that these inanimate symbols create atmospheres and moods that modify the persuasiveness of what is said in such places?

Consider the extent to which such symbols constrain and stimulate the expectations of listeners, and how the freedoms of speakers are affected. It was not by chance that Hitler often spoke in gigantic stadiums at night, with flags massed, torches flaming, and drums beating, or that bugles blared prior to his entrance into these carefully staged settings. Nor was it by chance that Mussolini always spoke from balconies, which in some cases he had built to order. Neither is it strange that speeches before mobs seem to get the most effect if delivered from elevated places above the crowds. The same words uttered in different settings acquire different meanings. What is it, then, that stadiums or balconies or raised speakers' platforms *say* above and beyond the speakers' words? And how far is it possible for a speaker to "unsay" or "contradict" the special messages given out by physical settings?

Come back to Figures 7, 8, 9, and 10. Is it *possible* to create a relationship of equals without altering the arrangements of Figure 7? What would be required to dimish or "informalize" the "authority" of a speaker in the setting of Figure 8? What would it take to develop a spirit of *cohesiveness* in the audience seated as represented in Figure 9? How does a leader "lead" in the setting of Figure 10? There are reasonable answers to these

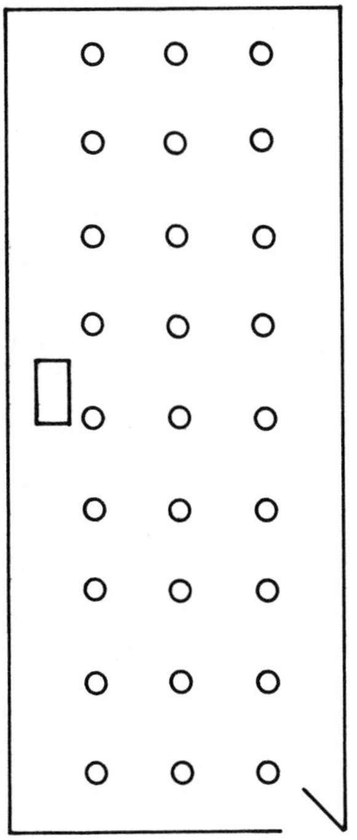

FIGURE 9.

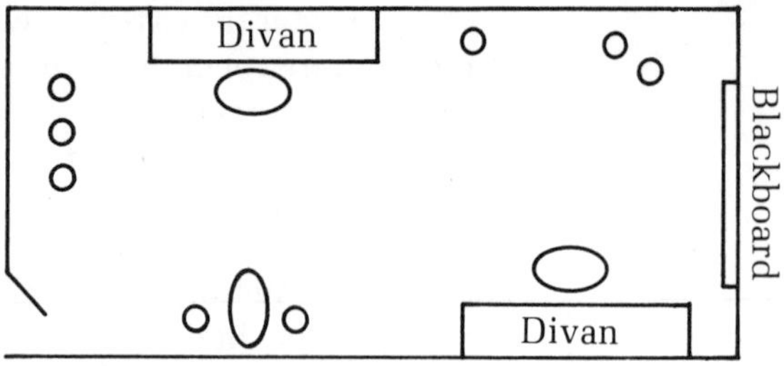


**FIGURE 10.**

questions. The defense of any answer must be drawn from what we have said in earlier chapters on locating and choosing ideas, organizing them, and choosing language.

The problems we have been posing are only partially problems of delivery: how you say things must conform to the kind of human relationship you try to create through speaking. But no one will create a relationship of equals in the conditions of Figure 7 by manner of delivery *alone*. To informalize the "authority" of a speaker in the situation of Figure 8 will require that linguistic style as well as manner of delivery be adjusted. Special address to special *needs* of listeners would be necessary to render the audience in Figure 9 cohesive. And only the most constructive *substance* could cause a leader to emerge prominently in the circumstances of Figure 10.

## SUMMARY

This chapter must end where it began. Delivery is a means to an end in speaking. For the most part, delivery can only reinforce or contradict the meanings of verbal communication. It is primarily the *reflection* of a speaker's attitudes toward self, subject, and listeners. At its best it is free but controlled response to thought and feeling fully experienced by the speaker. To repeat, delivery that is "good" helps listeners concentrate on what is being said; it does not attract attention to itself.

There are useful guidelines by which to regulate bodily and vocal action, and we have identified a number of them. But even these are, in the last analysis, only a *means* to freer, more open, more resourceful revelations of your ideas and your emotional meanings given to and for others in a particular place and time. The same is true of the physical things and spaces you share with others. They, too, are facts, just as your body and voice are facts. They, too, will "speak" something, just as your

voice and actions (or want of action) speak constantly. The issue for you is: can you organize all of this nonverbal "speaking" to serve your primary end—purposeful communication with others? You can if you remember that your body and voice, a desk, or a room are resources to *use*. If your purpose is clear and strong, and if you force all of these resources to *serve* that purpose, you will make them reflect your intentions. Then they can scarcely fail to support rather than contradict the verbal message you have brought to the rhetorical situation.

## EXERCISES

*Written*

**1.** Write a description of the bodily action used by one of the following:
   a. A professor during a lecture.
   b. A classmate delivering a speech.
   c. Your roommate as he goes about his daily activities.

**2.** Write an analysis of your voice after listening to a recording of it. Comment specifically on volume, rate, pitch, and quality.

**3.** Listen to a live speech delivered in person or over television. Write a description of the speaker's delivery with these questions in mind: What did the speaker do to support his ideas visually and vocally? What did he do with his body and voice which detracted from what he was saying?

**4.** Observe one of your classmates as he delivers a speech and during an informal conversation. Write a comparative account of his use of body and voice in these two situations. Note the similarities and differences in vocal and visual elements.

*Oral*

1. Prepare and deliver a three- to six-minute speech in which you explain some procedure requiring much action: how to do a dance, how to perform artificial respiration, how to handle a fencing foil, how to execute wrestling holds, how to direct calisthenics, or some similar process. Or, experiment in private with different ways you can physically (a) suggest and (b) demonstrate several movements this kind of speech would call for. Explore differences between what you do when only *hinting at* a movement or step in a process and when you *demonstrate* the movement or process. (Note: if you feel unduly nervous about speaking to a group, you will find a speech of the sort suggested here especially helpful in reducing your tensions.)
2. If bodily movement is not your "style" in communication, try some version of this exercise. Below are a series of common events that need at least *some* nonverbal communication, whatever you say about them. As a classroom exercise, put the items in some narrative or make an explanation that will allow you to use each idea; then give a brief talk in which you convey the meanings physically as well as by words. As a private exercise, stand before a mirror and make up different verbal-nonverbal communications of the idea in each statement. See how many different ways you can communicate the same idea and still "act like yourself."

   a. A man was out-of-doors and, for some reason, he *studied the sky.*
   b. *A small* cloud intrigued him. It seemed about the size (choose a size) and it was *shaped* like this (choose the shape and communicate it verbally and nonverbally).
   c. For some reason his thoughts drifted to air travel (perhaps he hears a plane), and he looked toward the horizon *somewhat to his left.*
   d. He had a thought of *great importance* (to you, to your audience or both). Perhaps it was about pollution, how small the world is, or whatever you choose.
   e. You would like *to offer us* your own interpretation of this thought.

   The italicized ideas are spots at which some kind of movement, if only of eyes, will be essential if you are to observe the speaking conventions of our culture.
3. Explain the "layout" of a supermarket. Tell your listeners, in your own words, that as one enters past the shopping carts into the main display area, the fresh produce will be on one side, the frozen foods will be on the other, the meat department will be in a far corner, etc. Try to suggest by vocal variety and action the spatial pattern of such a store. As a private exercise or with a partner, experiment with different ways of *suggesting* physically how the cash register is related in space to the fresh produce department (or use any other two sections of the store).

**4.** If using your hands in communication seems unusual or awkward for you, try this exercise. Let your topic be: "Some Geometric Figures We Couldn't Do Without." As a classroom exercise, give a two-minute talk on the subject, describing rectangles, an octagon, various types of triangles, or others. In private or with a partner, and using a mirror, see how many different ways you can *clearly* suggest and demonstrate the shapes of boxes, picture frames, different models of telephone handsets, etc.

**5.** Assign each of the following sentences to three or four members of your class. Ask each person to say or read his sentence with an emphasis different from that used by the person preceding him, changing the meaning of the sentence each time it is read. Following the readings, discuss the differences in volume, pitch, and rate employed to achieve the differences.

a. Whom do you suppose I saw in class today?
b. Oh yes I'd love to go.
c. You aren't really sure of that are you?
d. I've never seen such food.
e. There are always a lot of men at the movies on Saturday night.
f. It was the most spectacular yet peculiar race you ever saw.
g. There was the book just where I'd left it, rain-soaked and falling apart.
h. No I simply can't believe that that is so.
i. Whoever heard of a person doing such a thing.
j. Oh my dear what have you done?

**6.** Using the statements in Exercise 5 above, speak them before a mirror, experimenting with different ways you can reinforce meanings for them by (a) movements of your eyes and the muscles around them and (b) actions of muscles located around your mouth.

**7.** Paired with a classmate or with a friend, play the old game of charades—but with a slight difference. After each successful, wordless communication of a concept or term, stop to discuss *why* the successful communication *worked* for the person guessing. Begin with easy words and concepts like *chair, bed, stairway.* Then move to actions and processes such as *jogging, reading, riding.* Go on to more difficult things, concepts, and ideas comparable to: *the face of a clock, the front door of a house, serenity, madness,* etc. Whenever nonverbal behaviors succeed in communicating meanings, consider carefully which of the behaviors best suggested the hidden meanings. You will learn something about the role of extraneous and precise movements in non-verbal communication.

**8.** Record several different utterances of sentences like those in Exercise 5. Then play them back to analyze what vocal behaviors are changing the meanings. Pay particular attention to the special meanings that are introduced by *pitch* changes, by varying degrees of *loudness,* and by *pauses.* (This project can be undertaken by a small group assigned to investigate vocal patterns and report on correlations between pitch-loudness-pause variations and emotional meanings.)

**9.** a. Below is a list of words which are commonly mispronounced. Discuss their most common mispronunciations with your classmates and decide upon "acceptable pronunciations." You will find that most of the mispronunciations you discover result from addition, omission, or substitution of sounds and/or syllables.

across
athlete
believe
bosom
cement
enough
environment
err
escape
film
fire
genuine
library
orange
parade
poem
probably
room
stomach
umbrella
wash

b. Practice the acceptable pronunciations in private.

c. Make a list of additional commonly mispronounced words and be prepared to explain in class why the mispronunciations occur.

# APPENDIX
# The Biography of a Speech

Every speech has its own story—its own biography, so to speak. It is our practice as teachers of speech to make special assignments from time to time in order to emphasize the importance of careful planning and preparation and to enable students to recognize the development of their speeches from the first glimmer of an idea for a subject through the uttering of the final syllables on the platform. One such occasion produced this account.

This biography of a speech is chiefly composed of records by Randy Jill Cohn, made when she was a sophomore in a beginning course in public speaking at Herbert H. Lehman College.[1] We think reading it will enable you to see that the problems you encounter as you prepare and deliver speeches in your first course are not unusual but rather typical. Further, the materials will show you that with foresight and effort it is entirely possible for a college student to compose and present significant, interesting persuasive talk.

Ms. Cohn tells in the pages that follow how she readied her final speech in the course. Her speech, although not perfect, was, in the final analysis, a successful effort in oral persuasion.

As you read the history and text of Randy's speech remember that her experiences are not to be followed as a model. Continually ask yourself where Randy did well and where she could have done an even better job at the various stages of preparation. Ask yourself such questions as how you would have done it differently. What choices would you *not* have made? What choices are there here which would not have been right for you? Was her subject a good one for her audience? Were her methods of research sound? Was her final choice of arguments good in the sense that what she said encouraged the persuasive effects she was seeking? How well did she word what she said? Was her style appropriate to her audience? How good are her own self-assessments following the event? Read with a questioning mind and in a mood of speculation.

The diary Randy was asked to keep begins.

---

[1]Used with permission.

## Diary of Speech Preparation
## Final Speech—Speech 100

by

*Randy Jill Cohn*

*Discovers a topic and purpose; tests for appropriateness.*

The subject for my final speech came to me while in speech class. Prof. Wilson was speaking about how someone gave a speech on joining a certain organization, and as immediate feedback for his persuasive ability he passed out a sheet for people to sign if they wanted to join. This made me think of the donor program. I decided I would persuade the class to become organ donors (donation takes place at the time of death). This program involves filling out a card, in the presence of witnesses, stating that you will be willing to give your organs to those individuals in desperate need of them. I felt this subject choice was not only vital but proximate—something that would interest and also affect each member of the audience, but would also give me great satisfaction and immediate feedback. I decided to get out and see if I could get the donor cards, for without them my speech would not be what I had hoped it would be.

*Begins testing feasibility of speech plan.*

In March—even before I gave my Round IV persuasive speech—I telephoned Roger Smith of Grasslands Renal Dept. I asked Roger if he would please try and get me the donor cards and some information on the donor program. He said he would be glad to. I explained that I needed them for my speech in school and that I needed around twenty-five donor cards. He was agreeable as always.

I let the speech ride for quite a while, mainly because I was busy with my other subjects and also had two other speeches, scheduled almost one on top of the other, to work on (due to the fact that we never speak in the same position in any speaking round).

*First search for needed material fails.*

Three weeks later—approximately at the end of March or beginning of April—I telephoned Roger Smith and asked him if he had any luck in getting the materials for me. He had been unable to get the donor cards but had gotten two pamphlets. I thanked him and went and picked up the pamphlets the next day at the hospital. Unfortunately the pamphlets were not what I really had in mind for the speech, but they were interesting for me to read anyway.

*Trying new source of material apparently succeeds.*

Week of April 1st—I was pretty upset about not getting the donor cards and was determined to get them. I called up the National Kidney Foundation, located in Hempstead, Long Island. I explained to the secretary what I wanted. She said, "Sure. I'll send them out tomorrow."

*Success! Speech becomes feasible.*

Sure enough about three days later the pamphlets with donor cards attached arrived—third class mail, SPECIAL HANDLING. I counted them and found that she had sent thirty, which would be fine.

I was now able to relax a little because if I had not been able to get the cards I would have had to change my topic.

It was at this time that Randy was able to turn in her subject registration. Her teacher asked that each member of the class provide what he called a "choice of subject" paper in order to ensure that the content of the final speeches would be of high caliber and that students would not be listening to speeches that were unworthy of their time. Randy was one up on the game. The subject registration was due at least two weeks before the speech was to be delivered. Hers was submitted four weeks before actual delivery. This is what it looked like:

---

Prof. Wilson
Speech 100

Speech Registration

Randy Cohn

Choice of Subject for Final Persuasive Speech

*Subject*—The Donor Program: Transplantation.

1. I have decided to give my speech on the donor program. It deals with the accumulation of potential donors for organ transplants. I feel it is a timely and vital topic. It is a subject which each one of us should realize exists and

which needs our help. The transplant donor program can only exist if we all participate in it.

*Subject tested for appropriateness and importance; specific response from audience determined.*

Anyone over eighteen years of age can be an organ donor. This means that everyone in my audience is a potential donor. This will make the speech have a closeness to each member of the audience.

I am planning to pass out donor cards to everyone—as a source of feedback for me and also—and most important—as a way of gathering more donors. I know that there is a crying need for this program to succeed. Believe it or not, the dead can now give life to the dying.

2. Tentative Subject Sentence—

I am here to give you the chance of a lifetime, a chance to help mankind, a chance to give of yourself, a chance to give the greatest gift of all—the gift of life, by simply signing your name.

*Ideas for introduction mixed with subject sentence. Ambiguity will mar preparation and the speech.*

3. Tentative Main Points—
   Idea of gift of life
   How it is possible
   History of transplantation—brief
   Present status of transplantation—brief
   Requirements and provisions of transplant donor program

*Items are more informative than persuasive. What will be the result?*

4. Sources—
   *Interview:* *Person-to-person conversations with people awaiting transplants.*
   *Books:* Moore, Francis, *Give and Take*
   Warshofsky, Fred, *The Rebuilt Man*

Others to be gotten.

*Knows clearly where to begin research.*

---

Randy's diary continues as follows:

Once I was set with the topic, I started thinking about my speech at all sorts of times. It is hard to write down things like this. For example, Monday at 9 AM while taking a bath I was thinking of different types of wording and phrases—such as "gift of life," "dead give life to the dying," etc.—which I thought would be appropriate for the topic. Well, this is what I do with all my types of writing and speaking. I sort of plan them out and get little "brainstorms" here and there, and if I like the results or remember them, I fit them into my speech.

*Early choice of subject allows informal preparation at leisure.*

Being busy with other subjects, I did not do any more work on the speech, except for my "bathtub brainstorms" and "driving to school creative phrasing," until I went to the library on May 3rd. I made my famous trek to the card catalogue—subject division—and proceeded to look up "transplantation," "donor," "organ," and "kidney." Under "transplantation" I found four books. I filled out the cards and handed them in. Believe it or not, I was *unable to get three of them*, and one I didn't like! So I wasted that hour.

*Another search for material fails.*

On May 5th I went to the library in Scarsdale where I live. I went to the card catalogue and found five books that sounded good and a couple more that were so-so. I went to the 617.9 and 612.08 sections where the books were located and found them not only useful but very interesting. I took them out—four of them. (One book I thought would be good was out.)

*New research attempt succeeds.*

Between May 5th and May 8th, I read the chapters in the books which applied to the donor program and organ donations. One of the books was written in such an interesting manner that I decided to read other chapters. I found out a lot about the early origins of the transplant and its very old history, dating back before Christ. I found the accounts so fascinating that I felt I would include them in my speech.

*Finds unexpected interesting material.*

Oh yes—during the period between receiving the donor cards and getting the books out, I was trying to decide whether the speech should be persuasive or informative. I knew that before I made the speech I had to have my rhetorical purpose clear if I wanted my speech to be effective and clear to my audience. I decided on making it persuasive because it is my opinion that the persuasive speeches given in class were more interesting than any of the

*Ambiguity about goal still present; resolution still not exact.*

other types. Also in a persuasive speech the speaker can get more involved and emotional—and this is how I feel about the donor program (emotionally involved).

May 8th—I outlined my speech. I had previously phoned my boss explaining I would not be able to work May 8th due to a buildup of school work. This is an understanding we have, so there was no problem there at all.

*Prepares intensively; enough attention to what persuasion requires?*

I set my alarm and got up at 9:00 on Saturday. Started at 10:00 and did not complete my speech until 5:15. This included typing, too. I only took off about an hour at the most (for lunch)!! I like to get down to work and fininsh things (in one sitting). I began by getting the books I used together, with pages I wanted to use marked, along with some notes I had jotted down and the donor card pamphlet. Plopped down on my bed, I started to "create." I do this by writing directly in outline form. I knew I wanted to write an introduction which only hinted at the topic—making the statements "chance of a lifetime" and "gift of life" sort of attention getters. Then I would go into the interesting early accounts and to today's developments to show contrast; and then have the donor program reappear and the persuasion enter in to round out the opportunity previously (in introduction) presented. I typed up what I wrote after reading and fixing up phrases.

*Checks time for speech.*

I practiced the speech for my mother before typing it. It was 8½ minutes which I felt would be perfect. Then after typing it, I practiced again by giving it to my father (8½ min. again—by *stop watch).*

My grandmother and Aunt Madline came for dinner and were my next audience (8½ min. again).

*Refines outline for speech.*

During these practice periods I picked up any typing, spelling, or phrasing errors, which I corrected. My mother wanted to read it out of interest and found a few misspelled words and typing errors I had missed.

Sunday, May 9th. I typed the bibliography and title page. I clipped the speech together with an extra piece of paper at the end (looks nicer), and I sighed a sigh of relief. I put the speech in a safe place to be practiced at a later date.

The outline which Randy gave to her instructor on the day she spoke is more complete than many students would wish to compose. With the bibliography she attached, it follows here exactly as she submitted it.

**The Gift of Life**

Introduction

I. I am here to give you the chance of a lifetime.
   A. How often has each one of you said, "I wish there was something I could do" or "What good can just one person be?"
      1. This attitude is quite prevalent on today's campuses, as well as in our homes, clubs, and anywhere people can be found.
      2. This "What effect will I have?" point of view applies to littering, voting, ending pollution, as well as simply helping others.

(Central Idea)

   B. But, I am going to give each one of you, as individuals, a chance to leave an imprint on the world, a chance to give of yourself, a chance to do some good, a chance to give the greatest gift of all—the gift of life—by simply signing your name.

   (Transition: You are all probably saying, "What is this girl talking about, each of us give life? Doesn't she know life cannot be given to someone like a present?")

II. However, with the advances in medical research each one of you can give the gift of life by being an organ donor.
   A. Advances in medical science now make it possible to replace a variety of malfunctioning human organs.
      1. For example, since 1954 thousands of kidney transplants have taken place.
      2. Techniques for transplanting kidneys and corneas are currently the most advanced, but progress is also being made in overcoming problems connected with the liver, pancreas, heart, bone, and other tissue.
      3. Even teeth have been transplanted.
         a. A tooth with root and nerve was extracted from a thirteen-year-old boy's mouth, due to an overcrowding of his teeth.
         b. After six months in a refrigerated bank, this very same tooth replaced a recently lost tooth in another patient's mouth.
   B. So, you see, besides giving life to dying heart patients, and kidney victims, you can also make life more pleasant for those people suffering from eye problems, tissue deficits, bone disease, along with cosmetically helping the victim of a knocked out tooth.

(Transition: The donor program can only be effective if you and individuals like yourself participate in it.)

Body

**I.** I would like to give you some information on transplantation.

- **A.** The history of transplantation does not begin with today's headlines, but in the writings of Hindu physicians who practiced more than 1,000 years before Christ.
- **B.** The incredible accounts of transplants, preserved in legends, old wives' tales, and textbooks are so numerous that some doctors wonder whether or not they had basis in fact.
  - **1.** The first recorded techniques of transplant surgery were published in 7th and 8th century B.C. by an Indian surgeon named Sushruta in a textbook called the *Samhita*.
    - **a.** One account deals with repairing ear lobes.
      - **1.)** The ear lobes were split by the weight of the heavy earrings that the affluent Hindus wore.
      - **2.)** Sushruta wrote: (quote Warshofsky, p. 7).
    - **b.** Another transplant technique used by surgeons in India was the restoration of noses.
      - **1.)** This operation was necessary due to loss of noses in battle or removal in punishment for stealing.
      - **2.)** Sushruta states: (quote Warshofsky, p. 8).
      - **3.)** Quite advanced for the time, even if they were just legends.
  - **2.** Some of the most persistent of such legends are those of the twin saints Cosmas and Damian, who were beheaded in 303 A.D. for their medical practices.
    - **a.** Their most famous miracle is a leg transplant, allegedly performed in the Middle Ages, several centuries after their death.
    - **b.** A man afflicted with a cancerous leg found shelter in a church in Rome which had been named for the twin saints.
    - **c.** As he slept, Cosmas and Damian appeared to him in a dream, with drugs and surgical instruments.
    - **d.** One brother amputated the leg, and the other hurried to a nearby cemetery and severed the leg of a Moor who had died that day.
    - **e.** They proceeded to graft the Moor's leg onto the patient, then placed the cancerous limb in the Moor's grave.
    - **f.** When the man awoke the next morning, he found a healthy black leg instead of a cancerous white one.
  - **3.** This legend, referred to as the "black-leg" legend, became a favorite subject for Renaissance artists such as Fernando Rincon.
    - **a.** (Visual aid—Rincon's picture)
    - **b.** This painting was done around 1500 and is hanging in the Prado in Madrid.

**c.** Of course we all know that ninety-nine percent of all this is fiction, but today transplantation is real—as real as the organs working inside of you.

**d.** However, more than one-thousand years later the legend of the "black leg" became a reality, when Lapchinsky successfully transplanted a black hind leg onto a dog named Bratnik.

**II.** Today we know that the advances made in the area of transplantation are outstanding.

**A.** Dr. Barnard and his heart transplants.

**B.** Thousands of successful kidney transplants—2,400 per year.

**C.** Cornea transplants, allowing the blind to see, have become a perfected art.

**D.** Continuing research in this area has enabled the dead to give life to the dying.

(Transition: This brings me back to where I began.)

**III.** The Donor Program must live if the dying are to be saved.

**A.** Each one of you is a potential donor.

**1.** Anyone eighteen years of age or over, and of sound mind, may become a donor by signing a donor card, to be carried with him at all times.

**2.** Donation goes into effect at the time of your death.

**3.** Thousands die yearly because there just are not enough donors.

**4.** In signing a donor card, you can specify whether you wish to donate only certain organs, all needed organs, or give your whole body for anatomical study.

**B.** This may sound morbid to some of you, but we all must die sometime, so why not help extend the lives of others; you never know—some donor may prolong your life or the life of one of your relatives.

**1.** A donated organ, successfully transplanted, is literally the gift of life, your gift of life.

**2.** It is not necessary to register with any organization; and if you happen to change your mind, you can rip up your card, thereby selfishly destroying your beautiful gift.

(Transition: I am going to present each one of you with a card and pamphlet and hope you will think about the program and sign the card, remembering life is for the living.)

Conclusion

**I.** In conclusion, I would like to read to you what I consider a beautiful explanation of why you should join the Donor Program.

**A.** I quote: (Moore, pp. 129–30).

**B.** Isn't this gift a truly wonderful opportunity for you to do something for mankind?

**C.** Please give of yourself, so that more may live.

**Interviews:**

I have talked at length with a number of patients on hemodialysis, and thus have learned of the tremendous need for organ donors.

These people are living each day in the hope that someone whose life has come to an end will have been thoughtful and generous enough to offer his organs to these struggling victims of kidney disease.

**Books:**
Longmore, Donald, *Spare-Part Surgery: The Surgical Practice of the Future* (Garden City, N.Y.: Doubleday, 1968).
Moore, Francis D., *Transplant: The Give and Take of Tissue Transplantation* (New York: Simon and Schuster, 1972).
Schmeck, Harold M., *The Semi-Artificial Man* (New York: Walker & Co., 1965).
Warshofsky, Fred, *The Rebuilt Man: The Story of Spare-Parts Surgery* (New York: Thomas Y. Crowell Co., 1965).
**Pamphlet:**
*The Organ Donor Program*, National Kidney Foundation (New York, no date).
**Newspaper:**
"Two Senators Score Kidney Fund Cuts," *The New York Times* (October 25, 1973), p. 6.

During her rehearsal period, Randy made the following entries in her diary:

May 10th—Practiced speech two times—second time standing. This is a good idea because it gives you an altogether different feeling. First time—under hair dryer.

May 11th—Practiced speech—trying not to look at paper unless absolutely necessary.

*Rehearses first with, then without, outline.*

May 12th—Practiced three times: once over phone to member of class. Two times in front of mirror standing. Retimed—now ten minutes due to slower delivery—more relaxed.

On the day of her speech, May 13th, Randy was fourth and last speaker on the program. Her speech was recorded on tape. In the nine minutes and forty seconds Randy spoke this is what she said.

I am here to give each of you the chance of a lifetime! How often have each one of you said, "I wish there was something I could do?"

or "What good can just one person be?" This attitude is quite prevalent on today's campuses as well as in our homes, clubs, or anywhere people can be found. This "what-effect-will-I-have" point of view applies to voting, littering, ending pollution—as well as simply helping others. But I am going to give each of you, as individuals, the chance to leave an imprint on the world, a chance to give of yourself, a chance to give the greatest gift of all—the gift of life—by simply signing your name./[1]

*Introduction challenges and creates suspense as planned.*

Now, you're probably all sitting there saying, "This girl's really crazy! You can't give life to someone as though it were a present. Life is created." However, due to advances in medical research each one of you *can* give the gift of life by being an organ donor. Advances in medical science have made it possible to replace a variety of malfunctioning organs. For example, since 1954, thousands of kidneys have been successfully transplanted. Techniques for transplanting kidneys as well as corneas are most advanced, but progress is also being made in transplanting livers, pancreas, hearts, bone, and all other tissue. Even teeth have been transplanted: A boy of thirteen whose tooth with nerve and root intact was extracted—this was due to an overcrowding of the teeth in his mouth—was recently replaced—after six months in refrigerated bank—in the mouth of a patient who had lost a tooth. So you see, besides giving life to the heart and kidney patient you can also make life more pleasant for those people suffering from bone deficits, tissue disease, eye problems, along with cosmetically helping the victim of a knocked out tooth. The donor program, however, can only be effective if you and others like you participate in it./[2]

*Examples show development and extent of transplantation.*

I would like to give you some information on transplantation. It didn't begin with today's headlines or the donor program, but it did begin with the writings of Hindu physicians, over a thousand years before the birth of Christ. The incredible accounts of these transplants preserved in legends, old wives' tales, and textbooks are so numerous that many doctors today wonder whether they did have basis in fact./[3]

*Excellent, unusual historical examples, explanations, and anecdotes—are they developed to support Randy's purpose?*

The first recorded techniques of transplant surgery were published in the seventh and eighth centuries by an Indian surgeon named Sushruta in the textbook called the *Samhita*. One account deals with the repairing of ear lobes. This became necessary because the Hindu women have pierced ears, and they wore these very heavy earrings which split the ear straight through due to the heaviness of them. Sushruta wrote about this, and this was—has been—related to us in a book called *The Rebuilt Man* by Fred Warshofsky. The technique consists in slicing off a patch of healthy flesh from one of the regions of the cheeks and inhering it to one of the severed lobes of the ears which is more elongated on its interior side than the other./ [4]

Another technique which developed at the same time and was reported in the *Samhita,* is the repairing of noses, and this became necessary because they were lost in battle or else removed as a punishment for stealing. And quote:

> When a man's nose has been cut off or destroyed, the physician takes the leaf of a plant which is the size of the destroyed parts. He places it on the patient's cheek and cuts out of this cheek a piece of skin the same size but in such a manner that the skin at one end remains attached to the cheek. Then he freshens with his scalpel the edges of the stump of the nose and he wraps this piece of skin around the—from the cheek—around the nose carefully and sews it at all the edges. As soon as the skin has grown together with the nose, he cuts through the connection with the skin of the cheek./ [5]

And—this is quite an advanced technique for that time—even if it was just, you know, a legend—that even then it was thought of, y'know, quite advanced./ [6]

One of the most persistent of the legends of this time was of the twin saints Cosmas and Damian. They were beheaded in 303 A.D. because of their medical practices; but their most famous miracle is said to be a leg transplant. This was allegedly performed in the Middle Ages, which was several centuries after their death. It is said that a man afflicted with cancer found shelter in a church in Rome which was named for these twin saints. As he slept, Cosmas and Damian came to him in a dream bearing drugs and surgical equipment. One of the brothers amputated the leg while the other rushed to a nearby cemetery and severed the leg of a Moor who had died that day. They proceeded to graft the Moor's leg onto the leg of the patient with the cancer. And when the man awoke the next morning he found he had a healthy black leg in place of the cancerous white one. This legend was referred to as the "black-leg legend," and became a favorite subject for Renaissance artists such as Fernando Rincon. And I have a picture of this here. It's a little small. I hope you can see it. It was done in 1500, and it is now hanging in the Prado in Madrid. And here are Cosmas and Damian with their patient. Here, does this look like he's stark naked to you? This is his black leg which is taken off the Moor who now has a cancerous white one./ 7

Now, these legends as we know, are about ninety-nine percent fiction, but transplantation is real, as real as the organs working inside of each one of you. However, over a thousand years later the black-leg legend did become a reality when Lapchinsky transplanted a hind leg—a black hind leg—onto a dog named Bratnik. Today, we've all heard of many advances in the area of transplantations, and they are outstanding. We've read about Doctor Barnard and the heart transplant. Thousands of successful kidney transplants. Corneas—allowing the blind to see—and they've really become a perfected art by now. And other areas of research have enabled the dead to give life to the dying./ 8

*Could these ideas be reconstructed to serve Randy's persuasive purpose more directly?*

This brings me back to where I began—the donor program. The donor program must live if the dying are to be saved. Each one of you is a potential donor. Anyone who is eighteen years or over and of sound mind may become a donor by signing a donor card to be carried with him at all times. Donation goes into effect at the time of your death. Thousands must die yearly just because there aren't enough donors./ 9

In signing a donor card you can specify whether you wish to donate only certain organs, all of your organs, or give your body over to anatomical study. Now, this may sound morbid to some of you, but we must realize that we all must die sometime, so why not help extend the lives of others? You never know. Some donor may help prolong your life or the life of one of your relatives./[10]

A donated organ successfully transplanted is literally the gift of life, your gift of life. It is not necessary to register with any bank or organization. If you happen to change your mind you can rip up your card and thereby selfishly destroy your once beautiful gift. I am going to present each one of you with a pamphlet and a card, and I hope that you will think about the program and sign the card, remembering that life is for the living./[11]

*Could listeners be moved to action more directly?*

In conclusion, I would like to read to you what I consider a beautiful explanation of why you should join the donor program. It is written by Francis Moore, and it goes as follows, I quote:

> The biologist has long known that "I am a body, I have a soul" should be rephrased to "I am a soul dwelling for a time in a body." Each person's body is a complex machine housing the human mind and soul. When a person dies his mind is stilled. His soul is alleged to depart for other regions, and his body is consumed by fire or decay. Its many substances are then free to enter again into the living cycle of nature. Regardless of what becomes of his soul each person's body can claim a certain immortality in the recircularization and reutilization of carbon, minerals, and water. However, immediately after death when some portion of that body is replaced in another person, this recycling of nature occurs sooner than it otherwise would./[12]

Isn't this gift a truly wonderful opportunity for you to do something for mankind? Please give. Give of yourself, so that more may live!/[13]

The donor cards and pamphlets which Randy handed out to the members of her audience at the end of her speech are reproduced on pp. 241–242.

When the speech was over, there was a limited period for class discussion. Randy took note of what was said. She also received a criticism sheet from Professor Wilson. A reproduction of that critique is reproduced on pp. 243–244.

**Signed by the donor and the following two witnesses in the presence of each other:**

Signature of Donor | Date of Birth of Donor

Date Signed | City & State

Witness | Witness

This is a legal document under the Uniform Anatomical Gift Act or similar laws.

For further information consult your physician or

TEAR HERE TEAR HERE

KIDNEY FOUNDATION OF N.Y., INC.
432 PARK AVE. SOUTH
NEW YORK, N. Y. 10016

STAMP HERE

The National Kidney Foundation, together with its Affiliates, is the only voluntary health agency seeking the total answer to diseases of the kidney . . . prevention, treatment and cure. Its many-faceted program brings help and hope to millions of kidney sufferers through patient services, research, legislation, professional education, and public information. Activities such as the Organ Donor Program are made possible by the voluntary contributions of a concerned and generous public.

KIDNEY FOUNDATION OF N.Y., INC.
432 PARK AVE. SOUTH
NEW YORK, N. Y. 10016

**If you needed a kidney or other vital organ to live...**

THE ORGAN DONOR PROGRAM

Life is what it's all about.

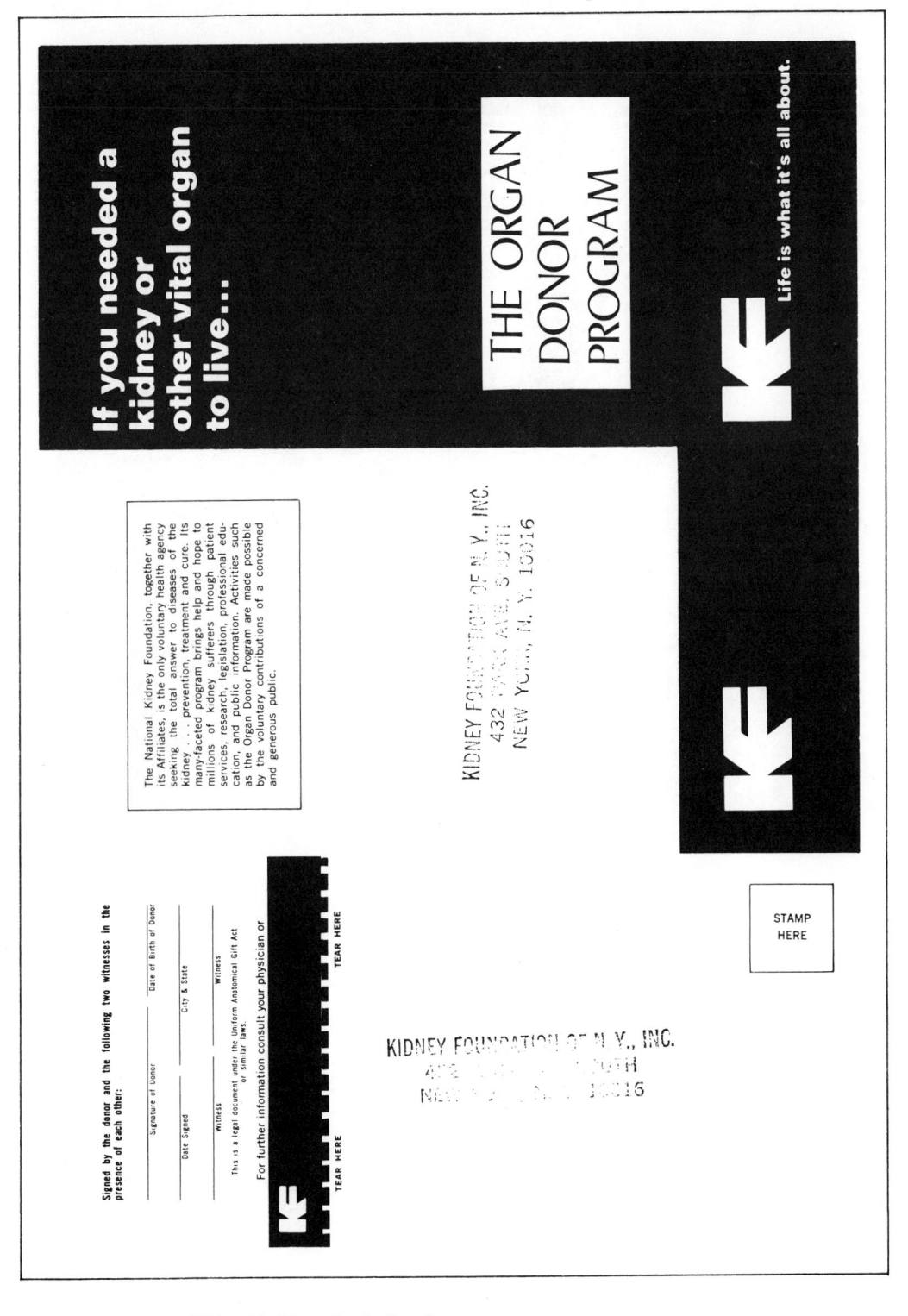

**IF YOU NEEDED A KIDNEY OR OTHER VITAL ORGAN TO LIVE . . . WOULD YOU BE ABLE TO GET ONE?**

This question can only be answered by first answering a number of other questions:

**WHAT IS THE PRESENT STATUS OF ORGAN TRANSPLANTATION?**

Advances in medical science now make it possible to replace a variety of malfunctioning human organs. For instance, since 1954 thousands of kidney transplants have taken place. Techniques for transplanting kidneys and corneas are currently the most advanced, but progress is also being made in overcoming transplantation problems connected with the liver, pancreas, heart, bone and other tissue.

**HOW ARE ORGANS FOR TRANSPLANTATION OBTAINED?**

They are donated by individuals like yourself, with the donation going into effect at the time of death.

**IS THERE A NEED FOR ORGAN DONORS?**

Yes. Thousands of lives every year are lost because there aren't enough donors of kidneys or other organs. A donated organ, successfully transplanted, is literally the gift of life — *your* gift of life.

**HOW CAN I BECOME A DONOR?**

Simply sign the attached card in the presence of two witnesses who also sign. Then carry the card on your person at all times.

You will note that the card offers several options:

(a) indicates that you contribute any needed organs or parts

(b) restricts the donation to the organs or parts you specify

(c) gives your entire body for anatomical study

**IS THERE AN AGE REQUIREMENT FOR DONORS?**

Yes. Any one 18 years of age or over and of sound mind may become a donor by signing the card. An individual under 18 years of age may become a donor if either parent or a legal guardian gives consent.

**DO I HAVE TO REGISTER WITH SOME AGENCY?**

No. Your signed and witnessed donor card is all that is needed.

**DO I HAVE TO MENTION THE ORGAN DONATION IN MY WILL?**

No. Your donor card is a kind of "pocket will" and is all you need. Mention it in your will if you wish. But obviously it's important to carry the card and also inform your family and physician to insure their cooperation.

**CAN I CHANGE MY MIND LATER?**

Yes. Simply tear up the card. Nothing else is necessary.

**CAN I BE SURE MY GIFT WILL BE USED?**

Yes, if circumstances permit and the organ donation can be used to benefit the health and life of another person.

**WHEN WILL MY GIFT BE USED?**

For purposes of transplantation, organs must ordinarily be removed within an hour after death. According to the Uniform Anatomical Gift Act (the "model law" that governs such matters in the states), the physician in attendance has the responsibility for determining that life has ceased and that the donor's wishes may now be carried out. The Act specifies, however, that the physician attending the dying person should not participate either in the removal process or in transplantation. That's the job of the hospital and the transplant team.

**WILL ORGAN DONATION AFFECT FUNERAL AND BURIAL ARRANGEMENTS?**

No. Removal of organs or tissues authorized by a donor will not interfere with customary funeral or burial arrangements. These remain the responsibility of relatives or persons in charge of the estate. If a person wills his body to a medical center for anatomical study (line "c" on the donor card), arrangements must be made in advance with the particular medical center.

**WILL MY ESTATE BE PAID OR HAVE TO PAY FOR ORGAN DONATION?**

No.

**WHAT ARE THE ETHICS OF ORGAN DONATION AND TRANSPLANTATION?**

Moral leaders the world over favor such donations as expressions of the highest humanitarian ideals. The gift of an organ essential to the life of another human being is consistent with principles of religious and ethical systems overwhelmingly held. If you have any question in this regard, you should consult with your religious leader.

**WHAT DOES THE FUTURE HOLD?**

As the problem of organ rejection comes under better control and as techniques for tissue-typing and organ preservation are improved, kidney and other transplants will become increasingly feasible. Thus, thousands of people who might otherwise die will live.

**WHAT ELSE CAN I DO TO ADVANCE THIS LIFE-PRESERVING PROGRAM?**

Acquaint others with the donor card program. The more donors available, the more this new and important medical science can be used for the benefit of mankind. Learn more about organ donation. Your Kidney Foundation will be happy to give you more information and to provide additional donor cards.

TEAR HERE

TEAR HERE

24 HR. EMERGENCY DONOR TELEPHONE 861-7370

**UNIFORM DONOR CARD**

OF ______________________________

Print or type name of donor

In the hope that I may help others, I hereby make this anatomical gift, if medically acceptable, to take effect upon my death. The words and marks below indicate my desires.

I give: (a) —— any needed organs or parts
(b) —— only the following organs or parts

______________________________

Specify the organ(s) or part(s)

for the purposes of transplantation, therapy, medical research or education;
(c) —— my body for anatomical study if needed.

Limitations or special wishes, if any: ______________________________

TEAR HERE TEAR HERE

FILL OUT BOTH SIDES OF CARD CARRY AT ALL TIMES

THE USE OF THIS REPLY CARD IS OPTIONAL • FOR INFORMATION ONLY

**PLEASE PRINT OR TYPE**

FULL NAME MR. MRS. MISS ______________________________

HOME ADDRESS ______________________________

CITY ______________ STATE ______________ ZIP ______________

DATE YOU SIGNED THE ORGAN DONOR CARD ______________

IF YOU CARE TO CHECK ANY OF THE ITEMS BELOW, WE WOULD BE PLEASED TO TAKE CARE OF YOUR REQUEST.

Send free information on:

- Additional Organ Donor Cards (quantity ..........) ☐
- The Kidney Foundation .......... ☐
- Kidney diseases .......... ☐
- 5 warning signs of kidney disease .......... ☐
- Artificial kidneys .......... ☐
- Kidney transplantation .......... ☐
- High blood pressure and the kidneys .......... ☐
- Childhood nephrosis .......... ☐

Please add my name to the Kidney Foundation mailing list to receive free publications as they are issued ☐

I would like to volunteer my services to help the Kidney Foundation in its activities .......... ☐

Contributors to the Kidney Foundation are eligible to become members. If you wish to become a member, please check here .......... ☐

NAME: Colx, Randy SPEECH NO.: final Symbols:
SUBJECT: The Gift of Life DATE: 5/13

X—No
✓—Yes
Grades:
Papers:
Speech: A
For the round:
Consult Instructor?

SUBJECT AND PURPOSE
Subject worthwhile? ✓✓
Purpose delimited? ✓

CONTENT AND ORGANIZATION
Introduction – a bit hard-hitting
Get attention? ✓
Needed information given? ✓
Purpose made clear? ✓

Samhita by Sushruta
I am here to give each of you the chance of a lifetime
Attitude – voting, littering, ending pollution
{Leave an impact on the world: You can give being an organ donor: heart, bone, teeth, cosmetic}

Development
Organization—soundly planned? ✓✓
—easily followed? ✓
—transitions effective? ok
—internal summaries appropriate? none

Donor program only effective--- transplantation

Supporting material—clear? ___
—interesting? ✓✓
—convincing? When and how will we know?
—enough of it? ✓
—visual aids effective? As you know—too small

[You're working a bit too hard.]

[Remember good art is unobtrusive and, therefore, disarming.]

Conclusion
Provide a note of finality? ✓
Whole speech in focus? ✓

ears
noses
legends—persistent: Cosmos & Damion

DELIVERY
Eliminate "I quote" or "quote" in presenting testimony

Mental Alertness
Realize each idea as uttered? ✓
Keen sense of communication? ✓

[How do you think the audience likes your historical run-down?]

Body
Eye contact adequate? ok
Posture acceptable? ok
Movement meaningful? ___
Gestures effective? ok+

[Is the historical background helping to persuade your audience?]

"Real—as real as organs working inside each one of you."

Voice Soften it some. A bit wavering at times.

Distinct? ✓✓

Vocal variety adequate? OK

Rate?__Pitch?__Volume? __

Fluency adequate? ✓+

LANGUAGE

Have good oral qualities? Good

Grammar correct? ✓

Convey ideas clearly? ✓

Pronunciation correct? ✓

Increase interest and impact? ✓✓

OVERALL EVALUATION

Adapted to situation and audience? ✓+

Purpose fulfilled? ?

Make good personal impression? ✓✓

Interesting? ✓ Emotional pull is good!

Each a potential donor
Sign card
Sounds morbid—extend the lives of others
Your gift of life
A pamphlet & card
Life is for the living!

NEXT TIME work especially for:

Another time in persuasion try to improve the proportion of argument for action in contrast to historical material.

---

The final assignment having to do with this final project asked for the students' final impressions. Randy's read:

Prof. Wilson
Speech 100

Randy Cohn
5/15

Response to Evaluation Sheet

Subject and Purpose:

*Teacher*—No comment.

*Class*—I feel that they enjoyed it. I got the feeling that they were listening and taking it all in. I hope some of them signed the cards. I know of a couple who did. If that results in saving a few lives in the long run, it was *worthwhile* in my opinion.

*Does Randy's analysis of listeners' responses show her goal was completely clear?*

Content and Organization:

*Teacher*—Prof. Wilson felt it was a "bit hard hitting." I felt quite strongly about the topic, and felt that I should make it just what you

*Relation of history to persuasion is in dispute. What is your judgment? What did Randy actually accomplish by her speech?*

said it was—"hard hitting." However, maybe it was a little much for the audience. Also commented on the fact that my historical information was not supporting my persuasive purpose. In answer to this, I placed this in this speech for a few reasons. First—to break up the monotony of my plea; second to compare the past knowledge to future and present advances to make it more poignant; and lastly to give it an uplifting, novel quality—more variety. I do not believe a speech which is constantly rephrasing "give," or "donate," in a million different ways, can be effective or interesting.
*Class*—One member felt that the historical information added to the persuasion due to reason number two above (contrast quality).

Delivery:

*Teacher*—Eliminate "I quote"—I had not said this while practicing and then I heard someone use it in his speech and assumed (incorrectly) that it was the correct method. Now I know!
Voice level—too intense and "wavering." I did not realize I was talking quite so loud. I imagine this was in reaction to my frustration, as a member of the audience, to having to strain to hear the speakers—and also due to nerves. I really was not feeling nervous and did not feel my voice wavering.

*What decides correct choice of words? Can you tell when you speak too loudly or too softly?*

*Class*—Felt voice was too loud. Guess I just have a big mouth. (Well at least the subway trains didn't block me out!)

Language

*Teacher*—Good (Thank you).
*Class*—No comment.

Overall Evaluation:

*Teacher*—Felt it was a difficult type of speech to give but that emotional pull was good. Not too sure how convinced the audience was—I felt they liked it; whether they were persuaded takes time. They are all young, and if they hear about the program again, they will have time to think and decide. At least they know of the possibility now.

*What is your overall evaluation of Randy's speech? What would you advise her to work on next time?*

*Class*—I feel they enjoyed it because it was a little different from the cut and dried, overused topics (pollution, schools, politics, alcohol, courts), and it involved them.

# Special Index for the Study of Types of Speeches

This index is designed as an aid to students and teachers who wish to structure the study or preparation of speeches around purposes for which speeches are made. The general section of the index identifies treatments of topics pertinent to all or to several purposes. Subsequent sections indicate the portions of this book which relate directly or with special relevance to a specific type of speech.


**I.** General
- **A.** Audience Adaptation: 41–61
- **B.** Determining the Response: 26
- **C.** The Sequence of Preparation: 38–39
- **D.** Choosing Subjects: 24–26, 64–67
- **E.** Subject Sentences: 27–28
- **F.** Support and Amplification: 113–130
- **G.** Disposition: 149–181
  - **1.** Introductions: 152–153
  - **2.** Bodies: 153–154
  - **3.** Transitions: 154–155
  - **4.** Conclusions: 155–156
- **H.** Outlining: 165–171
- **I.** Titles: 171
- **J.** Bibliographies: 171–172, 174–177, 235–236
- **K.** Style: 183–200
- **L.** Delivery: 32–34

**II.** Speeches to Inform
- **A.** Invention: 63–74, 133–137
- **B.** Disposition: 156 (Chronological); 156–157 (Spatial); 157–158 (Topical); 158 (Ascending-Descending Orders); 158–159 (Causal Sequences); 159–160 (Problem-Solution); 161 (Open Proposal); 163–164 (Monroe's Motivated Sequence); 164–165 (Elimination Order); Sample Outline: 172–175, 233–236

**III.** Speeches to Induce Inquiry
- **A.** Invention: 63–74, 142–144
- **B.** Disposition: 162–163 (Reflective Sequence)

**IV.** Speeches to Persuade
- **A.** Invention: 63–74, 136–142
- **B.** Disposition: 158–159 (Topical); 158 (Ascending-Descending Orders); 157–158 (Causal Sequences); 159–160 (Problem-Solution); 160–161 (Withheld Sequence); 161 (Open Proposal); 163–164 (Monroe's Motivated Sequence); 164–165 (Elimination Order); Sample Outline: 175–177

**V.** Speeches to Entertain
- **A.** Invention: 63–74, 144–146

**B.** Disposition: 156 (Chronological); 156–157 (Spatial); 157–158 (Topical); 158 (Ascending-Descending Orders); 158–159 (Causal Sequences); 159–160 (Problem-Solution); 161 (Open Proposal); 163–164 (Monroe's Motiviated Sequence); 164–165 (Elimination Order)

# Index


Accuracy:
of information, 133
of language, 188–190
Acting, speaking as, 6–7
Activity:
in delivery, 56, 207–210
in language, 56, 192
Adjacency, as attention-getter, 56
Advising, as goal, 69–71
Affixed words, 193
Age, of audience, 54–55
Amplification, 134
Analogy, 115–117, 135–136, 191
Anecdotes, 114–115
Anxiety, about speaking, 34–36
Argument, diagram of, 100–102
Aristotle, 52–53, 103, 190
Articulation, 213
"Artificial Kidney Machine, The," 150, 157, 172–175
Ascending order, 158
Assertions, 27
Assignments, violation of, 48–49
"Atlanta Exposition Speech," 116–117
Attention (*see* Interest, maintaining of)
Attitudes:
changing of, 51–56 (*see also* Persuasive speeches)
of speaker, 37, 204, 206
Attributes, basic types of, 71–72
Audience (*see also* Interest, maintaining of; Rhetorical situation)
adaptation to, 25, 42–45
characteristics of, 49–56, 209
demands of, 91–92
importance of, 7, 11, 41–42
and types of listening, 19–23
Audio-visual aids, 126–128

Bacon, Francis, 74
Bernstein, Leonard, 60, 130, 194
Bibliographies, 171–172
examples of, 174–175, 176–177, 235–236
"Big Fraud, The," 156, 175–178
Biography of a speech, 227–245
Bitzer, Lloyd, 13, 45
Bodily action, 22–23, 205, 207–210
Body of a speech, 153–155
Boorstin, Daniel J., 93–94
Brainstorming, 64–66
Breathiness, 216

Campbell, George, 137–138
Card catalogue, 81–82
Carmichael, Stokely, 119
"Case for the Non-Voter, The," 140
Causal sequences, 158–159
Central idea (*see* Subject sentences)
Change, effectors of, 51–56
Chester, Giraud, 44
Children, as audience, 209
Chronological pattern, 156
Cicero, 189
Clarification, tactics of, 113–128
Clarity, 190–191
Classification pattern, 157–158
Cohn, Randy, 91, 113, 114–115, 124, 150, 151, 152, 153, 157, 191–192, 197
biography of a speech by, 172–175
outline by, 227–245

Collins, Mary M., 156, 175–178
Communication, theory of, 9–10
Comparisons, 115–117, 135–136, 191
Completeness, 133
Comprehensive listening, 20
Concentration, 187–188
Conclusion of a speech, 155–156
Confidence, inspiring of, 92, 103–108, 134, 140–141
Conflict, as attention-getter, 57
"Conspiracy against Lefty, The," 145
Constructive information, 141, 142
Contrasts, 115–117
Conversation, vs. public speaking, 205–206
Covert action, 207
Credibility (*see* Confidence, inspiring of)
Criticism sheet, example of, 243–244
Crowell, Laura, 84–85

Definitions, 117–119
Delivery, 201–222
- as adaptation, 202–206
- and bodily action, 22–23, 207–210
- modes of, 32–34
- and rhetorical setting, 217–222
- role of, 5–6, 107
- and voice, 210–217

Demands, of audience, 91–92
Demeanor (*see* Delivery)
Descending order, 158
Descriptions, 119–120
Dike, Robert, 106
Direct sequence, 161
Disposition (*see* Organization)
Disraeli, Benjamin, 187

Economy of language, 191–192
Elimination order, 164–165
Encyclopedias, 77–78, 80–81
Entertaining speeches:
- disposition in, 156–161, 163–164
- invention in, 144–145

Etymological definitions, 118–119
Evaluation, 30, 240–245 (*see also* Feedback)
Exclusion, 150–151
Exemplifying, 121–122
Extemporaneous speaking, 32–33, 185
Eye contact, 204–205

Facts, sources of, 83
Fairness, 140–141
Familiarity, as attention-getter, 57
Fear of speaking, 34–36
Feedback, 41–42, 206, 214 (*see also* Evaluation)
Feelings, appealing to, 138
Field of experience, 9
Flesch, Rudolf, 193
Formulas, appealing to, 55–56
Furnishings, importance of, 218–222

"Gift of Life, The," 91, 113, 114–115, 124, 151, 152, 153, 157, 191–192, 197
- biography of, 227–245

Goals:
- in choosing language, 188–195
- determination of, 26, 67–69
- limiting of, 139–140
- review of, 90–91

Grammar:
- accuracy of, 189
- simplicity of, 193

Hanley, Theodore D., 215
Hitler, Adolph, 221
Humanizing ideas, 84–86
Humor, 58, 145

Impromptu speaking, 32–33, 34
Indexes to periodicals, 82
Indirect sequence, 160–161
Informative speeches:
- disposition in, 156–161, 163–165

invention in, 27, 67–68, 133–137, 163
sample outline for, 172–175
Inquiry, inducing of, 142–144, 162–163
Intelligence:
of audience, 53–54
speaker's claims to, 104–105
Intensity, as attention-getter, 58
Interest, maintaining of, 50–51, 56–58
in informative speaking, 135–136
through language, 191–195
Interviewing, 74, 75–76
Introduction of a speech, 152–153
Invention, defined, 89
Investigation, firsthand, 76–77

Jarrow, Charles, 140
Justifications:
combinations of, 108–110
personal, 92, 103–108, 134, 140–141
rational, 92, 95–103, 138–139
self-interest, 92, 93–95, 137–138, 141

Knowledge, role of, 5, 25

Lane, B. E., 54
Language (*see* Style)
Lecterns, 218
Lewes, George Henry, 184
Lewis, C. S., 115–116
Libraries, 77–78, 80–84
Lindsay, John V., 108–109
Listeners (*see* Audience)
Liveliness of language, 191–195

Main points:
phrasing and developing of, 153–154
placement of, 151
"Man with the Muck-Rake, The," 104–105
Memorization, 32, 34
Men, in audiences, 51–52
Metallic vocal quality, 216–217
Middle-aged audiences, 52–53
"Mingled Blood," 105
Monotony, 216
Monroe, Alan H., 163
Motivated sequence, 163–164
Mussolini, Benito, 221

Nasality, 216–217
Nizer, Louis, 20
Note taking, 78–79, 177–178
Novelty, as attention-getter, 57

Observation, firsthand, 76–77
Open-proposal sequence, 161
Opinions, changing of, 47–48, 51–54
Organization:
and listening, 22
main components of, 151–156
patterns of, 8, 29, 149–151, 156–165
role of, 8
Outlining, 29–30, 32, 165–172
samples of, 30–32, 172–177, 233–236
Overt action, 207

Passions, appealing to, 137–138
Patterns (*see* Organization)
Periodicals, 83
Personal-interest justifications, 92, 93–95, 137–138, 141
Personal justifications, 92, 103–108, 134, 140–141
Persuasive speeches (*see also* Attitudes, changing of)
disposition in, 157–161, 163–165
invention in, 27, 68–69, 137–142, 163–164
sample outline for, 175–179
"Philosophy of Social Justice through Social Action," 196–197
Pitch, 215–216

Planning (*see* Outlining)
Ponce, Felipe V., Jr., 116
Positioning of ideas, 151
Practice:
  suggestions for, 30, 37–38, 187
  value of, 3–4, 18–19, 187, 206–207
Preparation, sequence of, 29–30
Problems, defining of, 142–144, 162–163
Problem-solution sequence, 159–160
Proofs (*see* Justifications)
Propositions, 27
Proximity, as attention-getter, 56
Public speaking, defined, 2–3
Purpose:
  clarity of, 8, 134–135
  determination of, 26, 67–69
  review of, 90–91

Qualifications (*see* Confidence, inspiring of)
Quantifying, 124–126
Questions, defining of, 143–144, 162–163
Quotations, 122–123

Rate of speaking, 214–215
Rational justifications, 92, 95–103, 138–139, 141
Reading:
  as research, 74, 77–78, 83
  of speeches, 32, 34
Realism, as attention-getter, 57
Reasoning (*see* Justifications)
Reference librarians, 83–84
Reflective sequence, 162–163
Refutation, 141
Rehearsal (*see* Practice)
Rein, Irving, 5
Reinforcement, tactics of, 113–128
Relationships:
  as attention-getters, 50
  basic types of, 72
Reliability (*see* Confidence, inspiring of)
Repetition, 123–124
Research, 74–84, 139
Residues, method of, 164–165
Responses (*see* Feedback; Purposes, determination of)
Restating, 123–124
Revisions, 84–86
Rhetorical situation (*see also* Audience)
  alteration of, 47–49
  and choice of subject, 25
  and delivery, 217–222
  elements of, 10–15, 45–46
  and imagery, 42–45
  and organization, 150–151
  understanding of, 41–42, 46–47
Rockefeller, Nelson, 5
Romney, George, 5
Rooms, adaptation to, 217–222
Roosevelt, Franklin D., 84–85, 150, 187, 196–197
Roosevelt, Theodore, 104–105
Rosenman, Samuel, 150

Schalliol, Charles, 119–120, 122–123
Schramm, Wilbur, 9–10
Sears, B. O., 54
Self-interest justifications, 92, 93–95, 137–138, 141
Sense experience, as attention-getter, 50, 57
Sequence:
  of main points, 151
  of organization, 156–165
Settings, adaptation to, 217–222
Sex, and suggestibility, 51–52
Simplicity of language, 191, 193
Simplification, 55–56
Situations (*see* Rhetorical situation)
Spatial pattern, 156–157
Specificity, as attention-getter, 57
Speech mechanism, 210–213
Stage fright, 34–36
Statistics, use of, 124–126
Structure (*see* Organization)
Style:
  attributes of, 188–195
  improvement of, 184–188

oral vs. written, 195–198
role of, 5, 183–184
Subject, choice of, 24–26, 64–67
Subject sentences, 27–28, 90–91, 134, 143–144, 145, 169
Suspense, as attention-getter, 57

Themes, basic types of, 71–72
Thesis (*see* Subject sentences)
Thurman, Wayne L., 215
Timing, 37, 214–215
Title of a speech, 171
Topical pattern, 157–158
Topics, basic types of, 71–74
Toulmin, Stephen E., 99
Transitions, 154–155
in outlines, 169
Trustworthiness (*see* Confidence, inspiring of)

Unity, 133

Violation of assignments, 48–49
Vitality, as attention-getter, 57
Vividness of language, 57, 191–192
Vocabulary, 186
Voice, 205, 210–217
Volume, 213–214

Washington, Booker T., 116–117
"What Can We Prove about God?" 97–98, 100–102
Winans, James A., 203
Withheld-proposal sequence, 160–161
Women, as audience, 51–52
Writing:
to improve speaking, 186
vs. speaking, 195–198

Youth, as audience, 52

Zellner, Leon, 97–99, 121
Zimmerman, Ralph, 105